THE LHOTA NAGAS

THE LHOTA NAGAS

BY

J. P. MILLS, I. C. S.

WITH AN INTRODUCTION AND SUPPLEMENTARY

NOTES BY

J. H. HUTTON

GYAN

Published by

Gyan Publishing House
5, Ansari Road
Daryaganj, New Delhi-110002
Phone: 011-47034999, 9811692060
E-mail: books@gyanbooks.com

Distribution Network
gyanbooks.com
India, USA, Canada, UK, Australia

ISBN: 978-93-6433-010-7 (PB)
First Published, 1922

2nd Impression 2024

Printed at: Gyan Press, Delhi.

THE LHOTA NAGAS
Author: J. P. MILLS, J. H. HUTTON (INTRODUCTION AND SUPPLEMENTARY)

THE LHOTA NAGAS

The *Puthi* of Lakhuti in ceremonial dress

THE LHOTA NAGAS

BY

J. P. MILLS, I.C.S.

WITH AN INTRODUCTION AND SUPPLEMENTARY
NOTES BY

J. H. HUTTON, C.I.E.

HON. DIRECTOR OF ETHNOGRAPHY, ASSAM

Published by direction of the Government of Assam

MACMILLAN AND CO., LIMITED
ST. MARTIN'S STREET, LONDON
1922

PREFACE

I HAVE attempted in this monograph to give some account of the Lhota Nagas, a tribe whose dour attitude towards inquirers has caused them to be somewhat neglected in the past. Boasting no great knowledge of anthropology, I have avoided theories and confined myself to facts. During some three years' residence at Mokokchung as Assistant Commissioner I have had considerable opportunity of becoming acquainted with the habits and customs of this tribe, many individual members of which are now my personal friends.

The generosity of the Assam Government has made the publication of this monograph possible, and my thanks are due to my many friends who have assisted me in the preparation of it. But for the encouragement and advice of Mr. J. H. Hutton, Deputy Commissioner of the Naga Hills and Director of Ethnography in Assam, it would probably never have been written. He has helped me throughout in every possible way, and has contributed a most valuable introduction and notes. I am further indebted to Mr. Hutton for six photographs and a drawing, while for two other photographs my thanks are due to Mr. S. G. Butler. I have further to thank Miss A. M. Grace of Hove for the coloured frontispiece and Miss E. M. Paterson for the drawing of the median bands of the two types of *rükhusü*. Lt.-Col. J. Shakespear has been kind enough to do the index for me.

It is through the hearty co-operation of my Lhota friends that I have been able to make some record of their tribal customs and beliefs, and my thanks are especially due to Etsisao and Chongsemo of Okotso, Asao and Chamimo of Pangti, Santemo of Niroyo, Ranchamo of Seleku, Yanasao of Akuk, and Shambemo of Tsingaki. Tsansao, of the staff of the Sub-divisional Officer, Mokokchung, gave me invaluable assistance in recording folk-tales and typing my manuscript.

The only previous account of Lhota customs which I have seen is that given by Mr. Hutton on pp. 362–370 of *The Angami Nagas* (Macmillan, 1921). Other investigators of Naga customs have, as a rule, dismissed them with a few words. Dr. W. E. Wither's *Outline Grammar of the Lhota Naga Language* (Calcutta, 1888) I found most useful.

J. P. Mills.

CONTENTS

PART V

PART VI

PART VII

LIST OF ILLUSTRATIONS

MAPS

INTRODUCTION

WHEN I made over charge of the Mokokchung Subdivision of the Naga Hills to Mr. Mills in November 1917, I urged him to study in particular the Lhota tribe with a view to writing a monograph on them. The reason why I selected the Lhotas was that it appeared to me that they, more than any other tribe in the Naga Hills District, were beginning to lose their distinctive features and were in danger of early denationalization between the upper and the nether mill-stones of Christianity, as taught by the American Baptist Mission, and Hinduism, as practised by the Nepali settler or by the Assamese who are the neighbours of the Lhota on the plains side. It was already a very rare thing to see a Lhota in ceremonial dress, and it was a, to me, unpleasantly common thing to have Lhota ceremonies and the officials of the Lhota hierarchy spoken of in spurious terms of Hinduism. The Baptist Mission, with its headquarters at " Impur " in the Ao country, was at work in the north, and one of the first disputes I had to deal with when I went to Mokokchung in 1913 was a complaint from the village of Pangti that a missionary had been initiating his converts by immersing them in the village spring, to which the village elders objected both on sanitary and religious (or, if you will, superstitious) grounds on the lines of Tennyson's Churchwarden when he complained of the Baptists—

" They weshed their nasty sins in my pond, and it poisoned the cow."

The Hindu tendency was most noticeable in the south, and it was at Kohima that one of my Lhota interpreters, by his office the natural guardian and exponent of tribal customs, came to me to ask for leave, as his village was about to perform the "Lakshmi puja," by which he meant the *Rangsikam*.

I am happy in thinking that not only have Mr. Mills' efforts in investigating the customs and beliefs of the Lhota tribe succeeded in putting them on record while there was yet time, but they have also incidentally contributed not a little to revivify their observance. For there is no question but that they had begun to lose their hold. The prohibition of head-hunting alone was bound to act in that direction. In one small and decaying village (Lisio) Mr. Mills found that there had been no *Puthi*, and therefore presumably no communal ceremonies, for twenty years. There is now a *Puthi* and the ceremonial life of the village has acquired fresh vigour, and I have some hopes that the decay that had set in may be thereby staved off, for it cannot contribute to healthy life to be deprived entirely of all public and communal ceremonies, and to revive them may do good. Again, at Okotso, when I first knew it, about a third of the village had turned Christian: the remainder, having observed that no immediate disaster seemed to follow the forsaking of ancestral customs, but being in no wise desirous to take up the burden of the angel of the Church of Impur, who looks with disapproval on tobacco and the national dress and insists on total prohibition as regards fermented liquor, had lapsed into a spiritual limbo in which they observed no religious customs at all. The "morungs" had fallen into decay and the young men would not take the trouble to renew them; the village ceremonies, if observed at all, were observed in the most perfunctory manner, and the community as a whole took neither part nor interest, giving at best an apathetic conformity not perhaps entirely unparalleled in modern Britain. How far it is due to Mr. Mills' interest in Lhota custom I do not know, but the non-Christian population of Okotso has certainly reformed, rebuilt its "morungs," and re-instituted the *Oyantsoa* in its fullness.

The hill country in which the Lhota lives is a very

beautiful one indeed. I am sitting on the banks of the Dayang as I write, and if the Abana and Pharpar, the rivers of Damascus, are one whit as lovely as the Dayang and the Chebi, then verily had Naaman the right of it. But the Lhota himself has not been fortunate in his critics. From Lieut. Bigge, the first to make his acquaintance, in 1841, down to even Col. Woods, whose acquaintance with the Lhota ended in 1912, he has been stigmatized as surly, sullen, or sulky. Yet it is most undeserved. Absurdly sensitive to ridicule, and, partly no doubt for that reason, extremely reticent, he is not near so readily moved to hilarity as his neighbour the Sema, or even the Angami. Dour he is, and very canny; hardly could even Mr. Punch's Aberdonian better him in the virtue (or is it "vice"?) of thrift. If the Sema among Naga tribes be likened to the Irishman (I think the comparison is Mr. Mills' originally), then the Lhota is the Scot among them. He is far from inhospitable and I think he has been misjudged, because his critics, while having more than the casual acquaintance which is predisposed to be attracted by the manly hill man, and having discovered that he is not so delightful a person as one would like to believe, have never penetrated to the real intimacy which would have ended in a very mutual esteem. Possibly too they may have judged him in some cases from the point of view from which La Fontaine writes of his cat,

> "*Cet animal est méchant;*
> *Quand on l'attaque il se défend!*"

and it must be admitted that the Naga, suspicious of strangers as he is, is a little apt to defend himself before he has been attacked at all. However that may be, I can state without reserve that Mr. Mills, during the three and a half years in which he has had to decide their disputes and deal with the Lhotas in various ways, has fully gained their confidence—without it this book could not have been written—and has doubtless found them, as I have myself, very pleasant companions, particularly on the river or in the jungle or after dangerous game.

The Lhota occupies to some extent a midway position

among Naga tribes between the cultures typical of the north and of the south, and is particularly interesting as retaining very clear indications of the composite origin of the tribe. The main body are perhaps of the same origin as the Sangtams, and hence from the south, perhaps from the Chindwin valley in Burma to which the Southern Sangtams trace their origin. Thence there are traditions of Lhota sojourners at Kezakenoma (Keshur) and at Kohima in the present Angami country, and at Themoketsa and the extinct village of the hero Pembvo in the Rengma country. Indeed it is now no longer quite clear whether this chief was a Lhota or a Rengma, and whether he protected against the pursuing Angamis the rearguard of the Lhotas crossing the Dayang northwards, or that of the Rengmas migrating westwards to the Mikir Hills, but the Lhotas of the neighbouring villages jealously preserve his memory and all that touches him, while Chankerhomo, who is associated with him in legend and who slew in one day thirty Angami warriors of Phekekrima, only to be eventually captured and tortured to death by them, was undoubtedly a Lhota and the site of his execution is still shown. Indubitably the Lhotas have been subject to the influence of the same cultures as the Angamis, and it may be seen in their practice of the erection of monoliths on the performance of certain ceremonies, in the practice of burial and in the manner of taking omens, which both Angami and Lhota do by dropping chips cut from a reed instead of by the firestick like other Naga tribes. Like that of the Angamis too is the Lhota social organization into three phratries, though it is conceivable that in both tribes the use of the word *apfu* for mother, as in one phratry, is of southern or eastern origin and the use of *azo* or *oyo* by the others is of the western immigration from the plains of Assam, where *ayo* is still the Assamese word for 'mother.' The Rengmas, however, very like the Lhotas in many respects, and having a similar dual system, seem to have migrated generally from east to west, the bulk of the Rengma tribe having moved from the Naga Hills westward across the Dhansiri valley to the Mikir Hills only a hundred years ago.

Alongside the traces of immigration from the south we have the clear tradition among the Lhotas of an origin from the Himalayas and the plains of Assam, and the use of the cross-bow, the tradition of the *tsonak* and the strictly preserved *yanthang* "daos" alike connect the Lhota with the north bank of the Brahmaputra, or with the Singphos.

Thirdly, we have stories of fighting stones and of girls that came out of oranges or bamboo shoots [1] almost identical in form with stories told by the Khasis,[2] and traceable perhaps to Bodo or Mon-Khmêr survivals. The Lhotas too are prolific in families descended from "jungle men" taught and kept as slaves.

In the remaining pages of the Introduction I have endeavoured to give a general idea of the composition of the Naga tribes with a view to a better appreciation of the position among them of the Lhota tribe itself, and of the significance of many points in Mr. Mills' account of that tribe.

It is generally assumed in a vague sort of way that those tribes which are spoken of as Nagas have something in common with each other which distinguishes them from the many other tribes found in Assam and entitles them to be regarded as a racial unit in themselves. It has been asserted that the Naga tribes are marked by a very strong affection for their village sites in contradistinction to the Kukis and perhaps other tribes like the Garos and Hill Kacharis.[3] But this love of old sites, even if true of most Naga tribes, is certainly not true of all and really exists in a very marked degree rather among the Angamis than among Nagas as such, while even the Angamis can recount their genealogies back to a time when their tribe was still in that migratory stage still characteristic, more or less, of

[1] See *The Angami Nagas*, Pt. V., "The Story of Hunchibili."

[2] See Gurdon, *The Khasis*, p. 168, "The Story of U Loh Ryndi." The version of this story with which I met in the Khasi Hills in 1911 substituted an orange for the fish. Another Khasi story derives the origin of the Jyrwa Nongsiet clan from a girl who came out of a bamboo shoot, but I cannot find it mentioned by Col. Gurdon, and it may be a Lynngam or Synteng clan.

[3] So, too, in the Khasia Hills the Khasis live in permanent villages, hile Bhois and Lynngams are more or less migratory (Gurdon, *op. cit.*, 34).

Kukis, Garos and the Sema Nagas, and probably not far distant in the past of the Kacha Naga tribes. The truth is that if not impossible it is exceedingly difficult to propound any test by which a Naga tribe can be distinguished from other Assam and Burma tribes which are not Nagas.[1]

The expression "Naga"[2] is, however, useful as an arbitrary term to denote the tribes living in certain parts of the Assam hills, which may be roughly defined as bounded by the Hukong valley in the north-east, the plains of the Brahmaputra valley to the north-west, of Cachar to the south-west and of the Chindwin to the east. In the south the Manipur valley roughly marks the point of contact between the "Naga" tribes and the very much more closely interrelated group of Kuki tribes—Thado, Lushei, Chin, etc.

This area now occupied by the Naga tribes is known to have been subject to at least three great immigrations of races from different directions. Thus there is known to have been (1) immigration from the direction of Tibet and Nepal;[3] the Singphos are known to have come from this direction, and it is probable that the Akas, Mishmis[4] and other tribes of the north bank of the Brahmaputra did also, while the Bodo tribes—Garos, Mikirs and Kacharis—

[1] In prescribing rewards for the learning of languages the Local Government has assumed a similarity of language between the tribes classed as "Naga" by giving a reduced reward for passing a test in a second Naga language after one has already been learnt, but in point of fact the linguistic test breaks down as badly as the migration test, for Sir George Grierson, in classifying the languages of the area, groups some Nagas with Kacharis, Mikirs and others in the Naga-Bodo group, some with Thado and other Kuki languages in the Naga-Kuki group, and others in different groups, and it would really be far more logical to base the examinations on these groups than on the false supposition based on the present use of the term "Naga," which is really as inaccurate as the reputed divisions of the Hill tribes of Burma into "Tame Chins, Wild Chins and Ka-chins."

[2] *Nāga* is a corruption of the Assamese *Năga* (pronounced "Nŏga"), probably meaning "a mountaineer" from Sanskrit *Năg*, a "mountain" or "inaccessible place."

[3] *Gazetteer of Upper Burma and the Shan States*, I. i. ch. vii. (N.B., pp. 331 and 387).

[4] Mr. T. P. M. O'Callaghan tells me that the Linghi sept of Mishmis came from the south; so, too, the Sotia clan of the Miri tribe is reported by Mr. R. C. R. Cumming as claiming a southern origin, though in both cases the rest of the tribe came from the north. The Apar Tanengs are also believed to have come from the south, and they, unlike their neighbours, practise the cultivation of irrigated rice with a certain amount of terracing.

certainly came from the same direction. There has also been (2) immigration from the direction of Southern China across the valley of the Irawadi,[1] of which movement the Tai races—Shans, Ahoms, Tamans, etc.—formed part. And at the same time there has been (3) immigration from the south which has barely stopped now, for the Lushei-Kuki migration was still progressing northwards until 1918, when it was only just prevented from spreading into the unexplored area north of the Ti-Ho (Nantaleik) river by driving the newly-formed colonies on the north bank back across the river at the end of the rains in 1918 before the operations against the Kukis opened in the following cold weather. By that time the Kukis in their attempt to migrate north had already attacked Makware.

The Lushei, Thado and other Kuki tribes are perhaps themselves another branch of the northern immigration,[2] but if so they must have turned north again, for they drove up from the south in front of them both the old Kukis—possibly non-Kuki tribes [3] already subjected to Kuki influence—and that very different race which became the predominating factor in the Angami Naga tribe, and which has probably entered to a lesser degree into the composition of a number of its neighbours. The Angamis or the ancestors of a section of what is now the Angami tribe were undoubtedly located far to the south of the present Naga Hills.

In addition to these immigrants we have (4) still another element in the Kol-Mon-Annam occupation which almost certainly extended over part of the area now inhabited by Naga tribes.[4]

[1] *Gazetteer of Upper Burma and the Shan States*, I. i. p. 191 and ch. vi. *passim*.

[2] The origin of the Kuki-Lushai-Chin family is a matter of some doubt (see *Gazetteer of Upper Burma and the Shan States*, I. i. p. 451 *sq.*), but apparently they came originally from the north and are probably related to the Burmese and to the Singpho-Kachin group.

[3] Probably Bodo.

[4] *Census of India*, 1911. Part I. ch. ix. The Bodo race seems to have been widely intermingled with the Munda and Mon-Khmêr families, and though the latter is spoken of as an Austric race, it seems clear enough that the Bodos came into Assam from the north, and it may perhaps be questioned whether the Munda Mon-Khmêr races are not equally Turanian in origin, an origin which has also been claimed for the Polynesians and Melanesians in the Pacific. *Vide* Dr. George Brown, *Melanesians and Polynesians*, pp. 16, 17, 369, 370 (Macmillan, 1910).

There is evidence to support a contention that traces of all these race movements are to be found in the culture and composition of the tribes now occupying the Naga Hills and known collectively as "Nagas."

First of all we have the Naga traditions of origin themselves, indicating, as one would expect to find, almost all the points of the compass. From Tamlu northwards there are the various Konyak tribes, whose traditions of origin at least include an ascription of their origin to the hills to the north and to migration from the plains in the west or north-west as well, though others, perhaps with Singpho affinities, reached their present country from the north-east, while one or two Konyak villages, indistinguishable from the Konyaks generally in culture, claim an origin from the country to the south of them at present occupied by Aos. Like the Konyaks, the Aos claim a part origin from the plains to the north-west, though the bulk of the tribe claims an autochthonous source at Chongliemdi.[1] The Khoirao again, or some of them, for the Khoirao Naga villages are hardly uniform enough to be described as forming a tribe, claim a western origin from the plains of Assam, and this in particular is the case with Ngari and perhaps one or two neighbouring villages, who have been less affected by Memi Angami culture than the others, and of whose connection with the Semas there can be no doubt. The Semas trace their origin to the south, and may certainly be connected through the two villages called "Swemi" (one of which is still Sema though surrounded by Angamis) with the Khoiraos of Ngari and so with a western origin;[2] while a connection

[1] There are in Yacham and also in some Konyak villages to the east apparently definite traditions of an immigration from a place called Maibang of a clan which still preserves as heirlooms certain peculiar types of spiked armlets of bronze. "Maibang" is a Kachari place name = "Much paddy." Besides the Kachari capital of that name in the North Cachar Hills, there is said to have been a Maibang village on the outer Lhota range.

[2] But even the Semas themselves contain traces of a mixed origin; there are clans in Vekohomi who admittedly came from the country to the south-east across the Tizu. These it is true claim that they were an offshoot originally of the genuine Sema, but there is little, not even probability, to support their claim. All the northern and eastern Semas contain large and demonstrable admixtures of Ao and Sangtam blood, and it is likely that the original blood of the Sema invaders is excessively diluted and that not even all the chiefly families are of true Sema descent.

is to be traced between the Sema with this western origin, and the Kacharis, Garos, Lynngams and Bhois. The same probably applies to the Kezami–Angamis, though the infusion of Angami blood and culture has swamped the Sema characteristics. It is to be noted that Grierson classes the Khoirao language as Naga-Bodo, and Kacharis, while allowing Nagas, or at any rate Kacha Nagas, to eat and sleep in the porches of their houses, refuse to allow Kukis inside them at all, giving as their reason for this that the Kacharis and the Nagas were originally descended from two brothers, whereas the Kuki is an alien entirely. Possibly there may also be some connection between certain elements of these Bodo tribes and the Manö and Southern Brè tribes of the Karens in Burma. At the same time the Semas have absorbed numerous villages of Sangtams who trace their origin to the south or south-east, the Southern Sangtams putting it ultimately in Burma.

From the north-east or east, as has been mentioned, some of the Konyaks derive their origin. The Kalyo-Kengyu tribe, with perhaps Singpho affinities, trace their origin to the north in so far as can be ascertained from the two or three villages on the Ti-Ho river with which we are at present in contact. The Sangtam claim to a south-eastern origin has been mentioned. The Northern Sangtams merely point to the south, but the Southern Sangtams derive their origin from the Chindwin valley to the south-east of them, and have a vague tradition that their tribe has become separated into two parts of which one went apparently west, while remnants are believed to exist in the Chindwin valley still. It seems likely that the part of the tribe that went westwards may be represented to-day in the Lhota tribe, who have a similar if more definite tradition about the splitting of their tribe into two parts, of which one stayed behind at the time of migration. The Tamans, again, located round Tamanthi in the Chindwin valley were at one time located in the hills to the east of them and returned to the valley, leaving some of their fellow-tribesmen behind in the hills, and might possibly be connected with those same Southern Sangtams. In any case they trace their origin to China across the Irawadi valley, and the descendants of part of their tribe are presumably still somewhere represented among the Naga tribes.

Of tribes with a southern origin, the Angami is the principal if not the only representative, though here again we find strong indications of a mixed origin. To their present site they came from the south-east, having come into their present country from the Tangkhul country to the south of them, but unmistakable traces of terraced cultivation have been found far to the south in the Lushai Hills, and it is possible that the immigrants, who brought in this method of agriculture so peculiarly the attribute of the Angami and, though in a less perfect form, of their Tangkhul neighbours, came from further south still. While a spirit in the sky is regarded by Angamis as the ancestress of them all, one legend of their origin, a legend apparently of the *Kepepfüma* division of the tribe, derives the Memi Angamis from the daughter of a local god at Mekrima (Maikel) impregnated by a cloud that came out of the south, and while a common Angami tradition points to a village, in the Tangkhul country, known to them as Piwhema, as the remotest place known to have been a fount of the Angami tribe, a commoner legend still traces the two divisions of the Angami tribe, the *Kepezoma* and the *Kepepfüma*, to two brothers who emerged from the bowels of the earth at Mekrima just as the ancestors of the Ao tribe emerged at "Six-Stones" on Chongliemdi Hill. In Kohima itself, however, the biggest Angami village, one important clan, the Puchatsuma, came from the west like the Khoiraos, while another clan claims to have come from the south-west where the present country of the Kacha Nagas is. Part of the Chang tribe again claims an origin from the south, though part admits to a common origin with the Aos from Chongliemdi, perhaps due to the Ao blood incorporated with the Changs in the course of their extension westwards. They would seem also to have Konyak, Kachin, or Singpho affinities in some respects. But the Changs have a very clear and definite tradition of a complete change in their language, habits, dress and everything else having taken place a few generations ago.

Their immediate origin several tribes place in the south. The Rengmas thus migrated from the Kezami-Angami country, throwing out the Naked Rengmas eastwards to Melomi, and ultimately sending the bigger portion of the tribe westwards to the Mikir Hills. Tangkhuls point to the south or to the east, Lhotas to the south with Rengmas and Angamis, though there is one element in the Lhota country that points very definitely to the snows of the Himalayas seen far to the north-west as the home of their ancestors. All Naga tribes also have legends of clans descended from indigenous women out of caves or wild men caught in the jungle and tamed, whose descendants are now no longer distinguishable except by this tradition from the rest of the tribe. Thus there are many Lhota clans usually described as descended from jungle " spirits " [1] captured by men of their tribe; the Phoms have a clan descended from a woman with a child who emerged from a cave when they occupied the country; the Angamis of Kohima have a clan descended from a far-distant ancestor " of the wood-cutting generation " who was caught in the forest and tamed by one of the earliest Angami occupants of Kohima village.

Again, just as each tribe, almost, contains traditions which cannot be reconciled with a homogeneous origin, so marked differences of type and physique are everywhere traceable, not only as between different tribes, where they are in some cases most pronounced, but as between individuals in the same tribe. Of course within the tribe each village tends to form its own type, and after some experience of any tribe it is possible to locate with some accuracy the villages of persons met by the shape and appearance of their faces, but beyond this the physical types are different. The Angami is tall and well proportioned, the Tengima and Memi sub-tribes in particular having straight eyes and a

[1] In Assamese the Lhotas speak of them as "spirits," *deo*, but in their own language as "jungle-men," *orakyon*.

nose sometimes even aquiline,[1] but in any case features that are far more regular than the very Mongolian-looking Sema, whose tendency is most decidedly towards a flat nose and oblique eyes, combined with a figure shorter and squatter than the Angamis. Another distinguishing mark of the Angami among Naga tribes is the huge calves he has on his legs. This is so marked that it finds a place in Sema folk-lore and is a proverbial characteristic of the Angami. Yet one can see no reason in external circumstances for the development of the calf of the Angami leg any more than that of any other Naga leg. The Angami's mountains are no steeper than any other Naga's, nor does he descend and ascend them any oftener. The Kukis have a similar calf development, but it is not combined as a rule with the tall stature of the Angami. The Chang has the stature but not the breadth nor the calf, being rather curiously built on very marked lines of his own—tall, lean and narrow, though muscular enough.

In colour again there is much variation, and though the height at which a village is situated seems most definitely to affect the complexion of its occupants, it will by no means entirely account for the variation in colour to be found both between different tribes and again between different individuals within the tribes. Generally speaking three distinct colour types may be traced, corresponding more or less to the "straight-haired light brown race," the "wavy-haired brown race" and the "crisp-haired dark-brown race" into which Ratzel divides the races of Indonesia.[2] Generally speaking the predominating colour among the Naga tribes is red. A really dark skin, such as that of the Central Indian or Santali coolies who work on tea gardens, is spoken of with contempt and aversion, and the Changs go so far as to say that the only decent colour for a man is red, disliking white less than black, it is true, but nevertheless regarding it as decidedly unpleasing and classifying Nagas only as *Mat-mei*, "real men," of whom a red skin is an attribute. With this red or light brown

[1] So has the Kacha Naga, and the Phom to some extent.

[2] See Ratzel, *History of Mankind*, Vol. I. Book II., Map of the Races of Oceania.

skin wavy hair is usual. In villages at a high altitude the skin is often so fair that the pink of the blood can be seen in the cheeks and a blush is easily detected. On the other hand, a fair and sallow complexion and straight hair are often to be seen in all tribes and at all altitudes, being apparently independent of climate and little affected by it, but much more prevalent among Manipuris and Kukis, in Ao Nagas and in the Konyak tribes, than among other tribes. It is less common in Lhotas and hardly to be seen at all among the Angamis, who are a very pronounced red, while among the Semas, who are a darker brown than the Angamis though in some high villages very fair (when washed), the sallow type is rarer than among Lhotas. Everywhere and in all these tribes alike the children are apt to have rusty-coloured reddish hair, which usually turns black [1] as they get older.

Much rarer than the sallow type is that associated with a decidedly dark brown skin and fuzzy hair suggesting the Negrito type.[2] Individuals of this type may be met with occasionally in all tribes, but they are nowhere very common, though perhaps least rare among Phoms, Konyaks and Aos. The fuzzy hair is always a subject for derision, being regarded as most unsightly (straight hair is by all looked on as the most becoming), and more so perhaps even than a dark skin.

Cephalic indices, as far as data are available, suggest a connection between Aos, Manipuris and the Ahoms and perhaps some other sub-Himalayan tribes of Assam, which might be due to a common infusion of Tai blood.

One very marked line of cleavage between Naga tribes and their neighbours is to be found in the methods of disposal of the dead. Burning is practised in this hill area only by the Hinduized Manipuris to the south and by the

[1] The black of a Naga's or Kuki's hair is normally a dull brownish- or reddish-black rather than the blue-black of some races. Children with reddish, or even yellowish, hair are particularly common in Phom villages.

[2] In the Konyak villages of Shiong and Tang there appears to be a whole clan whose hair is of this type. The member of the clan whom I saw had *very* curly hair which stuck out fuzzily in all directions.

Singphos (or some of them)[1] to the north-east, but the other methods practised in disposing of the dead may be roughly classified as burial, exposure and, for want of a better term, desiccation.

Burial is practised by the Angami, Sema, Rengma, Lhota, Sangtam, Yachungr, Tangkhul and Kacha Nagas and by the Kukis, but the burial is not in all cases absolute. Thus the Kukis, in the case of rich or famous men, sometimes detach the head after decomposition and place it in a cleft or hole in the side of a cliff where it could be got at only with great difficulty. This practice is very rare, but certainly exists or existed among some or all clans of Thado Kukis. Again, the Yachungr and some of the Southern Sangtams bury their dead inside the house under the bed, and do not hesitate to disturb the grave and dig out the bones of its last occupant to make room for a new one. The Tangkhuls and some, at any rate, of the Naked Rengmas build small houses over their graves with little ladders up to them for the ghost to inhabit, while the Lhotas, Sangtams and Semas build thatched roofs over their graves, which perhaps suggests that they formerly exposed the bodies in the miniature houses, since Aos who have turned Christian, though they bury the body, build a thatched roof over the grave like that which would be put over a body exposed on a platform if they followed the custom of their unconverted fellow-tribesmen. North of the tribes mentioned exposure on a platform is the rule, the body being in some cases smoked first. Among Aos rich men are smoke-dried in their houses for two months. The platform usually consists of a bamboo shelf thatched over like a house and covered in at the ends, though some Konyaks use a wooden dug-out like a boat to contain the body, reminding one of the Lhota practice of using a dug-out boat-shaped coffin. In the case, however, of the tribes that practise exposure, the practice here again may be described as not absolute.

[1] The Maru. *Gazetteer of Upper Burma and the Shan States*, I. i. p. 386. The Lolos also burn their dead (*ibid.* p. 615) and put their ashes in clefts in the rock. In the Assam hills north of the Brahmaputra the Taroan and Miju Mishmis first bury, then exhume and burn their dead. The Khasi and Garo tribes also burn.

The Phoms and some Konyaks separate the head from the body, wrenching it off after decomposition, the latter in some cases collecting the skulls in pots in a separate place, and in others putting them out on stone platforms, while the Phoms put them in niches in the cliffs. Both Phoms and some Konyaks bring the heads of deceased men into their houses for a time (the Phoms for a year) and treat them while there with some ceremony.[1]

The Chang tribe occupies a midway position both geographically and culturally between the burying tribes and the exposing tribes, and practises both customs indiscriminately and in accordance with the fancy of the individual, though exposure is believed to be the newer form of treating the dead.[2]

To the north-east or east of the tribes already mentioned in this connection the Kalyo–Kengyu tribe, or part of that tribe, practises what I can only describe as "desiccation" of the dead. This custom of theirs has probably not before been placed on record. The dead are smoked in their houses for two months over a fire and then the smoke-dried body is retained as it is in a wooden coffin like a lidless box with a mat or bit of thatch to cover it, either inside the house or just outside the mat-work walling and immediately under the eaves at the point nearest to the hearth. Here it is kept until the next sowing, when on an appointed day all those who have died since last year's sowing are brought out, their withered bodies broken up, and their bones picked out and counted by a number of persons of both sexes, not fewer than a fixed minimum, slightly less for a woman than a man. The bones of each corpse are placed in an earthen pot and put at the back of the family granary, where they remain untouched till they dissolve into dust or

[1] In Yacham, a composite Ao–Phom village, each family has its own place of exposure where the bodies of its dead are exposed on a platform under thatch in the Ao manner, but smoked out of doors *in situ*, after which the heads are ultimately wrenched off and the bodies in their wrappings added to the heap in the clan burial tree.

[2] It possibly dates only from the comparatively recent absorption by the Chang tribe of certain Ao villages east of the Dikhu. Colonel A. E. Woods, touring among the Changs in 1900, states definitely that they bury their dead.

till the granary rots and falls on them, while the broken bits of body together with the coffin and its appurtenances are thrown away into the jungle, preferably over a steep place near the edge of the village.

When the implements and weapons of the tribes in the Naga Hills area are examined, it appears that while some are of marked northern form, others are clearly connected with Indonesian forms such as those in use among the Igorot of the Philippines, while other patterns seem to show a very clear connection with the Kol-Mon-Annam types. One type of northern origin is represented by the Kabui dancing dao and by a similar dao intended for real use. The latter is very rare, but I have one specimen picked up in a remote Kacha Naga village. It is precisely similar to a dao figured on page 190 of Major Butler's *Sketch of Assam* (Smith, Elder & Co., 1847) as a Bhutanese weapon. One kind of obsolete Lhota *yanthang* is also a northern type.[1] Both these kinds of Naga daos are remarkable for the way in which the iron of the tang, which fastens the blade to the wooden handle, projects beyond the hilt into a sharp point, the object of which seems to be to facilitate sticking the dao in the ground by one's side when sitting. The Garos use a similar type (and seem to be a tribe of northern origin), but so do the Khasis, and it is possible that the type may have some other source. In any case it is very marked and distinct from any kind of dao in general use among Naga tribes. Of weapons suggesting relationship with Philippine Island tribes there is a type of spear with ornamental barbs curving outwards from the shaft, of which some Angami patterns closely resemble the Igorot spear, while I have an old Kacha Naga spear with a head identical in shape with Igorot spear-heads. This barbed type seems not to occur north of the Angami country, though the Aos may at one time have used miniature imitations of such spears for money, and I have an obsolete Konyak spear-head with straight barbs closely

[1] Mr. Mills tells me that all these obsolete Lhota *yanthang* seem to be connected with the partial migration from the north as opposed to the general immigration from the south.

resembling the straight-barbed Igorot type. Again, there is a rare Tangkhul dao with a long projection behind resembling a common type of Igorot dao, while the stone hammer used by all Naga smiths could scarcely be distinguished from a similar hammer from the Philippines.[1]

With the Kol-Mon-Annam family the shouldered hoe (see Gurdon, *The Khasis*, p. 12) has been intimately associated. The Yachungr Naga hoe (*thoù*), obtained from a tribe hitherto almost entirely isolated from regular intercourse with its neighbours, is almost identical with the miniature Khasi hoe used for hoeing sweet potatoes, and is very similar to the Mikir hoe of the same type, while Mr. Peal found shouldered hoes of a squarer type among some of the Konyak Nagas. Both these types closely resemble some Battak hoes from Sumatra in the Leipzig Museum of Ethnology (Ratzel, *op. cit.* I. p. 429) and are much the same shape as the Easter Island obsidian tanged blades.[2]

The question of the use of the bow is also to be considered. While the cross-bow is the weapon of Singphos, and has been adopted from them apparently by the Naga tribes of the north-east in direct or indirect communication with them, it is not in general use among the Naga tribes.[3] The simple bow is also not the natural weapon of a Naga. While the Kukis, before they acquired guns, relied, like the Khasis, principally on the bow, the Naga rarely uses it. The weapon was known to the Semas and is still employed by children as a toy, and the Angamis have learnt the use of the pellet-bow, possibly from the Kukis, and use it for

[1] The story of people created with their noses upside-down so that they could not go out in the rain, because it ran off their foreheads down their nostrils, is not the sort of story that one would expect to occur spontaneously to different peoples in different parts of the world. It is reported from the Bila-an in the Philippines (Frazer, *Folk-lore in the Old Testament*, Vol. I. p. 16) and is found in the Naga Hills among both Changs and Semas. The Angamis have the story in which the Semas and Changs introduce the incident, but do not, apparently, relate this particular tradition.

[2] Stone hoes (or axes), both roughly shouldered and with very carefully squared shoulders, are to be found in various parts of the Naga Hills, and are regarded as thunderbolts.

[3] The Lhotas are to some extent an exception. They know and use the cross-bow, though their Ao, Rengma, Angami and even Sema neighbours do not. North of the Brahmaputra both the long-bow and cross-bow are in use, and one tribe uses the former for shooting fish, special long arrows being used for that purpose.

killing small birds, but as a serious weapon the bow is not used by either tribe; and though the Semas believe that their ancestors used it, the Angamis appear never to have done so, a fact which is interesting in view of the apparent absence or scarcity of the bow in Borneo, Sumatra, and the Celebes (*vide* Ratzel's Map, *op. cit.*, Vol. I. p. 145).

Another point to be noticed is the use of the war drum. Sangtams, or rather Northern Sangtams, Aos and the Konyak tribes, and probably the Yachungr and Chang tribes in some degree, make enormous drums out of a whole tree hollowed through a narrow slit in the top, and the ends carved usually with a mithan head and hornbill tail respectively. This drum, when beaten by the young men who can line up to twenty or thirty or more on each side with drumsticks like dumb-bells, will send a challenge, a pæan of victory, or a dirge for the dead, for miles. But the Southern Nagas—Lhotas, Semas, South Sangtams, Rengmas, Angamis etc.—do not make these drums at all.[1]

Diversity of origin on the part of the Naga tribes is suggested again by a number of miscellaneous considerations. Most Nagas for instance reap with a reaping-hook, but the Sema, like the Manö and Southern Brè (Karens) of Burma,[2] and like the Garos,[3] use their hand only, stripping the grain from the stalk straight into the basket, a most painful method if it does save threshing.

The use of terraced cultivation forms a very marked point of distinction between Naga tribes. The various branches of the Angami tribe practise it in its most elaborate form, followed closely by some Khoirao and Kacha Naga (Nzemi) villages very strongly dominated by Angami culture, and followed in a quite appreciably less elaborate way by Naked Rengmas, Tangkhuls and Maram Nagas. Other tribes do not use irrigated terraces at all, if we except the Semas, among whom it has been deliberately introduced by Government, and who still only practise this form of cultivation in

[1] The Wa of Burma make drums of this sort (*U. B. and S. S. Gazetteer*, I. i. p. 502).

[2] *Upper Burma and Shan States Gazetteer*, I. i. p. 535.

[3] Playfair, *The Garos*, p. 34. So too the Lynngam and Bhois (Gurdon, *The Khasis*, p. 40).

a very small degree, save in a few villages who have adopted Angami culture in general. At the same time, even among the Angamis, the Chakroma villages have no terraces. It may be noted that the Angami system of terraces produces physical features exactly like the system of the Bontoc Igorot in the Philippines.

Among the tribes that jhum there is a marked difference in the method of sowing rice. The more southern tribes—Angami, Lhota, Rengma, Sema—sow carefully, digging a little hollow and dropping in the grain. The Aos and Changs, on the other hand, sow anyhow, just chucking the seed down broadcast, and so do the Konyaks, in so far as they sow rice at all. The amazing fact about the latter is that *taro*, not rice, is the staple crop, and in spite of excellent land for rice cultivation, they only sow very little. They prefer *taro* (*Colocasia antiquorum*).[1]

Closely associated with terraced cultivation is the custom of erecting megalithic monuments. The erectors of the most numerous monoliths are the tribes practising terraced cultivation, though Kacha Nagas (Lyengmei) and Kabuis put up little dolmens and occasional monoliths, while the Lhotas and Rengmas proper, also having no terraced cultivation, yet erect monoliths and alignments of monoliths in all their villages. North and east of the two latter tribes, however, few Nagas seem to put up either, and the place of stones in ceremonial is apparently taken by wooden and Y-shaped posts, used by Semas, Sangtams, Kalyo–Kengyu, Chang and possibly other tribes, while the Ao uses round-topped posts or posts with a divided top.[2] The Garos, it may be noticed, also use the Y-shaped post, while the similarity of both the Y-shaped Sema post and the round-topped Ao post respectively to the bifurcated and round-topped stones left by the old Kachari kings at Dimapur is too close for mere coincidence. It should be added that Mr. Mills tells us that Lhotas occasionally substitute a Y-shaped post for a

[1] The Konyaks also have the custom of blackening their teeth like the Brè Karens of Burma (*U. B. and S. S. Gazetteer*, I. i. p. 534).

[2] Phoms and some Konyaks put up a single erect stone with flat stones round it as a place for the exposure of enemy heads in front of the clan "morung."

stone in their ceremonials where no stones suitable for erection can be found, while there is a kindred of a clan in Yekhum village which migrated from further east and which habitually erects posts, as it is not allowed to erect stones.[1] In building, again, while the Angamis, Tangkhuls, Semas and other tribes south of them build on the ground, the Aos and other tribes to the north build on a bamboo platform or " machan." The Lhota method is a sort of compromise, as when he builds on a " machan " he covers the floor with earth.

Even more than their customs the social constitution of several Naga tribes suggests a diversity of origin. In more than one tribe we find traces of a dual division crossed by a triple one, and indicating a division into three elements, either as three separate groups or as two primary groups, one of which is again split making three. In addition to these there are odd clans descended from " men caught in the jungle " and others, as already mentioned. Thus among the Aos are found two linguistic groups, Chongli and Mongsen, existing side by side in the same villages though retaining frequently their different languages, and always, among the women, their differences of tattoo and of hair-dressing. The word for " mother " in the one of these two Ao languages is *ocha* (Chongli), in the other *avu* (Mongsen). Across this dual division of the Aos we get a triple division into three clans, Pongen, Langkam and Chami, which are nominally at any rate exogamous and which run through both the linguistic groups, though the nomenclature varies, and though the whole exogamous system is somewhat complicated by subdivision and by adoption from one group to

[1] The reason given is that this kindred has never been allowed to carry the village *oha* (sacred stones) at the time of migration, or indeed to touch them at any time.

The Khawlthang sept of the Haokip clan of Thado Kukis also uses Y-shaped posts (*vide* Col. Shakespear's *Lushei-Kuki Clans*, p. 65).

The Angami uses them only in the case of the *Lisü* " genna " performed in Kohima villages only. At this " genna " the spirit of fertility is caused to perambulate the village, symbolized by a Y-shaped and by a phallic post, the former pulled by chaste boys, the latter carried by a man, and representing respectively the female and male organs of generation. It has been already pointed out that the Puchatsuma clan in Kohima has a western origin.

another. Of the three groups mentioned Pongen is generally recognized as *doyen*, while the social position of Chami is usually regarded as decidedly inferior to the other two. Again, among the Southern Konyak villages at any rate there seem to be two linguistic and tattoo groups (one of which tattoos the face of the warrior and the other the chest only) called *Thendu* and *Thenkoh*, while there are said to be also three social divisions running through both groups, of which the first, called Ang,[1] corresponds to the Ao "Pongen" and provides hereditary chiefs in those villages which possess them, though in the case of the Konyak chief the heir to the chieftainship has to be of Ang blood by both parents, contrary to the prevailing exogamous system. In the Rengma tribe we have again two linguistic groups, as among the Aos, existing side by side sometimes in the same village, and called Inseni-Kotsenu and Tseminyu respectively. Of these two groups the latter apparently are again divided into two parts distinguished by the use of different terms for "mother" (*avyo* and *apfsü*).[2] The Angamis are again divided into two groups commonly known as Thevoma and Thekronoma (or Cheroma) or Solhima, using the words *azo* and *apfu* respectively for "mother," although the former term only is in use among the numerous Chakrima sub-tribe of Angamis, though the distinction between the Thekronoma, called by them Solhima, and the Thevoma is recognized. These two divisions of the Angamis may be spoken of as *Pezoma* and *Pepfüma* respectively according to the terms they use for "mother." The *Pezoma* group appears to be also subdivided into Sachema and Thevoma, two divisions of more or less equal status, though the former is actually the senior. Nowadays, however, the Sachema group, which is very small indeed numerically as compared with Thevoma, has been

[1] In some cases the *Ang* has really no political influence at all, and seems to be kept as a sort of "fetish" rather than anything else. Thus Kamahu in 1920, having never had an *Ang*, obtained one from Wanching, "because it was good to have one."

[2] They also have different words for "father," *aphu* and *apyu*, like the Tengima Angamis *apo* and *apvu*. The present census shows a practical equality of those Rengmas using *apfsü* for "mother" with the total of the Tseminyu using *avyo* and the Inseni-Kotsenu using *azao*.

virtually lost sight of, and "Thevoma" includes the whole of the *Pezoma*. It should be added that according to tradition the Thekrono division was originally the elder, but was cheated of its birthright by the first ancestor of the Thevo division. The word *Solhima*, used ordinarily by a large part of the Angami tribe for the Thekronoma division, means "alien" or "stranger."[1] In the Memi group of the Angamis we have again a third division, called Cherhechima in some villages, which is regarded as socially inferior to such an extent that the other Memi will not intermarry with it. This division seems also to be regarded as the source of some unlucky emanation which has an evil influence on any who fall under it, though the neighbouring Tengima, Dzunokehena and Kezami Angamis have no objection at all to intermarrying with the Cherhechima. The Lhotas seem to be divided like the Angami into two phratries using *oyo* for "mother," with a third using *opfu*, and, as in the case of the Angamis, the use of the distinct terms does not extend throughout the whole tribe, but seems to be dying out.[2]

[1] The word is distinct in meaning from *Teprima*, a foreigner from the plains, including Assamese, Bengalis, Europeans, etc. The proportion, as worked out, during the 1921 census, of *Kepezoma* to *Kepepfüma* in the Angami tribe shows a nearly three to one majority of the former among the Tengima and Dzunokehena groups, and a nearly two to one majority in the Chakrima group of the "Thevoma" over "Solhima." This excludes the Kezami and Měmi sub-tribes, of which the former seems to be wholly *Pezoma* and the latter wholly *Pepfüma*, at any rate as far as the terms used are concerned, though the division may exist in fact but have disappeared from the terms of address as in the case of the Chakrima. The bulk of the Memi group are in the Manipur state and were therefore outside the scope of the inquiry. The total figures actually returned from those groups in which the inquiry was made were—

	Kepezoma.	*Kepepfüma.*
Tengima	13,516	4,748
Chakrima	11,051	5,771
Kezami	4,670	—
Memi	—	1,099
Total for those Angamis in the Naga Hills District	27,239	11,618

The census for the Ao tribe showed the Chongli Aos 16,276 souls against 5,809 Mongsen Aos.

[2] The Sema clan of Chishilimi was perhaps originally organized on a dual basis, the clan being descended from two brothers, Chesha and Chishi, and the descendants of one brother being regarded as superior. Here again there was a dispute as to which was the superior division, the descendants of Chishi eventually establishing their claim by chicanery, though Chesha was the elder brother.

Turning to the polity of the village, different tribes have very different customs. Among the Semas a system of hereditary chiefs exists, each chief having an almost feudal position as lord of the manor of his village, a system which seems to have obtained among the Kacharis, as the remnants of it are still perceptible among the remote Kachari villages of the south-west of the Naga Hills. The Changs have a system of chiefs very like that of the Semas, and both may be compared in this respect to the Thado Kukis, though among the latter the system is more elaborately developed. The Konyaks too have hereditary chiefs in the Thendu section of the tribe, though not in the Thenkoh division, but among the Konyaks the priestly side of the chieftainship seems more prominent than among the other Naga tribes with chiefs.[1] On the other hand, the Ao and Tangkhul villages are governed by bodies of elders representing the principal kindreds in the village, while the Angami, Rengma and Lhota and apparently Sangtam villages are run on lines of democracy, a democracy so extreme in the case of the Angami that, in view of his peculiar independence of character, it is difficult to comprehend how his villages held together at all before they were subject to the British Government. The Angami has, however, hereditary priests, office descending in the line of the first founder of the village in question.

In the eschatology of the different tribes there is, on the one hand, a belief apparently universally accepted which regards the souls of the dead as inhabiting butterflies or other insects after death. Concurrently with this we find a belief in an existence in a future world in which the shades of the dead go on living just as they did in this world. Most tribes place this world underground and indicate

[1] Mr. Mills has pointed out to me that the *Ung* clan among the Changs is priestly, and that there must be one of this clan in every Chang village. As the Ung clan is usually spoken of with contempt it doubtless represents a conquered population acquainted with the gods of the soil, at any rate in the Chang country. Chang *Ung* probably = Konyak *Ang* in any case, and the Changs seem to be largely invaders in Phom, Ao or Konyak territory.

some mountain [1]—usually one formed as it were in a succession of rises vaguely suggesting steps from a distance —as the path by which this under-world is approached. The Angamis, however, believe that the souls of the dead who have conformed to the best (Angami) standard of life spend their future existence in the sky in the company of the ancestress or creatrix of all life. Other tribes, though believing in the existence of a sky world, or at any rate of sky spirits, do not locate the home of the dead there. Along with these a third belief is also to be found, as among the Semas, according to which the spirits of the good dead go to the East and those of the unsatisfactory dead to the West.

Among other points worth notice are the fact that lycanthropy practised by the Semas and other tribes to the north of the Angami country is never resorted to by Angamis, though they know of the existence in the belief and even believe in the common origin of the tiger and man.[2] Similarly the Khasis seem to have heard the theory from the Garos, but do not claim ever to practise it themselves.

In folk-lore some stories seem common to nearly all tribes and to the Kacharis too, while the story of the girl who comes out of an orange and the stories of fighting stones and the belief that the human race is becoming gradually smaller and will so continue till it is small enough to climb up a chili plant, are common both to Nagas and to the Khasis.[3]

[1] So, too, the Garo dead point to the peak Chikmang (Playfair, *The Garos*, p. 103). North of the river Brahmaputra the hill tribes are said to have no beliefs as to transmigration into insects.

[2] Mr. Mills has pointed out to me that the Lhota word for a familiar spirit is *Sonyo*, and the familiar usually takes a leopard form, while the Ao word *Chonyu* means "leopard" pure and simple. The Chang word *Saonyu* = "tiger."

The Thado Kukis, while not practising lycanthropy, believe very strongly in vampires and are extremely afraid of offending persons with the reputation of being such. The vampire sends his soul to suck the vitality of other men's souls during sleep. The Meitheis also believe in vampires, but I have not met the belief in any Naga tribe.

[3] The Semas have a story of a stone at Champimi which fought with Tukahu (Japvo) mountain. The Aos have several stones that fight or fought, and the Lhota stories are given by Mr. Mills. It may be noticed that the Aos, like the Khasis, have the practice of divining by breaking eggs and observing the fall of the fragments of shell.

On the other hand, there seem to be certain groups of stories which are not common to the Angamis in the south and to the Changs and their neighbours in the north.

Linguistic considerations are notoriously dangerous in their application to ethnography, but even here it is impossible to pass over without remark the very decided cleavage between the vocabularies and numerals of the languages classified by Sir George Grierson as Western and Central Naga, and the vocabularies and numerals of the Konyaks and Changs to the north-east, though the Aos have words characteristic of both groups. This north-eastern group seems in fact to approach quite appreciably nearer to the Kuki and Bodo languages of the southern tribes than to the languages of the Central Naga tribes in between the two.

Emphasis has sometimes been laid upon an affection for old sites, or an aversion to migration, as characteristic of Nagas, distinguishing them from the migratory Kuki, who, like the Hill Kachari, moves his village by preference, whereas the Naga only moves his under compulsion. This, however, as has already been pointed out, cannot by any means be applied to all tribes at present designated Naga.

A perhaps trivial point is the belief that neglect of washing causes illness, and the concomitant habit of personal cleanliness which is so much more marked in the Angami tribe than among its neighbours to the north, though the Lhota seems to have it in a greater degree than the Rengma, Sema, or Ao; the Angami dwelling, on the other hand, is frequently filthy as compared to those of the other tribes mentioned, principally owing to his habit of keeping his cattle in the front room.

Such are the more outstanding facts of the case, and it is almost superfluous to state the more obvious conclusions to be drawn from them, that no Naga tribe is of pure blood, but the area which they inhabit has been the scene of a series of immigrations from north-east, north-west and south, and that the different stocks introduced in this way have entered into their composition.[1] Indeed, in view of the struggles that have taken place for the fertile plains of Burma to the east and India to the west, it is inevitable that some elements of the races worsted in these struggles should have been pushed up into the hills. In particular the line of the Dikhu and the Ti-Ho rivers would seem to mark more or less the point of contact between movements southward from the north and northward from the south, roughly marking as it does, except indeed for the Ao tribe, the line south of which dead are always buried,[2] and also the marked cleavage between the languages of the Western Nagas and of the North-eastern Nagas, the latter bearing more resemblance perhaps to those of the Kukis in the south than to those of their immediate neighbours. The immigration of Singpho elements from the north and Tai elements from the east are absolutely clear.

The other conclusions I would suggest are some of them frankly speculative, but are perhaps not at variance with current views on the history of Indonesia in general. I should deduce a stage at which some race of Kol-Mon-Annam or Mon-Khmêr affinities was in occupation, leaving traces of that occupation in certain implements, weapons and perhaps in some folk-tales. I should describe the immigration from the north-west or west as definitely Bodo in character, and ascribe to this origin the erection of Y-shaped posts [3] and the practice of reaping by hand, and the indications of the more recent existence of a matrilineal system. Beyond this, whatever the Singphos and Kacharis may be, an admixture of Tai blood from the east is beyond dispute. It is the nature of the immigration from the south which is most intriguing. No one who has had much to

[1] McCulloch, quoted by Hodson (*The Meitheis*, pp. 68, 73), records a Manipuri tradition of the composition of the Manipuri people from different clans that came from the south, the east and the north-west. Mr. Hodson also suggests that the existing population was already located as at present in A.D. 1431 (*op. cit.* p. 74 note).

[2] But north of the Brahmaputra again burial is the rule.

[3] These Y-shaped posts are also used by the Wa of Burma to commemorate the slaughter of buffaloes (*Gazetteer of Upper Burma and the Shan States*, I. i. p. 505), whose village defences (*ibid.* p. 504) must closely resemble those of the Angamis and Kacha Nagas.

do with the Angamis could fail to perceive the difference of disposition and character between them and the other Naga tribes, though it is very difficult to state in what it actually consists, and it is certainly not so great as to constitute an entire distinction between the Angamis and the rest of their fellow-Nagas. My own view is that the Angamis contain a very much greater proportion of blood bequeathed by a mixed body of immigrants from the south (some of them at any rate nearly related either in blood or culture or both to the Igorot of the Philippine Islands), who already consisted perhaps of two races of which the weaker and less numerous was a race of settled habits and developed civilization, while the stronger was of more barbarous but warlike type.[1] The inhabitants they found already in occupation would be either absorbed into one of the two divisions of this mixed tribe or make a third class where they survived in sufficient numbers, and to this source I would ascribe the social institutions of the Western Naga tribes. I would ascribe the elaborate system of terracing to the more civilized of the southern immigrants, and to these southern immigrants in general the use of elaborate stone-work in building and the erection of stone monoliths and perhaps the practice of burying their dead—the Angamis even bury the heads of their enemies—and also perhaps the use of ultra-democratic institutions. If these deductions be correct I should regard the Semas as having received chiefs from the more barbarous of the southerners, and in the Lhotas I should see the result of a more intimate contact of both southern elements with the tribe at present represented by the Sangtams, who seem to have at one time occupied much more of the Naga Hills than they do now that a large and still increasing proportion of their tribe has been absorbed by the more virile Sema. The Khoiraos, Kacha Nagas, Tangkhuls and Marami have all been much more strongly influenced by the culture

[1] It might, of course, be possible to contend that this fusion took place as a result of two consecutive occupations of the Naga Hills themselves, but in my opinion all the evidence points to the fusion having taken place at any rate before the Angamis occupied their present sites. The barbarian element may have been Tai in origin.

of these southern immigrants, than have the other tribes north of the Angami country, and have accepted their culture to varying degrees.

To return to the Lhotas, this tribe is divided into three phratries—the *Tompyaktserre*, the *Izumontserre* and the *Mipongsandre*, meaning respectively "Forehead-clearing men,"[1] "Scattered men" and "Fire-smoke-conquering men." The expression "Forehead-clearing men" I do not attempt to explain,[2] but the phratry corresponds to the Angami *Kepepfüma*, which I have taken to represent the weaker but more civilized section of the southern immigrants. Among the Lhotas it is to be noticed that this phratry is the superior. Among the Angamis it is the inferior, with the tradition, however, that it was once the elder. Its women are addressed by their children as *Apfü* (Angami) or *Apfu* (Lhota). The Lhotas, however, have no terraced cultivation. The clans of the "Scattered-men" phratry use *oyo* for mother in some cases, *opfu* in others, but *oyo* predominating on the whole; but the name suggests a tribe of very different habits to the community-loving Naga, and would better suit a people like the Kacharis or Garos, living in small moving settlements and perpetually shifting from one place to another, a few houses at a time. In the "Fire-smoke-conquering-men," so called from the villages they burnt in warfare, one may see the influence of the more barbarous element of the (? southern) invaders, and the bulk of this phratry uses *ayo* for "mother" like the *Kepezoma* of the Angamis.[3]

I therefore conclude that in most if not all Naga tribes traces are to be found of the Mon-Khmêr and Bodo races, the Tai race, and a fourth race of southern origin akin to

[1] I am indebted to Mr. J. P. Mills for this explanation of the names of the Lhota phratries, which reached me long after I had formed the conclusions which they appear in some degree to strengthen.

[2] The meaning of the Lhota word is, I am told, very doubtful. If correctly interpreted it might perhaps refer to some habit of hairdressing. The Angami, in contradistinction to tribes to the north, brushes his hair up off his forehead; so does the Tangkhul.

[3] I take *azo* and *ayo*, Angami and Lhota respectively for "my mother," to be the same word.

some of the inhabitants of the Philippines and Borneo and other parts of Indonesia.

For the history of this corner of the earth is yet to be written, and, if ever it is done, it is to studies such as Mr. Mills has given us that future investigators will turn, for the tribes themselves will have vanished past all recognition. Has not the very *mingetung* of Phiro hidden its grim fruit in the folds of its own bark, lest the village forget that the days of the head-hunter are gone? Education and Litigation, doubtful apparitions, are usurping his place; the old beliefs wither under the shrivelling touch of Civilization, and the voice of the Missionary is heard in the land. The axe is laid to the root of Igdrasil; the Jötunn are climbing into Asgerd.

J. H. H.

KHORO,
April, 1921.

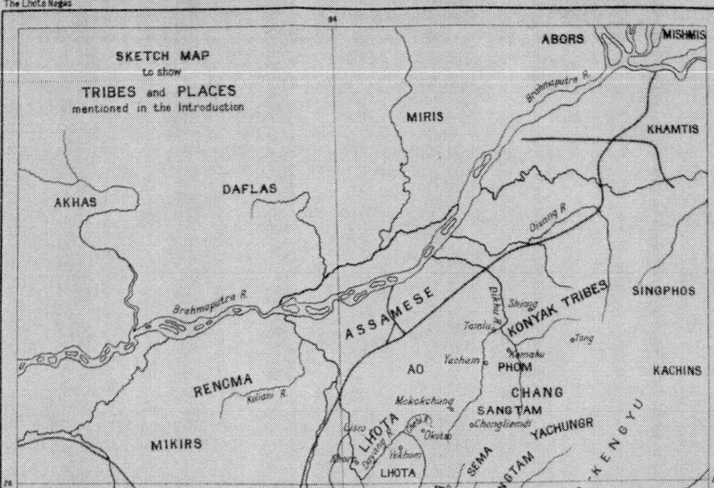

John Bartholomew & Son Ltd. Edin.

THE LHOTA NAGAS

PART I

GENERAL

Introductory—Origin and Migrations—Appearance—Dress—Ornaments—Weapons—Character.

THE Lhota Nagas are a tribe numbering some twenty thousand souls which occupies a piece of territory that may be roughly described as the drainage area of the Middle and Lower Doyang and its tributaries, down to the point where it emerges into the plains. Their land can show extremes of climate, from the high spurs of Wokha Hill, where frost is not unknown, to the malarious foot-hills bordering on the plains, where the heat radiated from the sandstone makes life almost unbearable in the hot weather. They call themselves *Kyŏn*, meaning simply "man," the name Lhota, of which I have been unable to discover any derivation, being that by which they are known to Government. They have long been in contact with the Assamese. Many villages even possess grants of land in the plains given by the Ahom Rajas, on the understanding apparently that the Lhotas in return for the land would refrain from taking Assamese heads. This agreement was loyally kept, and villages such as Khoro, who had no hostile Naga neighbours whom they could raid, used to content themselves with waylaying and killing an occasional Mikir on his way to or from market in the plains. There is no record of any fighting between Lhotas and Assamese, save a raid in 1685 on some villages of the plains near the Doyang by Nagas,[1] who were probably Lhotas: Akuk and Lakhuti claim to have met and defeated a force of Burmese at the time of the Burmese invasion of Assam.[2] The first recorded meeting between a European and Lhotas is that of Lieut. H. Bigge in 1841, who apparently did not like what little he saw of them. He calls them "a sullen race," and says that they "are alike filthy in their persons and habits, and have a pompous mode of addressing one which might in some cases be interpreted as insolent."[3] Evidently the gallant officer found the contrast between the suave, sleek plainsman and the easy-going, unwashen hillman rather startling. Captain Brodie, however, the first Englishman to visit the Lhota at home, was more fortunate. He marched along part of the Lakhuti range in 1844 and was given a most friendly reception.[4] In 1875 Captain Butler when in charge of a survey party was ambushed by the village of Pangti and mortally wounded. The truth of this disaster is as follows: Captain Butler arranged to march from Lakhuti to Pangti, and ordered the former village to supply men to carry his baggage. Lakhuti, which had old scores to wipe off against Pangti, decided to lay a trap for them, and sent a message asking them to attack the head of the column, while promising that they themselves would throw down their loads and attack the rear. Pangti fell into the snare and ambushed and speared Captain Butler. Lakhuti did nothing, and of course got off scot free, while Pangti was burnt. Naturally Pangti has never forgiven Lakhuti for this piece of treachery. In 1878 a stockade was established at Wokha and all the

[1] Gait's *History of Assam*, p. 162.

[2] The Lhota villagers on the outer range relate that the Burmese visited them in a horde which moved on from village to village, looting everything they could find and eating all the food supplies and defiling the houses in a very Prussian way before leaving, the Lhota inhabitants having fled to the jungle on the approach of the Burmese. One Lhota, who related this to me, said that the Burmese (*mān*) must, in his opinion, have been some sort of spirit or godling, but another contradicted him, saying that he knew well that the *mān* were men like themselves.—J. H. H.

[3] *Journal of the Asiatic Society of Bengal*, No. 110, 1841, p. 162.

[4] *Selection of Papers regarding Hill Tracts between Assam and Burmah and on the Upper Brahmaputra*. Bengal Secretariat Press, 1873, pp. 295 *sqq*.

Ndrung villages,[1] *i. e.* those on the left bank of the Doyang, were annexed. The rest of the tribe was annexed in 1889.

Origin and Migration.

The problem of the ultimate origin and composition of the Naga tribes still awaits solution. It will be sufficient if I give here the main Lhota traditions of their origin and early migrations. These are various and mutually inconsistent. One, but not the commonest, states that the Lhotas and plainsmen were once one people who migrated from a place called Lengka somewhere north or north-west of the Naga Hills, the exact site being unknown. They soon split up into two bodies, one of which became the plainsmen of the Brahmaputra valley and the other the Nagas of the hills. The curious long-hafted daos called *yanthang*, a few of which are still kept as highly-prized heirlooms, are specially connected with this tradition, and are said to have been given to the Nagas by their " brothers " of the plains. Some at any rate are not of Naga manufacture. One which was shown me at Okotso, for instance, was ornamented with brass bands. The usual tradition, however, gives the Lhotas an autochthonous origin, and is almost identical with that told by the Angamis of themselves. The story goes that three brothers, Limhachan, Izumontse and Rankhanda, the ancestors of the three phratries of the tribe, came out of a hole in the earth near the miraculous stone at Kezakenoma. If one load of rice were dried on this stone it became two loads. Owing, however, to the indecent behaviour of a man of the tribe the virtue went out of the stone,[2] and the Lhotas set out on

[1] Lhotas living left of the Doyang are known as Ndrung, and those on the right bank as Liye. The division of the tribe into two sections by a river which is unfordable for a great part of the year has led to slight diversity of dialect and custom.

[2] The following is the Lhota version of how the miraculous properties of the Kezakenoma stone were destroyed: In order to put an end to the quarrels of the brothers as to whose turn it was to dry, and double, his paddy, an old woman, who had no husband, and an old man who had no wife, were selected and these two had connection lying on the stone. This

their migrations, taking with them a little piece of the stone, which is still preserved at Pangti. Yet another tradition says that the common ancestors of the Lhotas, Southern Sangtams, Semas and Rengmas, came from somewhere near Mao. The first to split off were the Southern Sangtams, with whom the Lhotas claim close affinities.[1] It is said, for instance, that many generations ago a Lhota from Lungitang, knowing that his forefather had left "brothers" south of the Tizu, somehow made his way through the Sema country and brought back with him a Southern Sangtam, whose last descendant, by name Ezanyimo, died at Wokha about ten years ago. Old men say that specimens of the round brass ornaments (*pyabi*) which Southern Sangtams wear on their "lengtas," and of axe-shaped Sangtam daos, were preserved as heirlooms in some Lhota houses to within living memory. From Mao the tribe migrated slowly to Kohima, and from there, with the Angamis pressing them in the rear, reached the neighbourhood of Lozema, where the Semas are said to have split off. Thence they moved slowly on till they reached Themoketsa Hill, known to the Lhotas as *Honohoyanto* (fowl-throat-cutting-village). Here the mist begins to clear a little and most Lhotas claim to trace their descent back through nine or ten generations to some ancestor who lived at Honohoyanto. At this point the Rengmas split off and occupied their present country, while the Lhotas pressed on, one body through Phiro and Saki to the Lower Doyang, fighting the Angamis as they went, and another body to Wokha Hill, where a huge village called Lungcham is said to have been founded a little to the north of the present

destroyed its miraculous properties. Possibly the idea was that the sexual act between these old people was bound to be sterile and that this sterility should be communicated to the highly prolific stone. The Rengmas have this story as well as the Lhotas. In *The Angami Nagas* (pp. 19 and 362) I have recorded other accounts, both Rengma and Angami, of the manner in which the stone was rendered unfruitful, and suggested that the methods aimed rather at offending or hurting the spirit in the stone, an explanation perhaps equally applicable to the Lhota version.—J. H. H.

[1] The languages of the Lhotas and Southern Sangtams are very closely akin.

site of Niroyo. So vast was the crowd of warriors that at feasts and "gennas" there was never enough "madhu" to go round, though each man was only given one cock's spurful as his share. It was clear that they must split up or starve, so they began to move off and found villages, sometimes ousting the Aos, who were once in possession of almost the whole of the present Lhota country, and sometimes occupying vacant sites to which they were led by various omens. A common story, told to account for the founding of Lungsachung, Lotsü and several villages, runs as follows: A man had a sow which wandered off one day and could not be found. He tracked it for miles, till he found it lying under a big tree, where it had littered. He at once decided to found a new village on the spot, and the tree where the sow had littered became the head-tree.

Ceremonies connected with the founding of a new village.

But the days of expansion are over now, and in many a village abandoned house sites and "genna" stones all overgrown with jungle show how the tribe is shrinking. Yet attempts are still made from time to time to reoccupy the sites of old villages wiped out by malaria, and the ceremonies connected with the founding of a new village deserve to be described. Having selected a site with a good water supply and a tree suitable for a head-tree (*mingetung*), the would-be founder [1] cuts a branch from a bush on the site. If the cut is a clean one and no leaves fall the omen is good. If the branch is not cut through with one blow or leaves fall the omen is bad. The omens being good he and his fellow-colonists select a man to be priest (*Puthi*) of the new village, and while still retaining the old village as their headquarters, set to work to clear the jungle on the new site. Before doing so, however, the *Puthi* throws a cornelian bead into the spring which is to supply the new village with water, and prays that the young men and maidens of the village may be strong. After the jungle has been cut the founder makes

[1] A village was not always founded by one man. It was quite common for two men of different clans to join at founding a new village, each bringing his quota of families. Each clan would supply wives for the other, and the inconveniences of marriage outside the village were thus avoided.

new fire with a fire-stick [1] (*mi-hm*). The *Puthi* then spears a small boar, which must not be singed in the fire, and cuts the throat of a cock, from the entrails of which he takes the omens. The pig is cut up, and the *Puthi* makes a little square of sticks on the ground. In the middle he puts an egg and on each side thirty tiny pieces of pork. All eat the rest of the pig, the pot in which the meat was boiled being turned upside down on the ground and left behind. The jungle having been burnt and a small "morung" constructed, houses are built. When the village is ready for occupation the colonists go to it from the old village in ceremonial dress and fully armed, taking with them a branch stolen from the *mingetung* of the old village. This they stick in the ground under the head-tree of the new village. To ensure a good water supply in their new home they must bring water in a freshly-cut section of bamboo from the spring of the old village and pour it into that of the new. If they are lucky enough to be able to steal them they also put under their *mingetung* and in their "morung" luck-stones (*oha*) from the old village, thereby ensuring good fortune for their new home. About a month later the ceremony of *oyantsoa* (village-making) is performed. This will be described later in connection with the institution of a new *Puthi*.[2]

Appearance.

In colour the Lhota varies from light to medium brown, the inhabitants of the low ranges tending to be darker than those of high villages. The complexion even of the fairest girls is sallow, and the almost rosy cheeks one sometimes sees among the Angamis, and more rarely among the Semas, are unknown in the Lhota country. The hair is as a rule

[1] The fire-stick of the Lhotas is precisely similar to that of the Semas and other Naga tribes. A small piece of dry wood is split and a little stone put in as a wedge. The fork so formed is laid over some cotton wool or whatever is used as tinder, the operator holding it in place with his foot. A strip of dry bamboo is put under the fork, which is notched to keep it in place, and pulled backwards and forwards till the friction causes the tinder to smoulder.

[2] See pp. 122 *sqq.*

AN ELDERLY MAN OF LUNGITANG WEARING *LUNGPENSÜ* AND BIG EAR-PADS

YOUNG MARRIED WOMAN (OF OKOTSO)

[To face p. 7.

straight, though wavy and curly hair is often seen in the villages near the Ao border, in which there is almost certainly a considerable admixture of Ao blood.[1] The hair of a Lhota child is brown, with a distinct rusty tinge, becoming black in the adult. Young men usually pluck out the hairs of the chin with the nails of the thumb and forefinger, but middle-aged and elderly men sometimes have considerable beards, particularly near the plains, where types may occasionally be seen hardly distinguishable in outward appearance from Sylhet Mahommedans. The eyes are brown and slightly oblique in many individuals, the scantiness of the outer half of the eyebrows accentuating the Mongolian appearance of the face. Men average about five feet eight in height and women some three inches less. In build the Lhota is slight, but strong and wiry, though he has not the enormous calf development of the Angami. The hands and feet are small and well formed. The big toe is set rather far apart from the others, and a Lhota talking will often pick up a stone in his toes and tap the ground with it, just as a European might pick up a pencil in his fingers and fidget with it.

The style of hair-cutting resembles that of the Semas, Aos and other tribes. The back and sides of the head are shaved all round up to a point level with the top of the ears, the hair on the crown of the head being left long enough to reach to the top of the shaven portion.[2] When asked why they have adopted this style of hair-cutting they say that their forefathers used to wear their hair long, but took to cutting it in the present fashion because it kept getting into their eyes and catching in the jungle. The custom obtaining in the Southern Sangtam village of Phulangrr perhaps gives the clue to the real origin of the fashion. There no man is allowed to shave the back and sides of his head till he has killed an enemy in war. Till then he wears his hair cut more or less like a European. Little Lhota girls have their heads

[1] Wavy hair is common among the Aos and Konyaks, and curly hair far from rare.

[2] In villages near the Rengma border individuals are often to be seen who have adopted the Rengma custom and shaved their heads so high up all round that practically nothing but a small cap of hair is left.

completely shaved till they are about seven years old, when the hair is allowed to grow. Women wear their hair in an untidy bun on the nape of the neck, tied round with a bunch of strings of their own hair.

Baldness and grey hair are both uncommon and disliked, and old men sometimes hide their scanty locks under a wig of black goat's hair on a bamboo frame. All children have the lobe of the ear pierced at the conclusion of the birth "genna." At the first *Ramo*[1] "genna" he attends a boy has a hole pierced in the upper part of the helix. This is done with a pointed piece of bamboo, and no special ceremonies are attached to the operation. Among the Southern Lhotas, and occasionally among the Northern, another hole is pierced in the middle of the concha at the next *Ramo*. The holes in the helix and concha are for the cotton wool with which the ear is adorned and often become much distended in the case of elderly men.

Circumcision is not practised and neither sex is tattooed.

Dress.

Clothes. The one garment never discarded by a man in public is the *rive*, commonly spoken of in Naga-Assamese as "lengta." This consists of a long narrow piece of stout cloth ending in a broad flap. In putting it on the narrow piece is wound once round the waist so that it joins at the back and forms a belt. It is then brought through between the legs from the back, and up through the belt, the broad flap being allowed to hang down in front. The result is a garment which is both serviceable and entirely decent. The flap is either white or dark blue, with horizontal red stripes, broad among the Northern Lhotas and narrow among the Southern. In the old days a dark blue *rive* could only be worn by a man who had done the head-taking "genna," but this distinction is being rapidly dropped. A boy's first garment, assumed without any ceremonies when about seven or eight years old, is the flap of one of his father's discarded "lengtas" hung from a bit of string tied round his waist.

[1] *Vide* p. 108.

The skirt (*sürham*) worn by the women is about twenty-two inches deep. It is bound tightly round the waist and the overlapping top corner tucked in in front of the left hip. The edge which shows is often ornamented with iridescent beetle wings or bits of yellow orchid stalk. Among the Northern Lhotas the *sürham* is of dark blue cloth with narrow horizontal red stripes in threes, and a band of paler blue embroidered with red three inches broad running round the middle of the cloth. The skirts worn by Southern women have no red stripes, and the pale blue band is broader and nearer the top of the cloth. When about five or six years old a little girl puts on her first skirt (*khondrosü*). This is about ten inches deep, white with a dark blue border and a little red embroidery in the middle.

When working in the fields, or in the hot weather even when lounging about at home, a man usually wears nothing but his "lengta." When visiting his friends, however, or to sit about in the shade, or for a journey he always wears a body-cloth measuring about four feet by five feet. Usually such a cloth is simply wrapped round the body under the right armpit and over the left shoulder. But for any occupation such as hunting, where both arms must be left free, and whenever a cloth is worn at any "genna," it is tied on to the body as follows: The cloth is flung over the back, and the two top corners are brought round, one under the left arm and the other over the right shoulder, and tied across the chest. The two bottom corners are then brought up outside the cloth which is hanging over the back, and crossed and tied on the chest, one passing over the left shoulder and the other under the right arm.

The body-cloths are of various patterns and indicate the number of social "gennas" [1] performed by the wearer. The first is *sütam*, a white cloth with broad dark blue horizontal stripes. This is worn by boys [2] and men who have

[1] For description of social "gennas" see Part IV.

[2] As is the case among the Semas, a boy may if he likes wear any cloth to which his father is entitled while he lives with him. When he marries, however, and sets up house on his own, he may only wear those cloths to which he is entitled in his own right.

performed no social "gennas." A man who has performed the first social "genna" may wear the *phangdhrap*. Among the Northern Lhotas this is a dark blue cloth, edged with broad stripes of red with a broad strip of white cloth running across the middle of the cloth parallel with the red stripes. Among the Southern Lhotas the red stripes are narrower and a pale blue band near the top of the cloth takes the place of the white band. A Northern Lhota who has performed both the first social "genna" and the head-taking "genna" wears a cloth called *chamthe*, which is exactly like the *phangdhrap* of his section of the tribe, save that the median band is pale blue instead of white. For the performance of the second social "genna" no cloth is awarded, but the Southern Lhotas put on the *ethasü* after performing the third social "genna." This is a dark blue cloth edged top and bottom with four red bands, the body of the cloth being ornamented with little squares of red embroidery. Finally, a man who has completed the series of social "gennas" by dragging a stone wears a handsome cloth called *lungpensü*, which is dark blue with five bands of light blue about one inch broad, and three very narrow lines of light blue at top and bottom A man who has dragged a stone more than once has four or rarely even five narrow lines at the top and bottom of his cloth, which is called *eshamsü*. The *rükhusü* ("enemy-frightening-cloth") of the Southern Lhotas is rarely worn nowadays, and can only be assumed by old warriors of note. It consists of a *lungpensü* or *eshamsü* with a broad median band of white cloth ornamented with highly conventionalized representations of men drawn on cloth with black gum. These bands are made by Rengmas, never by Lhotas. The *rükhusü* of the Northern Lhotas is exactly similar to the cloth ordinarily worn by rich Aos, and is dark blue with six very broad red stripes, set closely together at top and bottom. The median band, which is always bought from the Aos, is about two and a half inches broad, and ornamented with a conventional design representing human heads, mithan horns and tigers.

Like the men, the women usually leave the upper part of

Drawing by Miss E. Paterson.]

ORNAMENTATION OF MEDIAN BAND OF *RÜKHUSÜ*.

Top, Northern Lhotas. *Bottom*, Southern Lhotas. The former contains combination of mithan and human heads, and the latter represents a row of warriors in full dress.

[To face p. 10.

the body bare, though filthy waistcoats are nowadays commonly worn by both men and women in villages near the plains. When body-cloths are worn by women they are either flung loosely round the body so that the top outer corner lies over the left shoulder, or bound tightly under the armpits. Among the Northern Lhotas an unmarried girl usually wears a plain dark blue cloth (*muksü*). On the night of her marriage, however, when she goes to her husband's house, she puts on a very pretty cloth called *loroesü*, dark blue, with big squares of narrow white and red lines, giving a sort of tartan effect. When her husband has dragged a stone she may exchange her *loroesü* either for a *lungpensü*, which is almost exactly similar to his, or for a *charaksü*, a cloth closely resembling *loroesü*, but with the tartan squares outlined with much broader red lines. Among the Southern Lhotas unmarried women and wives of men who have not yet dragged a stone wear a cloth called *süpang*, dark blue, with a broad light blue horizontal band near the top. When her husband has dragged a stone a woman wears a *lungpensü*.

In wet weather men and women wear slung on their backs light rain-shields (*phuchyo*) made of broad leaves carefully arranged between two layers of basket work, and strengthened by an edging of thin split bamboo.

Ornaments.

Apart from the finery in which he decks himself on ceremonial occasions, the well-to-do Lhota usually wears certain ornaments on any occasion when he wishes to be well dressed. In the holes in the helix and concha of his ear are tufts of cotton wool. Usually these are quite small, but old men in villages near the Sema border often wear big wing-shaped pads of cotton wool like those worn by their Sema neighbours, Some small ornament, such as a little brass wire spiral, is worn in the lobe of the ear, or in some villages an ornament formed of two or three porcupine quills, bound with yellow orchid stalk on to a bit of cane boiled ebony black in pig's fat. Like Semas and Aos,

Lhotas wear above the elbow armlets (*koro*) consisting of sections sawn from an elephant's tusk. Formerly the sole supply came from elephants killed locally. Now Angami traders buy ivory in Calcutta and Benares and sell armlets ready sawn. Only old men may saw up a tusk. For a young man to do so would be very unlucky. A man who cannot afford real ivory will sometimes wear an armlet made of white wood smoothed and rounded to resemble the real article. Wristlets (*khekap*) of cowries sewn on cloth may be worn by anyone who has done the head-taking "genna." [1] A man who has got first, second or third spear in at the killing of an enemy has a little cross of cowries at the top of his wristlets. Those worn by the Northern Lhotas are identical with the Sema type. They are bought from the Aos and are composed of cowries filed down till they are very narrow and sewn close together on to a cloth foundation. A red hair fringe (*khezi*) is worn, on the wristlets, ordinarily short, but of long hair in the case of a warrior of note. A man who has been in at the death of a tiger has little bunches of black hair in his red fringe. The wristlets of the Southern Lhotas are of unfiled cowries and the red hair fringe is rarely worn.

The commonest form of necklace is one composed of four or five strings of black beads made from the seeds of the wild plantain (*eshe*). Sometimes they are worn loosely round the neck, and sometimes are in the form of a tight necklet, the rows being kept in place by narrow pierced conch-shell supports. These supports are sometimes bought from Angamis and sometimes prepared by the Lhotas themselves, with the aid of a primitive but effective pump-drill, with a point made from a piece of an old umbrella stay. To do the head-taking "genna" entitles a man to wear a neck ornament of one or two pairs of wild boar's tushes (*soho*), with their bases bound with red cane, and

[1] What appears to be the original form of this ornament is still worn in some Eastern Chang villages. It consists of a long string of white wild Job's tear seeds, which is made for and given to a man by a girl with whom he is carrying on a flirtation. Further to the west the seeds are sewn in rows on to a cloth wristlet, and among the Aos cowries take the place of the seeds.

Photo by J. H. Hutton.]

SOUTHERN LHOTAS IN FULL DRESS

Both are wearing leggings and gibbon hair wigs, and the one on the left is wearing a double tail.

Photo by J. H. Hutton.]

CHAMIMO OF PANGTI

A Northern Lhota with his two wives standing by the stone he has dragged. He is wearing the cloth called *rükhusü*.

[*To face p.* 13.

fastened with a square conch-shell button with a cornelian bead in the middle.

The women's ornaments are few and simple, and the magnificent strings of cornelian beads worn by Ao and Sema women are rarely seen among the Lhotas. In the lobe of the ear is some simple little ornament such as a bunch of the crest feathers of the kalij pheasant bound round with red wool or yellow orchid stalk. Round the neck the usual plantain seed necklace is worn, sometimes with a big conch-shell pendant (*lakup*) in front. Above each elbow is a thick round pewter armlet (*tiwo*), and on each wrist four or five small flat brass bracelets (*rambam*). The armlets and bracelets are bought ready-made from the plains.

The full dress of the Lhota warrior closely resembles that of the Sema and Ao. Besides the ornaments already mentioned, he wears on his head a wig (*thongko*) either of the long hair from the neck and shoulders of the Himalayan black bear, or of the fur of the arms of the male gibbon. In his wig he may wear three king-crow feathers (*yizememhi*) if he has done the head-taking "genna" once, or if he has done it more than once, one hornbill tail feather (*reching'mhi*) for each occasion. On his ears he hangs big pads of cotton wool, and sticks in the lobe of his ear an ornament (*tera*) of drongo and scarlet minivet feathers. If he has ever in his life raided enemies working in the fields and carried off their property, he adds to the *tera* little brass chains of Assamese, or very rarely Lhota, manufacture, which he loops over his ears. Across his chest he wears one, or, if he has dragged a stone, two baldricks (*ritsen*), which are really glorified strings for supporting the "tail," which in turn is an elaboration of the "panji" basket. The Northern Lhotas wear baldricks bought from the Semas, made of blue cloth embroidered in scarlet with dog's hair, and edged with a deep fringe of scarlet goat's hair, with a line of yellow orchid stalk at the base of the fringe. Those worn by the Southern Lhòtas lack the fringe and are usually embroidered with wool bought from the plains. The human hair "tails" are of two types, one (*tsichap*) in which the hair falls straight from the little basket, and the other (*tsongotsichap*) in which the hair forms a deep fringe hanging from a piece of wood sticking out behind with a slight upward curve. In the old days the hair for tails was obtained from women killed in raids, but this source of supply being now closed, it is bought from any woman who is willing to sell her tresses. I am told that one lady can produce two good crops, but that the third crop is apt to be coarse. A warrior of note may wear either on his chest or between his shoulders at the back an ornament called *rüho* (enemy's teeth). This consists of a flat piece of wood, about ten inches long and five inches deep, covered with fine plaited work of red cane, with a border of cowries and a fringe of scarlet goat's hair at the ends and bottom. It is supposed to represent the head of an enemy, the red cane being the tongue and palate, the cowries the teeth, and the fringe of red hair the blood pouring out of the mouth. A man who has dragged a stone may wear between his shoulders at the back the head of a Great Indian Hornbill, a bird regarded by the Lhotas as symbolical of wealth. The true Lhota cowrie apron (*phuhorive*), which is now being rapidly ousted by the bigger one worn by Semas and Aos, is about fourteen inches deep and twelve inches broad, the bottom two-thirds being covered with closely set rows of cowries. A man who has been first, second, or third spear at the killing of an enemy may have the plain cloth above the sheet of cowries ornamented with little crosses of cowries. An old ceremonial apron preserved as an heirloom by Ovungtheng of the Chorothui clan in Nungying village is possibly a specimen of the original type of this garment. The tradition is that the apron in question, which is a square of red cloth measuring ten inches long by eight inches broad, ornamented with two little circles flanked by little stars of cowries, is an exact copy made two generations ago of the original apron worn by the ancestor of the clan when he came down from the sky.[1] The original was preserved till the time of Ovungtheng's grandfather, when it was destroyed in a fire. To within living memory small round brass plates (*pyabi*) with a perforated boss in the centre were worn with cowrie

[1] See p. 91.

A LHOTA WARRIOR IN FULL DRESS

(Ranchamo of Seleku)

[To face p. 14

aprons. Exactly similar plates are worn by Changs and Southern Sangtams at the present day. These plates were worn not only at dances and on ceremonial occasions, but also at the ceremony of calling a sick man's soul. For dances the Southern Lhotas wear huge, bulging Angami leggings (*chori*) of plaited red cane, with a pattern in yellow orchid stalk worked in them. The Northern Lhotas wear a different type, which fits much more closely to the leg. These they buy from the Aos, who in turn get them from the Changs, to whom they are sold by the makers, the Northern Kalyo–Kengyu.

Weapons.

Easily first in importance is the dao (*lepok*), which is used for every variety of purpose. With it a Lhota can slay his enemy or cut up a chicken, fell a forest tree or pare down the finest strip of cane, dig a hole for a post or cut a thorn out of his foot. Villages near the plains usually buy their daos from Assamese smiths. These weapons consist of a straight-edged blade about twelve inches long, and four inches broad at the top, narrowing down to an inch or less at the haft, which is fitted into a bamboo handle tightly bound round with cane. Like all Naga daos the blade is ground on one side only, so that a perpendicular stake can only be cut by a downward blow from the right or upward blow from the left. The daos made by the Northern Lhotas are practically identical with those bought from the Assamese. Those made by the Southern Lhotas are far heavier weapons. The blade is about twelve inches long. At the top it is five inches broad, narrowing down to one and a half inches at the haft. Both edge and back are slightly curved and the junction of the edge and top is prolonged into a small beak.

Two obsolete types of dao require mention. One is the axe-shaped dao called by the Lhotas *tšonak*, the use of which is now confined to the Southern Sangtams and other Trans-Tizu tribes. Lhotas, however, state quite definitely that they formerly used these daos, and old men say that when they were young they talked to old men who could remember the days when a few were still preserved.[1] The other obsolete type is that known as *yanthang*. These are supposed to have been brought from the north-west in the olden days, and a number of them are still kept as heirlooms. They vary much in shape, but usually have very long, narrow blades and always terminate in a long haft which must have passed right through the wooden grip, as it does in the case of the Kabui dancing dao. These daos are much treasured and are only produced at "gennas," when they are stuck upright, haft down, into the ground. The most famous is that of the hero Ramphan which is preserved at Akuk.[2]

Daos are carried in a wooden holder (*lechap*). This, like that of the Aos and Semas, consists of a solid block of wood some eight inches long by two and a half inches broad, pierced from top to bottom by a slit about six inches long and broad enough to admit the blade, but too narrow to let the handle slip through. The holder is carried at the back attached to a loose belt (*lechapsü*), which may be either dark blue or white, and in the case of a man who has done the head-taking "genna" is embroidered with red.[3] The dao, of course, hangs blade down, but whereas all other tribes carry their daos with edge to the left, the Lhota carries his with the edge to the right.

Next in importance is the spear (*otso*), which is always thrown, and never used for thrusting, the extreme effective range being about thirty yards. The length of the whole weapon is usually about six feet or rather more. The favourite wood for the shaft is "nahor" (*mesna ferrea*), but palm and other woods are also used. The shaft is

[1] The Changs say they gave up the use of these daos three generations ago. The Aos probably did so about the same time, but they still keep a few as heirlooms, and the leader of the dance at a big feast holds one in his hand.

[2] Some villages seem to regard this particular dao only as *yanthang* and either do not know, or refuse to admit, the existence of a whole class of daos called by that name.—J. H. H.

[3] I was told in Yimbang that though the red embroidered *lechapsü* was worn originally for taking part in a raid, it may now be worn by "anyone who has ever carried a load for Government," *i. e.* by all able-bodied Lhotas.—J. H. H.

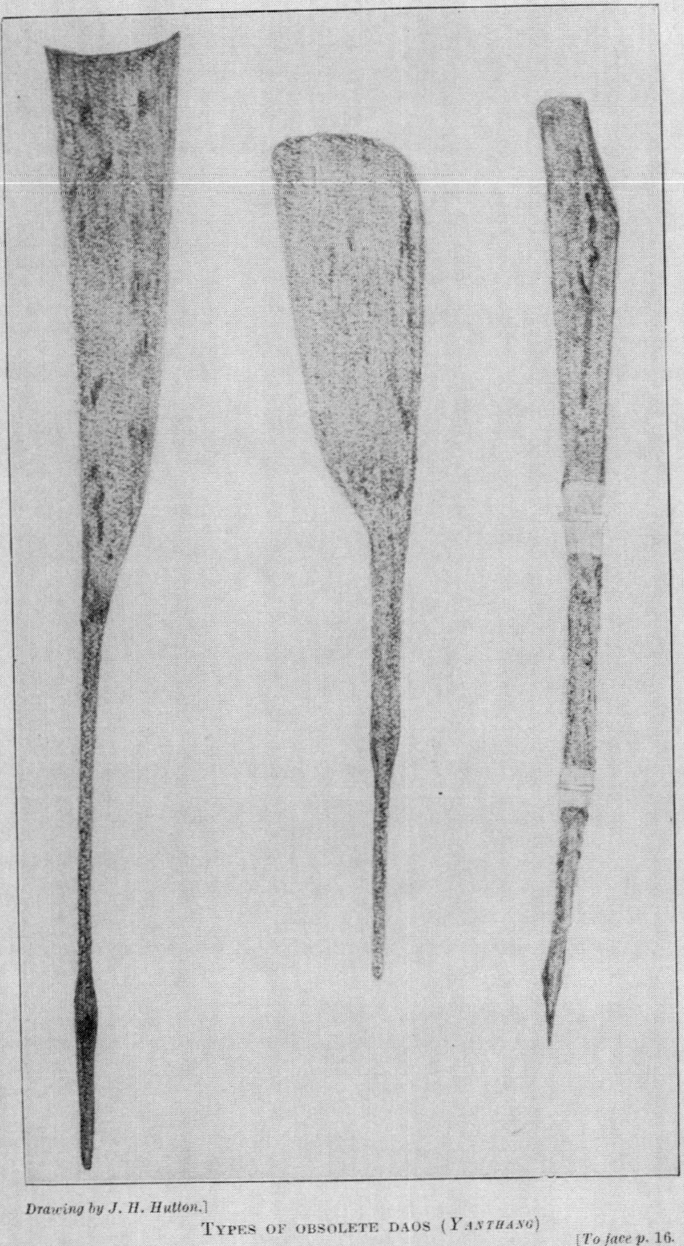

Drawing by J. H. Hutton.]

TYPES OF OBSOLETE DAOS (*Yanthang*)

[To face p. 16.

tightly fitted into a socket in the head without binding of any kind, and terminates in a sharp, socketed butt. No counterpoise is used. Occasionally spears are made of one piece of iron—head, shaft and butt. These are especially useful in tiger hunting, where the animal is liable to bite off the shaft of any spear that wounds him. Among the Northern Lhotas the blades are usually of the elongated lozenge type. They are both bought from the Aos and made locally. The Southern Lhotas usually buy Rengma-made blades of the Angami type, which are leaf-shaped with two short flanges at right-angles to the mid-rib. The average length of the blade is about ten inches, but on some ceremonial spears they may be seen up to two feet in length. A big blade with long barbs such as Angamis sometimes carry (*noringtso*) is occasionally used in Moilang and the neighbouring villages. There are several kinds of decorated shaft. That of the ceremonial spear (*phui*) carried by religious officials, such as the *Puthi* and *Wokchungs*, is covered throughout almost the whole of its length with long black goat's hair. The doing of the head-taking "genna" entitles a man to carry a spear the shaft of which is ornamented with scarlet goat's hair, bound on with string and then clipped short till it resembles very coarse velvet. If he has also been in at the death of a tiger there will be one or two narrow bands of black hair inserted in the scarlet. None of these red shafts are of Lhota manufacture. The northern section of the tribe buy theirs from the Aos, who in turn get them from the Changs. One type, called *kamang*, is only covered with red pile for about a foot of its length from the top. In the other type (*chovemo*) a space for the hand separates two long pieces of pile, the bottom one of which terminates in a deep fringe of red hair. The Rengmas supply the Southern Lhotas with their red shafts. One type, called *tandhro*, resembles *kamang*; another type is very like *chovemo*, but has no fringe and is called *rophutung*.

The cross-bow (*olo*) is still used for shooting birds and monkeys. The stock, made of hard wood, is about twenty-seven inches long, with a groove to keep the arrow in place.

When strung the string, which is of twisted *tchhütsang* bark, catches in a piece of notched bone inserted in the stock near the butt. Underneath is a trigger, which on being pulled tips the string forward and releases it. The bow itself, which is about five feet long and tapered off at the ends, is usually made of bamboo. To be strung the bow has to be held on the ground with the foot with the stock pointing upwards, and the string pulled up to the notch with both hands. An arrow (*lotsi*) is then placed in the groove. The arrows are merely pointed slips of bamboo about a foot and a half long, with a little bit of "hair-brush palm" (*shawo*) or bamboo leaf-sheath fixed in a slit at the end as a feather. They are carried in a small bamboo quiver (*lotsiphu*). The weapon is amazingly effective up to about eighty yards. Poison is never used.

In the old days shields (*otsung*) were always carried in war and are still used at tiger and leopard hunts. Usually they are of strong bamboo twilled pattern matting, but hide shields (*tsungkuk*) are also used. Sometimes a piece of buffalo skin is simply cut to the right shape and dried in the sun, and sometimes a piece of bear skin is stretched over a bamboo matting foundation. Shields are of two types. Those of the Northern Lhotas are about four and a half feet long and twenty inches broad, with a rounded top and parallel sides. Those of the Southern Lhotas are of about the same length, but have a square top and are only some fourteen inches across at the bottom, broadening out to twenty inches at the top. In battle shields were always carried held well away from the body, for though they were not tough enough to turn a spear thrown directly at them, they would check any spear which pierced them sufficiently to prevent it reaching the body.

Stout cane war-helmets (*kiven*), about six inches high in the crown, are still worn by the Southern Lhotas as a protection for the head at tiger hunts, and also at dances, when they are often ornamented with serow horns. Among the Northern Lhotas only a very few now exist, and these, gorgeously ornamented, are only worn by *Puthis* and very senior warriors at the dance connected with the building of a new "morung." They are covered with a coarse cloth made of scarlet dog's hair, with long strings of the same material hanging down behind. On the covering are sown pairs of boar's tushes, each pair forming a circle, while two long flat pieces of wild mithan horn, shaved down to the thickness of cardboard, fixed one on each side complete the effect.

Character.

Writers in the past have, as a rule, either ignored or maligned the Lhota. Captain Butler speaks of "the surly Lhota," and Colonel Shakespear dismisses them as "uninteresting people with dirty persons and villages." [1] They are reserved and do not readily open their hearts to a stranger, but they are not surly. Their sense of humour is well developed and they are always ready with a laugh, but, like all Nagas, they hate being laughed at and believe that misfortune or sickness is likely to fall upon anyone who is the object of derision. Though the tribe contains a few habitual criminals they are, on the whole, very honest. Petty theft is rare, and a man can leave his spear and cloth by the side of a village path knowing that he will find his property untouched when he comes to pick it up on his way home. In warfare they were probably no more cowardly than their neighbours, and when hunting tigers and other dangerous game they show extraordinary pluck. For an expedition they will supply carriers unequalled for steadiness and discipline by any other tribe. The standard of morals varies in a curious way from village to village, but the Lhota husband does not imitate the habitual unfaithfulness of the Ao, nor does he, like the Sema, boast of his immoralities and decorate the grave of a deceased Don Juan with a tally of his liaisons.

Children as they grow up and marry leave their old parents to fend for themselves in what seems to us rather a heartless way, but at a pinch they are usually ready to help to support them. In this the Lhota stands midway between the

[1] Col. L. W. Shakespear, *History of Upper Assam, Upper Burma and North-Eastern Frontier*, p. 202.

Konyak, who regards it as one of his chief duties in life to live with and help his aged parents, and the Ao, who usually never thinks of supporting his old father or mother, and even if he does so turns him out at last to end his days in a miserable little hut, "lest he should defile the house by dying in it." Towards animals the Lhota, like all Nagas, adopts a curiously inconsistent attitude. At times he will punish them cruelly as if expecting them to understand the difference between right and wrong. For instance, I heard of a Lhota who climbed a tree after a badly wounded monkey. The monkey clutched his hair, so he tore it loose and cut its hands off while it was still alive—"as a punishment," he said. At other times animals are treated as if they were incapable of feeling pain. Frogs are often kept overnight with their legs broken to prevent their getting away, and old men look back with regret to the good old days when mithan at a sacrifice were beaten to death with sticks and the valuable hair of goats and dogs was plucked from the living animals. A remarkable trait in the Lhota character, wherein they differ from all other Nagas with whom I am acquainted, is the extraordinary readiness with which they commit suicide. Often the reason is trivial in the extreme. I have known a man hang himself because the elders of his village fined him fifteen rupees—a sum he could well afford to pay. Usually, however, a love affair is the cause, and cases of lovers, who for some reason cannot marry, taking poison together are common. Little though he knows or cares of the details of the life hereafter, the Lhota never doubts that there is such a life, and lovers die professing their sure faith that they will be united beyond the grave.

PART II

DOMESTIC LIFE

The Village—The "Morung"—The Head-Tree—The House—The Contents—Manufactures—Trade—Loans—Agriculture and the Ceremonies connected with it—Live-stock—Hunting—Fishing—Food—Drink—Medicine—Drugs—Games—Music.

WITH the exception of those situated on spurs running down from the great mass of Wokha Hill, a Lhota village is invariably built on the very top of a ridge. The two essentials of a site are that it must be easily defensible from a Naga point of view, and near a spring. Unlike the Sema, the Lhota rarely calls a village after its founder. An almost unique example is Mangya, which is said to have been founded by Mangyasang. More usually some peculiarity of the site, or incident connected with the village, gives it its name. Seleku is so called because many flying squirrels (*selek*) were found when the site was cleared. Niroyo is the place of a plant with red berries called *niro*. Lungsa (*olung* = stone, *osa* = platform) is so called from a flat-topped rock near the eastern entrance of the village. Okotso is said to mean the place where the pigs of Pangti were eaten by tigers (*woko* = pig, *tso* = eat). Villages captured by the Lhotas from the Aos, such as Yimbang, Akuk, Mekula, still retain their Ao names only slightly corrupted. Often a village retains the name of its parent village, with Yanthamo ("new village") added, *e. g.* Are Yanthamo. To defend his village the Lhota used neither masonry walls like the Angami, nor hedges of living cane like the Konyak. The outer defence was a ditch cut across the ridge in a conveniently narrow place. The bottom and edge of this were studded with "panjis," and it was crossed by a rough-hewn plank which was taken up at night,

Position and defences.

or in case of attack. The inner defence was a stout fence of sticks and bamboos, also bristling with "panjis." This was carried right round the village except in places where the steepness of the ground gave adequate protection of itself. The door was of bamboo, studded with "panjis." A few sticks are still stuck up along the line of the old fence every year at the *Pikuchak* "genna," and whenever the village performs the *Oyantsoa* "genna." Huge trees stand at the entrance to most Lhota villages. These were preserved to form a wind-screen for the village and to provide convenient look-out posts for sentries. War between Lhota villages was rare, and a powerful village surrounded by friends would regard defences as unnecessary. Similarly nowadays Tuensang, the most powerful village of the Changs, has no village fence. It is situated in the middle of a circle of friendly Chang villages. The warriors of Tuensang emerge from the circle to smite their foes, and then retire behind their friends again. Woe betide the friend who is so remiss as to let a party of avenging enemies into the circle.

A Lhota village is as a rule built along a ridge and has a main entrance at either end, with smaller paths running down to the fields from the sides of the village, and may contain anything from a dozen to 350 houses. The entrance to the World of the Dead being on Wokha Hill, the spirits of the dead must leave the village in that direction. The path leading towards Wokha Hill is accordingly known as *etchhilan* ("dead man's road"). It is a curious sight, flanked with offerings to the dead (*s̆ochipen*) and bamboo erections (*nritangpeng*) showing the prowess in war and hunting of those recently deceased.

Communication.

From village to village there are narrow permanent paths along which men can only go in single file. As far as possible they keep along the very top of the ranges, for in the old days to use a path running under the shoulder of a hill would have been to risk having a spear thrown at you from above. Where the rock is soft sandstone, as it is near Tsori, toe-holes are cut in very steep ascents. Where the rock is hard a notched pole helps the traveller up the bad places.

A Lhota Village—Humtso

Photo by J. H. Hutton.]

The Doyang River from below Changsü.

[*To face p.* 23.

Small streams and ditches are bridged either by a single big tree or half a dozen stout poles laid side by side. Across broader streams, such as the Chebi, cane bridges are constructed. Long pieces of cane are stretched across from convenient trees on either bank. Between these a V-shaped cradle of cane is constructed, on which are laid long bamboos to form a foot-way. Long cane tie-ropes up and down stream prevent the bridge from swinging. The far-seeing Lhota often plants young trees of a suitable kind near the bridge-head trees to provide substitutes in case the old trees are washed away or die.

The village.

A village usually consists of one long street with a line of houses on each side facing inwards. In the middle of the street are the "genna" stones standing opposite the houses of their owners. The somewhat limited space is further crowded with old fallen "genna" stones, graves and stacks of firewood. The villages are swarming with pigs, dogs and cattle, and the state of the street in wet weather can be better imagined than described, though some attempt is made to keep the actual doorways of the houses clean by scraping away the filth with shovels (*mirothenga*) made of the shoulder-blades of cattle or mithan. Sanitary arrangements are non-existent. Pigs and dogs do the necessary scavenging in the jungle surrounding the village. In every village one piece of jungle is strictly reserved for men and another for women. Not all villages consist of one long street. At places such as Yekhum, where the ground slopes awkwardly, the houses are built according to the lie of the land and are in broken lines. Similarly at Pangti, which is on a fairly broad, level site, there are several rather badly defined streets and the houses face in all directions.

Unlike the Angamis, the Lhotas do not keep their rice in their houses but in little thatched granaries (*osung*) of bamboo which are raised on posts above the ground and stand in neat little groups just outside the village. By this arrangement the food supply is generally saved even if the village be burnt. It is absolutely forbidden to spread clothes to dry on the roof of a granary. To do so would cause all the rice to go bad.

The "Morung."

Every village, except the very small ones, is divided into two or more "khels" (*yankho*). Sometimes, but by no means always, a little strip of open ground marks the division between "khel" and "khel." In some villages these "khels" mark the divisions of clans. For instance, at Tsingaki there are two Kikung "khels" and one Nguli "khel." But this is not common. Usually a "khel" appears to be nothing more than a convenient division of a village in which men of various clans live. Sometimes some feature of the site gives the "khel" its name, e.g. *Hayili* ("level") khel in Akuk. Sometimes, as in the *Wokhayankho* ("Wokha men's khel") in Pangti, the first inhabitants have given a name to the "khel." Usually a man lives and dies in the "khel" in which his forefathers lived and died before him. But he is perfectly free to go to another "khel" if he wants to. In every "khel" there is a common bachelors' house or "morung" (*champo*),[1] a building which plays an important part in Lhota life. In it no woman must set her foot. At the *champo* raids were planned and discussed, and to it all heads taken were first brought. It is the sleeping-place of every Lhota boy from the time he first puts on his dao-holder till he marries, this rule being only relaxed in the case of boys who are allowed to remain at home and nurse an ailing and widowed mother, or when the *champo* falls into such a state of disrepair that it is no longer habitable. In the latter case boys are allowed to sleep in a separate room in their parents' house. The *champo* usually stands at the end of, and facing down, the village street. Though not to be compared with the huge "morungs" of the Aos and Konyaks, it is the best architectural effort of which the Lhota is capable. In length a typical *champo* extends to forty feet, with a breadth of

[1] It may be noticed that while the Lhota word for "morung," *champo*, seems allied to the vocabulary of the north-east (*e. g.* in Chang *chăm* = house, and some Konyaks use the same word), the word for "house," *oki*, is that of the western Naga vocabulary (Sema *aki*, Angami *ki*).

The Bachelors' House is an institution common to most of the tribes in Assam, and is also found among the Oraons of Chota Nagpur, a Kolarian (or Mon-Khmêr) tribe. *Cf.* S. C. Roy, *The Oraons of Nagpur* (Ranchi, 1915), p. 211.—J. H. H.

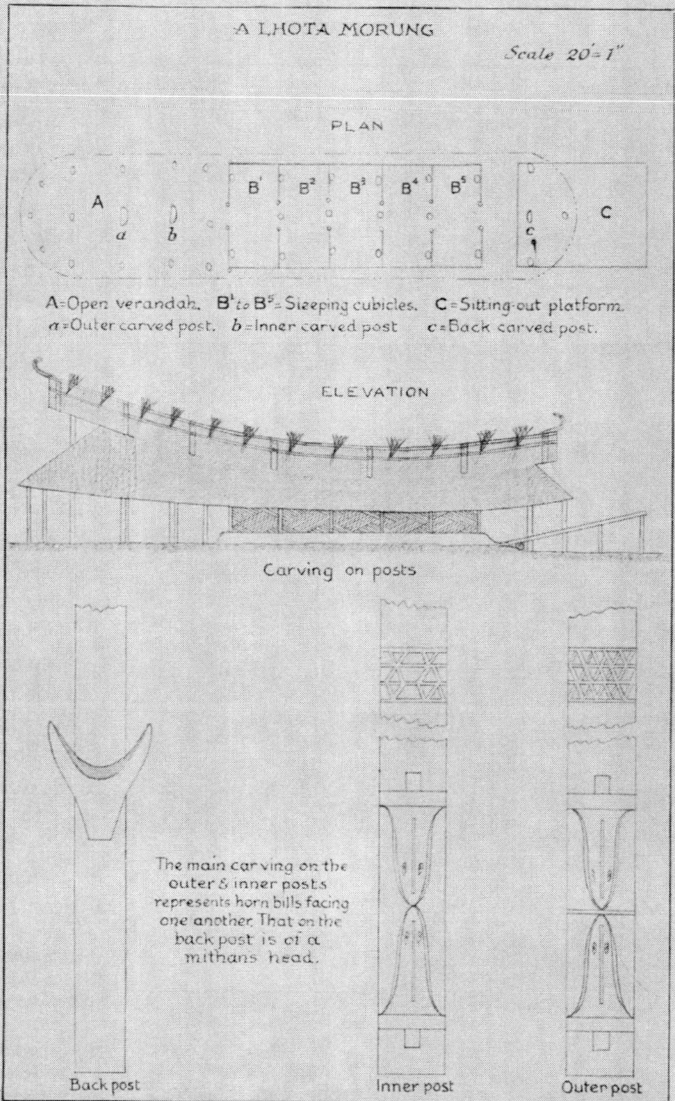
A LHOTA MORUNG
Scale 20′ = 1″
PLAN
A
a
b
B1
B2
B3
B4
B5
c
C
A = Open verandah. B1 to B5 = Sleeping cubicles. C = Sitting-out platform.
a = Outer carved post. b = Inner carved post c = Back carved post.
ELEVATION
Carving on posts
The main carving on the outer & inner posts represents horn bills facing one another. That on the back post is of a mithans head.
Back post
Inner post
Outer post

[To face p. 25.

fifteen feet at the front and twelve feet at the back. The roof-tree is low in the middle, and curves up to gables at the front and back, that at the front being about sixteen feet high and that at the back a foot or so lower. Two specially fine bamboos are selected for the roof-tree. Part of the root is left on them and forms a horn-like projection at each end of the roof-tree. To each horn is fixed a little cross-piece, from which are hung tassel-like ornaments of reed-stem. The house is thatched with either thatching grass or the leaf of a small palm called *oko* (*Levistonia assamica*). The eaves reach almost to the ground and are brought forward in a half-circle in front to form a sort of verandah roof. In the middle of the space covered by this verandah roof stands the front post (*humtse*), which is elaborately carved with conventional representations of mithan heads and hornbills, and is carried through the roof up to the high gable. Behind it is another carved post (*humtse tachungo*). At the base of this post are the *oha* stones on which the good fortune of the *champo* depends, and to it used to be fastened a piece of skin from the first head taken after a new *champo* was built. This piece of skin is called *humtse lama* ("post warmer"). It was believed that it brought strength to the post and luck to the village. So strong was and is this belief, that as late as 1913 Tsingaki was punished for buying a piece of a head to be used as *humtse lama* from the independent Sema village of Satami.[1] At the back of the *champo* is another carved post.

The interior of a *champo* is not attractive. It is dark, dirty, smoky, stuffy and full of fleas. Yet a Lhota talks of his happy *champo*-days much as an Englishman talks of his schooldays. The floor is sometimes levelled earth and sometimes a bamboo platform raised about two feet above the ground on posts. The walls are of bamboo. There is a door at each end and a passage about two feet

[1] Konyaks, after rebuilding a "morung," immediately go into the jungle and try to kill a monkey, the hand of which is tied to the main post. Failing a monkey, anything, even a little bird, will do, but something must be killed, and the hunting party returns home singing as if they had taken a head.

wide down the middle, in which fires are lit on cold nights, the smoke finding its way out as best it can in the absence of chimneys or windows. Where the floor is of bamboo four logs are laid down to form a square, the interior of which is filled in with earth rammed firmly down. On this the fire is made. On either side of the passage are cubicles with bamboo partitions, along the sides of which are sleeping benches of rough-hewn planks, or bamboo "machans."

The time varies in different villages, but a *champo* is generally rebuilt every nine years. Almost invariably it falls in ruins before the time is up, but on no account must it be rebuilt till the due period has elapsed. The ceremonies connected with the rebuilding are interesting. The *Puthi* having announced that the rebuilding will take place in so many days, the boys of the *champo* collect bamboos, thatching grass, posts, tying-bark and whatever is needed. If a new carved post is required the best carver in the village gets to work on it. Every *champo* has land belonging to it. With the rice from this land a pig and a big cow are bought. These are killed on the day before the work of rebuilding is begun, and the carcases kept in a little hut specially built by the side of the *champo*. Next day is the first of five days' *emung*,[1] which must be kept by the whole village. During these days no one may work in the fields, or weave cloth or make pots or bring into the village meat from a tiger's kill. If a stranger enters the village he will probably be ill, and he cannot leave it till the five days' *emung* are over. On this day the ceremonies begin. The *Puthi* formally begins the breaking down of the old *champo*, by pulling a piece of thatch off the roof and throwing it onto the ground. The *Puthi's* attendant (*Yenga*) then removes the *oha* stones from in front of the *humtse tachungo* and lays them down a little distance from the *champo*. The roof is next carefully cut in two lengthways and laid on the ground in such a way that the two halves lean up against one another and form

[1] The word *emung*, which corresponds exactly to the Ao term *amung*, means literally "gathered together." On an *emung* day no one may go down to the fields to work, or go farther from the village than is necessary to get water and firewood.

a shelter. Under this the boys of the *champo* must sleep that night. The posts are pulled out and laid on the ground, the whole building is dismantled and the site cleaned and re-levelled. The work of rebuilding is then begun. This again the *Puthi* initiates by a formal act. Beginning with the *humtse tachungo* he digs a little hole with the butt of his spear at the places where the three carved posts are to be set up, and pours or spits a little "rohi madhu" into each hole. The posts are then put up, new ones being substituted for any which may have decayed, and the *champo* is rebuilt as quickly as possible. Before leaving the work for the night the *Puthi* places a little ginger sprinkled with "madhu" on two crossed leaves at the foot of the *humtse tachungo* in order to keep away evil spirits, to whom ginger is particularly obnoxious. Thatching alone is left till next day, which is a day of less work and more play. Everyone feasts and puts on his best clothes, the men wearing full dancing dress. The first bunch of thatch having been put in place by the *Puthi*, the braves of the village dance, some on the ground and some on the roof of the "morung," all singing the *pangashari*, a slow chant in which the war-like deeds of the village in the past are recounted. This song goes on all the time the thatch is being put on. A similar dance on the roof is performed by the Konyaks of Namsang and Tamlu when a "morung" is rebuilt. The thatching being finished the *oha* stones are replaced by the *Yenga* at the foot of the *humtse tachungo*. All the men, led by the *Puthi*, then slowly dance in a rough column of fours formation round the village, ho-hoing as they go. The chant is called *yanungshari*. The carcases of the pig and cow are taken out of the little hut in which they have been kept and cut up and distributed to all males, the *Puthi* receiving as his share half the head of the cow split longitudinally. A feature of this, the second day of the ceremonies, is the dog-killing which takes place. Every *champo* in the village kills a small dog. That belonging to the *champo* which is being rebuilt is carefully fattened up beforehand and tied up in front of the *Puthi's* house. When the time comes to kill this dog an admiring throng gathers round while the oldest man of the "khel" sits by the dog and gives it a bone to keep it quiet. He then covers it with his cloth. Opposite to him stands the man reputed to be the finest warrior in the "khel," and the following dialogue takes place. Warrior: "Move away." Old man: "Will you take care?" Warrior: "I will take care." Old man: "Do not hurt the dog." Warrior: "I will kill it quickly." At these words the old man uncovers the dog and moves aside. The warrior then attempts to split its skull exactly in two with one blow of his dao. When the dog falls about a dozen bucks and boys dance round and round it chanting, "He has killed it, he has killed it." The head is cut off and brought to the *champo*, where it is carefully examined to see if it has been well and truly split. If the blow is found to have been a crooked one, the man who killed it is laughed at, told he is no warrior, but a boaster and a wind-bag. The head is then thrown away by the old man who attended at the killing.[1] In the evening a mock fight takes place between the young men and women of the village, both married and unmarried. The women pretend to try to push their way into the *champo*, while the young men keep them out. This mock fight is believed to increase the fertility of the women who take part in it. On the third day the slow dance round the village is repeated while the *yanungshari* is again sung. Most of the day is spent in feasting and drinking. On the fourth day the dance and chant are again repeated, but very few men put in an appearance, presumably because most of them have bad headaches after two days' heavy drinking. The chief performers are a few hard-headed bucks and irrepressible small boys. On the fifth day, the last *emung* day, everyone rests.

The Head-tree.

Perhaps the most conspicuous object in a Lhota village is the head-tree, *mingetung*, generally a magnificent specimen of *ningetung* (a tree of the Ficus family). It is usually situated on a mound well in the middle of the village. Against its branches were leant the long bamboos from which were hung the heads of enemies taken in war, and at its

[1] In some villages the head and trunk of the dog are tied up on the main post (*humtse tachungo*) of the "morung" and left there to rot.

roots are kept the mysterious *oha* stones. These are counted and a fence is put round the tree whenever the *oyantsoa* "genna" is performed. The fortune of the village is regarded as in a way dependent on the *mingetung*. So sacred is it that in some villages it cannot be photographed. To break a twig off it would entail the performance of the *oyantsoa* "genna" (village renewing "genna"), which must also be performed if the *mingetung* dies or a branch falls. The place of the *mingetung* can never be changed. That at Lungla has been blown down. A small tree close by is being used instead till a new *mingetung* can be induced to grow on the old sight, a vain hope, as the old site is a mound of shale without so much as a blade of grass on it. When a new village is founded a site is always selected on which there is a tree suitable for use as a *mingetung*. Under the new tree must be put a twig stolen from the *mingetung* of the parent village, though the parent village makes every effort to prevent this theft, as it entails the performance of the *oyantsoa* "genna" and is very likely to bring bad luck to the parent village. A curious belief is prevalent in Phiro. Skulls which had fallen from their strings were often picked up and jammed into interstices in the bole of the head-tree. At Phiro the *mingetung* is growing round and gradually covering these old skulls. This is regarded as a sign that the days of head-hunting are gone, never to return.[1]

Water supply.

Springs issuing from the side of the hill below the village supply Lhotas with their water. Sometimes it is drawn from a muddy pool of unappetizing greenish water, but often there is a good flow into a basin dammed up with rough masonry. Small fish have been put into the Niroyo basin, and are carefully preserved in order that they may keep the water clear of scum. At almost all springs there is a small dam, and over it a low fence so that women who draw water stand below and not in the supply from which they draw. Unlike the Ao, the Lhota does not fancy water after the village have washed their feet in it. When the

[1] Lt.-Col. R. G. Woodthorpe's sketch on Pl. XVIII., Vol. xi., of the *Journal of the Anthropological Institute*, 1888, shows what the *mingetung* of Phiro looked like in the old days.

path from the fields does not happen to pass near a stream, water is often led to it in bamboo pipes from a long distance in order that men coming up after the day's work may have a drink and a wash.

The Lhota House.

Description. A Lhota house varies in size from the wretched hovel of some old widow to the house of a rich man which may measure thirty feet long by eighteen feet broad—a limit far exceeded, however, by Aos, Semas and Angamis. To build a fine house as a show of wealth a Lhota would regard as great waste of money, and a Lhota likes to waste nothing. The walls are of bamboo and the roof of thatch (*lishu*) or palm-leaf (*oko, Levistonia assamica*). The front of all but the poorest houses is semicircular, with a door in the middle of the semicircle. The roof of the front semicircular room (*mpongki*) slopes up to the roof of the main building like the roof of the semicircular apse of a church. The upper roof-tree of the main building is carried forward over the roof of the *mpongki* with a slight upward slope, and is decorated with a little mock roof of thatch forming a sort of flying gable. In the middle of the *mpongki* is a bamboo post, which is carried through the roof of the apse to meet the projecting roof-tree of the main building. The interior of a Lhota house strikes a stranger as very cramped and uncomfortable. Unless one is very careful one bumps one's head at every step. There is none of the spaciousness which one notices in the house of a rich Sema or Ao. Where the ground is suitable and bamboos are plentiful there is a machan (*khantsung*) for sitting out at the back. Sometimes the whole floor of the house is simply levelled earth, as in a Sema or Angami house. More usually, however, a step made of a short, thick log leads up from the *mpongki* to the doorway of the main building, the floor of which is raised above the ground on short posts and made of stout bamboo matting on a framework of whole bamboos, the matting in turn being covered with a layer of beaten earth to keep the draught from coming up from below. The floor of the sitting-out platform at the back is of bamboo without

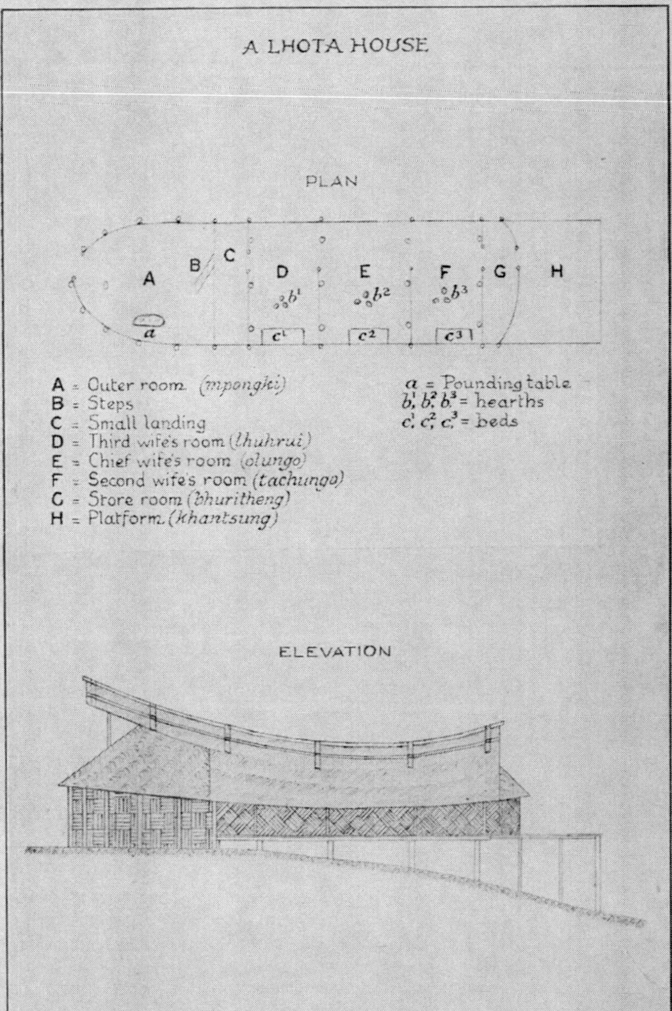
A LHOTA HOUSE
PLAN
A B C D E F G H
a
b1 b2 b3
c1 c2 c3
A = Outer room (mpongki)
B = Steps
C = Small landing
D = Third wife's room (lhuhrui)
E = Chief wife's room (olungo)
F = Second wife's room (tachungo)
G = Store room (bhuritheng)
H = Platform (khantsung)
a = Pounding table
b1, b2, b3 = hearths
c1, c2, c3 = beds
ELEVATION
Scale 20' = 1"

[*To face p.* 31.

any covering of earth. The pattern of the floor of this platform varies according to whether the owner of the house has or has not dragged a stone. In the former case a mat of split bamboos interlaced in a simple chequer pattern is laid over a foundation of whole bamboos laid at right angles to the back wall of the house. In the latter case the place of the mat is taken by split bamboos laid at right angles to the bamboo foundation.

In a Lhota household each wife has a separate sleeping cubicle with a fireplace (*nchü*) in the middle. A well-to-do Lhota usually possesses three wives. The main building of his house therefore contains three sleeping cubicles and a little store-room (*bhuritheng*) at the back. The cubicle nearest the *mpongki* is called *lhuhrui* and is occupied by the third wife. The middle one is called *olungo* and is the abode of the chief wife. The back cubicle is called *tachungo* and is used by the second wife. Daughters sleep with their mother or, if she is dead, with the step-mother they like best. Servants, if there be any, or a bridegroom working for his bride in his father-in-law's house sleep in the *mpongki*, either on mats on the floor or on the pounding bench. Guests sleep on mats on the floor of the store-room or in one of the cubicles.

A step up from the *mpongki* and a door close to the wall (usually the right-hand wall) lead into a narrow passage running the whole length of the house onto the platform at the back. On the left, assuming the passage to be on the right of the house, are the cubicles, the partitions of which stretch about two-thirds across the house, and up to the beams (*khokang*), the partitions between the *mpongki* and the first cubicle, and between the store-room and the sitting-out platform, going right up to the roof. The roof is supported on centre-posts (*tirhupu*), a bamboo one being placed in the middle of the *mpongki*, and a roughly-squared wooden one at each partition, and corner-posts (*okinge*) at the corners of the main building. Small posts in the walls help to support rafters (*khirong*). There is no chimney and the smoke finds its way out as best it can. The cubicles are lighted only by their fires.

Construction.

When a Lhota builds a house he sets about it as follows. After the harvest is in he chooses a site and touches the ground with his hand. Then he goes off to a dreamer (*hahang*), of whom there are two or three in every village, with a small present of food, and asks him to dream that night and tell him in the morning if the site will be a lucky one. Dreams of springs, gourds, cucumbers, leaves, daos and spears, among other things, are good. To dream of digging, hair dyed scarlet and black thread forebodes death. If the dreamer has a vision of frogs, crabs, or tortoises the man who builds a house on the site which is being tested will be ill. If the dreamer reports visions of good omen (and he generally does, for a seer of evil dreams does not keep his clients long) the builder of the house calls his friends and relations together and work is begun. The positions of the corner-posts are first marked out, the length and breadth and diagonals being carefully measured. These posts are then put in, and after them the centre-posts and side-posts of the walls. If the house is to have a raised bamboo floor this is now made. Long bamboos or poles are then laid along the top of the side-posts of the walls, which are notched to receive them, and tied in position with *yhandra* bark. This bark is taken from the tree in long strips and dried in the sun for some days. The strips are twisted and wetted when required for use. On the top of the skeleton wall thus made are laid and tied bamboo cross-beams in pairs, each pair enclosing one of the wooden centre-posts, to which it is firmly tied. There is no cross-beam across the *mpongki*. The tops of the wooden centre-posts are then notched and a bamboo roof-tree (*mhongki*) is put in place. This stretches out far in front of the main building. At its junction with the centre-post standing between the *mpongki* and the first cubicle it is broken half through and carefully bent down, for the projecting end of it will eventually form the centre rafter of the semicircular roof of the *mpongki*. The rafters (*khirong*) are then put on. To enable them to be tied they must necessarily project and form a series of forks along the top of the roof-tree. On these forks is laid another roof-tree, which is not bent down like the first, but projects right out above the *mpongki* and is supported by the bamboo centre-post. Further to strengthen the rafters and prevent them lifting in a high wind, two other roof-trees are placed in position in the side forks on either side of the main roof-trees. These side roof-trees project beyond the main building and are bent down like the under one to form rafters for the *mpongki*. Partitions inside the house are now built and purlins (*sütesüyo*) are put on, all being so bent as to form purlins for the *mpongki*. The bottom pair of purlins are so made that the projecting ends can be bent to meet and be tied. This gives the outline of the semicircular apse of the *mpongki*. Posts are put in to which the bottom pair of purlins are tied in position. The projecting ends of roof-trees and other purlins are then brought down and tied to it, and the framework of the house is complete. Chequer pattern bamboo walls are quickly put up and the thatching is begun. Sections of thatching about six feet long are prepared as follows by men on the ground, and handed up to men on the roof, who put them in position. Thatch is carefully bent double over a thin bamboo about six feet long, care being taken to see that it forms a fringe without gaps. Then to keep the thatch in place two more bamboos of the same size and length are placed on either side of it about five inches below the first bamboo. These are firmly tied together through the thatch with strips of bamboo. With palm leaves the top bamboo is omitted, a fringe of overlapping palm leaves being held in place by the two thin bamboos, one on either side. These fringes are then tied on to the rafters and purlins, beginning at the eaves and working upwards so that each fringe overlaps the one below it. Finally, thatch is doubled over the upper roof-tree and fastened down with two long bamboo wind-ties. This last layer of thatch extends to the end of the upper roof-tree, forming a sort of flying gable where it projects over the *mpongki*. Light bamboo doors are then made. These are not attached to the door-posts in any way and can be lifted and laid aside. Two crossed bamboos are attached to the door by a loop of bark string and jammed behind the door-posts to keep it in place. A man who has dragged a stone more than once can decorate his roof with crossed bamboos representing mithan horns, but this is considered rather a snobbish display of wealth and the privilege is rarely taken advantage of. In some Southern Lhota villages the *Puthis'* houses have the roof decorated with crossed bamboos of which the ends are split and splayed apart. This is a conventional representation of human hands, and the right to have the roofs of their houses ornamented in this way was formerly confined to men who had succeeded in bringing the fingers or toes of an enemy home from a raid. Rich Aos decorate their roofs in a similar way.

Before such a house can be occupied lurking evil spirits must of course be dealt with. For this the oldest of the men who helped to build the house is called in to act as *tsandhramo epang* ("driver away of evil spirits"). Having mixed ginger and "rohi madhu" in a new "chunga," he sprinkles the inside of the house with the concoction and says, "We are going to stay here. You go away." He then throws away the "chunga," which must never be used for anything else. The old man then marks out the places for the hearth-stones, which the owner places in position. The owner then either lights a fire with a fire-stick or fetches fire from another house—any house will do. Matches are never used by Lhotas for ceremonial fire-making. A meal is now cooked and partaken of by the owner and his household and friends and the old man, who then takes the omens. He holds in his hands a small chicken called *kichakro*, which each member of the household touches with his or her left hand. This he strangles and disembowels, taking the omens from the entrails. After which he cuts it up and, holding eight pieces of meat in each hand, takes his seat with the male members of the household on his right and the female members on his left, and swings his hands backwards and forwards four times with an underhand bowling action, counting the number of swings aloud. The chicken is the old man's fee, and he takes it away, returning in the morning to report whether he has had dreams of good or evil omen. A man may not act as *tsandhramo epang* for more than one household on the same day. The only restriction placed on occupants of a new house is one forbidding them to allow men from another village to enter the house till the earth which has been put on the bamboo floor is dry. A house of which the floor is mother earth may be entered by strangers as soon as the above ceremony has been performed.

The contents of the house.

In the front room of the Lhota house are kept heavy articles, such as the pounding table (*tsampo*), liquor vat (*ochen*), and pigs' feeding trough (*wokochakpfu*), the last being merely a log split in two and roughly hollowed. The pounding table is hewn from one piece of wood. In the top, which is slightly concave, one, two or three holes about six inches in diameter are burnt. In these the rice is pounded with heavy poles—an arduous occupation at which the daughters of the house spend a good deal of their time. The liquor vat consists of a log hollowed out from one end. Trees for this are carefully chosen, but a very large proportion of vats split or spring a leak before they are finished. On the wall of the front room are hung the feet of game which the owner of the house has killed. Spears are always kept stuck in the ground in front of the big wooden post. Along the sides of the inner cubicles are the small plank beds of the household. According to Lhota ideas a single thickness of cloth spread on the bed makes quite a soft enough mattress. Round the fire are little wooden stools about six inches high cut from one piece of wood. Floor space being limited in a Lhota house, most things are kept on rough bamboo shelves (*theka*) fixed to the beams of the house. Here are kept bundles of salt wrapped in leaves, cooking pots, baskets of yeast, traps, carrying baskets, and a thousand and one things. For cooking rice and meat Naga-made earthen pots are generally used, but for heating "madhu" shallow iron pots from the plains are popular. In them the brew can be stirred easily and without risk of an upset. Lhota houses contain very few drinking cups. Villages on the Sema border obtain bamboo cups from their neighbours, and nowadays cheap German enamel and aluminium ware are often used. But the true Lhota cup is a folded plantain leaf. It is really an astonishing sight to watch one's hostess fold a piece of plantain leaf into a cup with one hand, while she talks hard to one guest and pours out "madhu" for another, either from a gourd or, more commonly, an old beer bottle. The usual type of dish is a shallow wooden one, with no legs, called *opyi*, many of which are made in Lungsa. Some households also use a wooden dish on a raised stand, rather like a dessert dish, called *pyikhyu*. In the bamboo matting of the walls are stuck daos, bamboo spoons and many odds and ends. The hollow bamboos in which water is carried up from the spring are kept leaning against the walls. Over the fire is suspended a bamboo platform about five feet square. This prevents sparks flying up to the roof and also serves as a convenient place on which to dry meat, and keep such pots and spoons and things as are in continual use. The little store-room at the back is comparatively free from smoke and in it ceremonial ornaments and spare cloths are hung.

Manufactures.

Spinning. Spinning like dyeing and weaving, is performed entirely by women, and every Lhota woman is expected to weave the cloths of her husband and family. The thread is spun as follows. Home-grown cotton—the Lhotas are great cotton-growers—is cleaned of its seeds by being rolled on a flat stone with a small stick, used like a rolling-pin. This cleaning is a tedious process which generally falls to the lot of the old widows of the village, who eke out a scanty livelihood thereby. The cleaned cotton after being fluffed out by being flicked with the string of an instrument (*loko*) like a miniature bow is then gently rolled between the hands into "sausages" about nine inches long, after which it is ready to be spun into thread. The Lhota spindle (*humtsi*) is a very primitive affair and is similar to that of the Aos, Semas and Angamis. It consists of a thin penholder-shaped stick of hard wood about eight inches long, tapering to a fine point at the top, and about the thickness of a pencil at the thickest point near the bottom. Just above the thickest point is fixed a whorl made of soft black stone. This is made by rubbing on other stones till it is flat and round a piece of the soft stone used for the purpose. To make the hole in the middle a man holds it between his toes and twiddles a spear on it between his hands till the iron butt of the spear goes through. For spinning the tip of the spindle is wetted with the tongue. The spindle is then spun clock-wise with the right hand against the outside of the right thigh, the base of the spindle being kept in bounds by a conveniently cup-shaped piece of broken pottery covered with a bit of rag. The "sausage" of cotton is held in the left hand, and the end of it laid against the wetted tip of the spindle till it catches and the thread (*oying*) begins to form. When about a yard has been spun it is unwound from the tip of the spindle and rewound just above the stone whorl. The spindle is then worked as before, the cotton being held in the left hand, and thread accumulates above the whorl till the spindle becomes full, when it is wound off onto a wooden frame (*kukung*), shaped like a double T, and another spindleful is begun, and so on till the *kukung* is full. The thread is next hardened by being steeped for about five minutes in hot rice-water, after which the skeins (*yingsak*) are strung on a stick (*phutsi*) to dry. It is forbidden for a man to eat the boiled rice from which this rice-water has been taken. When the thread is required for weaving it is wound into a ball (*yingtso*), the woman who is sitting winding keeping the skein stretched round her knees.

Three colours, red, dark blue and light blue, are used Dyeing. by the Lhotas. Red thread is generally bought either from a shop or from an Ao village, for red dyeing is considered a risky occupation likely to bring on dysentery, and therefore only suitable for old women, who are of no value to the community. The industry, however, is carried on in a few Lhota villages, such as Changsü and Okotso. To make red dye the root of *Rubia sikkimensis* (*karung*) is pounded up, and another leaf (*'ntawo*) is pounded and added. The mixture is then boiled with water, and the thread put in while the water is boiling. The pot is then lifted off the fire and allowed to stand for three days, when the thread is taken out and dried.

Dark blue dye is made from the leaves of *Strobilanthes flaccidi-folius* (*tchemo*), pounded up and boiled with water. The thread is steeped in the mixture for half an hour and is then dried. This gives a colour like navy blue. To make light blue the leaves which have been already boiled and used for making dark blue dye are drained and dried and kept for a year. They are then broken up fine and mixed with cold water and the white ash of burnt bark, and put to stand till next day, when the thread is put in and left there for a day, or for two days if the dye is weak. It is then taken out and dried.

Dyeing is exclusively performed by women, who when they are so occupied must refrain from sexual intercourse and must not eat beef, goat's flesh, dog's flesh, dried fish, or that horrible vegetable known in Naga-Assamese as "stinking dal" (*nyingtyingtsing*), in fact any food with a strong smell. If any man were to dye a piece of thread he would never again have any luck in fishing or hunting. No one but the dyer must look on while thread is being dyed or the colour will be patchy and bad.

Like the Semas and Aos, the Lhotas use a simple single-heddle tension loom (*tsirochunglung*) which is set up and operated as follows. A beam (*tsikam*) of bamboo about three feet long is securely fastened to the wall of the house or any other suitable firm support in a horizontal position and at a height of about two feet from the ground. On this are slipped two loops (*tsisü*) of bark string, in which is put the other bar (*ncho*) of the loom. The loops are set at a distance apart equal to the breadth of the piece of cloth to be woven. The lower bar (*ncho*) is notched at either end, to enable the weaving belt (*ephi*) to be attached to it. This belt is of woven cane or bamboo and is worn by the operator in the small of her back. By it, as she sits in front of the loom, she can keep the necessary tension on the warp. Both the beams being in position and a strain having been taken on the *tsisü*, each *tsisü* is crossed by the lower string being pulled up and the upper down and a thin stick of bamboo

Photo by Mr. Butler.]

SPINNING

Photo by Mr. Butler.]

WEAVING

[*To face p.* 39.

(*yingyi*) is put in position. This is naturally held firmly in place by the downward pressure of the lower strings and the upward pressure of the upper. Then, working towards the weaver, the lease-rod (*chunglung*) is put in close to the *yingyi* without crossing the strings. Below the lease-rod the sword (*tsitam*) is inserted, the strings being crossed as in the case of the *yingyi*. The twine which is to form the heddle-loops (*ena*) is now tied loosely onto the left end of the sword and laid along it. This twine is sometimes thick cotton thread and is sometimes made from the twisted bark of a creeper called *enazü* (*Pineraria Thungbergiana*). Two balls of thread are then taken and their loose ends twisted together and joined. One ball is held in the lap of the weaver while the other is passed over the *ncho*, under the *tsitam* and the *ena* which is lying along it, over the *chunglung* and under and then round over and under the *yingyi* and then over the *tsikam*, from whence it is brought straight back to the weaver under the loom. The second ball is then passed under the *ncho* and over the *ena* and under the *tsitam* and *chunglung*, and under and back over and under the *yingyi* and over the *tsikam*, and is brought back to the weaver under the loom. The process is repeated till all the warp (*elomo*) has been set. The result is that the *ena* forms a series of heddle-loops and the *yingyi* (the object of which is to shorten the upper side of the shed made by the lease-rod) is entirely encircled by each warp. Unless the loom be a very small one the weaver cannot reach the *tsikam*. She therefore generally has an assistant, who can be a man, to pass the warp thread over and under the *tsikam*. The two ends of the warp thread, when all has been set are turned back across the warp and woven into the material. The shuttle (*yingshü*), which is simply a thin piece of bamboo, is filled from the ball by being spun against the right thigh. This process and that of setting the warp are the only two in which a man may take part. Before weaving can begin the *tsitam*, a flat piece of hard wood, is turned on edge and the heddle (*natyung*) is slipped in alongside it so as to take up the heddle-loops formed by the *ena*. The *tsitam* is then removed. The object of substituting the sword for the heddle while the warp is being set is to ensure big enough heddle-loops. The *tsisü* are then removed, and the lease-rod is moved down close to the heddle thus giving the warp enough strain to keep the latter in place. In weaving the shuttle is shot backwards and forwards by hand, the heddle being raised every alternate pick. To increase the shed the sword is put in for each pick and turned edgeways. For the check pattern so common in women's body-cloths both warp and weft (*mpyo*) are changed. For ornamentation little bits of red wool or yellow thread bought from a shop are worked in by hand as the weaving progresses, the warp being manipulated with a porcupine quill. Ordinarily the first weft-element passes alternately over and under a single warp-element, the second passing over those under which the first passed. A variety of pattern is that in which a single weft element passes alternately under and over pairs of warp elements. Another variety is that in which a single weft element passes under and over alternate pairs of warp elements and is returned under those under which it passed before, giving a pattern of interwoven pairs of warp and weft elements. Four pieces of cloth about one foot broad by five feet long go to make an ordinary man's cloth. These strips are sewn together along their long sides. The Lhota needle (*otyam*) is simply a piece of bamboo sharpened at one end. To the head is attached by wax a piece of thread about two inches long known as *otyam emhi* ("needle-tail") onto which the thread used for sewing is twisted. The broad stripes of light blue seen in so many Lhota cloths are invariably separate strips, sewn between two of the main strips of the cloth. A woman in the old days was forbidden to weave while her husband was absent on a raid, as it might cause him to trip over creepers in the jungle and fall into the hands of the enemy.

Though foreign articles are being used more and more Lhotas still make most of their own pots. They are round, and slightly contracted at the top, with a curved rim by which they can be lifted off the fire. The only ornamentation used is a string pattern which is applied by patting the pot while still wet with a flat piece of wood covered with coarse string binding (*khuzü*). The clay is obtained from the banks of small streams. Two kinds are used, grey (*linyikcho*), which is the best, and red (*linyocho*), which is not so good. Only women can make pots, but the industry is not restricted to old women. The clay is broken up and kneaded on a stone with a little water. After being left over-night it is again moistened and kneaded. A round base is first made by hand. A wall of clay is built onto this and kneaded well onto the base with the left hand, the wall being supported on the outside by a small stick (*phutamphen*) held in the right hand. The pot is then shaped with the left hand and stick, and put to dry in the sun while other pots are being made.

After the pots have been dried in the house for three or four days a rough platform of wood is built on the ground outside the village. On this the pots are laid upside down and twigs and rubbish and rice straw piled on them and fired. In this kiln the pots are left till next morning, when they must be taken away before dawn. Certain precautions have to be observed. The woman making the pots must refrain from sexual intercourse, and must not eat any strong-smelling food, such as beef, goat's flesh, dog's flesh, dried fish or "stinking dal," while she is so engaged, for to eat these things would cause the pots to "ring" badly. Anyone may watch the clay being kneaded, but no one must look on while the pot is being shaped, and only those helping the woman by carrying the pots or collecting fuel may be present at the burning. Were a man to see the pots being fired they would all crack. Nor must any dog come near, for should so much as a single hair of a dog touch a pot before it is finished the pot would have a hole at that very place.

The trade of a blacksmith is regarded by the Lhotas as a very unlucky one, and is restricted to the families members of which have been blacksmiths in the past. It is believed that no blacksmith lives long after he stops work. It is therefore not surprising that Lhota blacksmiths are few and far between. Nor is there much need for them. Villages near the plains buy all they require from Assamese smiths.

The Rengmas are great blacksmiths and make all the weapons and implements required by the Southern Lhotas of the inner ranges, while the Northern Lhotas are supplied in a similar way by the Aos. The few Lhota blacksmiths there are use foreign tools bought from the plains, though an indigenous type of bellows (*yongphophen*) is still in use in places. This consists of two sections of bamboo set up perpendicularly side by side in a clay base. Into each of these is fitted a piston bound all over with hen's feathers with their thin ends down. The downward stroke of the piston being against the "grain" of the feathers and the upward stroke with the "grain," quite an efficient valvular action results. These pistons are worked alternately by an assistant who holds one in each hand. At the bottom of each piston-case is a hole, to which is attached a bamboo tube (*zendro*). These tubes emerge together at the fire. Only soft iron is used. This is obtained from the plains in the form of old tea-garden hoes. Formerly iron is said to have been found and worked at Khoro Ghat on the edge of the plains, by a village of the Thangwe clan according to one tradition, or by Shans or Burmese according to another.[1] The finished article is tempered by being dipped in water. This tempering is not meant to be final. The purchaser after using the dao, or whatever the article may be, for a time, heats it in a fire of the slow-burning bark of a certain tree (*lepokriphu*) and tempers it in salt and water, or bamboo-pickle and water to his taste.

So impregnated with misfortune is the whole trade of the blacksmith that no house is ever built on the site of an old forge, though the forge is allowed to be built inside the village. To bring a piece of dross from a forge into a house would cause all the inmates to fall ill. With this in mind a woman in Yemkha in 1919 left a piece of dross as a parting present when she ran away from her husband.

[1] The spot where this was done is called *Rāmăkātī* or *mān yōnchopfĕ́* the latter meaning the "Burmese iron-foundry." It is a small outcrop of very shaly coal. Possibly the ancestor of the Thangwe Eni clan caught in the jungle by the Eni who adopted him was a Burman, like the ancestor of the Tephri-Methama sept of the Methama clan in the Angami village of Chichama.—J. H. H.

Living in a land where cane and bamboo are plentiful the Lhotas are naturally expert basket-makers. Every man can make his own household baskets, but the manufacture of difficult things such as cane helmets (*kiven*) is generally left to experts. No woman is allowed to do any basket-work of any kind. For rough baskets strips of fresh bamboo are used. Cane is far more valuable and is reserved for articles which are meant to last a long time. It is left to season before being used. For rough work a chequer pattern is generally used, but for shields (*otsung*), cane helmets, and grain baskets a twill pattern is used. A pretty cross-warped pattern with wefts parallel to each other and passing over and under the same afternate warps is used for the outside of rain-shields (*phuchyo*), giving an open-work effect rather like the cane seat of a bedroom chair. **Basket-work.**

Rough planks are hacked out with a dao, a most wasteful method, as the whole thickness of a tree has to go to make each plank. Wooden dishes are cut out of single pieces of wood with an adze (*ophü*). They are then dried in the rough and rubbed smooth with stones and a curious rough-surfaced leaf called *phukirongti* (*Clerodendrum serratum*). Small " madhu " vats and very occasionally wooden shields are made in the same way. The posts of " morungs " (*champo*) are carved in relief with conventional representations of hornbulls and mithan heads. The work is done with the dao and is as a rule very rough—far inferior to the carvings of Semas and Angamis, who in turn are much behind the Konyaks. **Wood-work.**

Nets like big landing-nets are made out of twisted strips of bark from the *erhingya* tree. They are fitted onto a circular frame to which a long handle is attached, and are used to land the stupefied fish which come to the top when a river is " poisoned." They are made by men, never by women. The maker must remain chaste the previous night. **Nets.**

Among the few indigenous beads of the Naga Hills are the little black beads (*eshe*) made from the seeds of a species of wild plantain (*sheyu*) by the Lhotas. The industry is **Beads.**

confined to women and exists chiefly among the Southern Lhotas. The seeds are tough, and both ends of each seed have to be laboriously chewed off. They are astringent, and "bead chewing" becomes a perfect habit with some women. The seeds are then pierced with a bamboo needle and strung, and the strings rolled on a flat stone till the beads become cylindrical and a good polish has been obtained. They are used for necklaces and look exceedingly well against a brown skin.

Hides. No process of tanning is known. Skins which are required for shields or any other purpose are merely cleaned and dried in the sun.

Trade. There is no tradition of any old form of currency, such as beads, or gongs, though thin key-shaped pieces of iron (*chabli*) such as the Aos used to use as currency are occasionally owned as heirlooms. Trade was apparently always carried on by barter in the days before the British coinage came into use. Even nowadays cotton which is taken down to the plains is almost invariably bartered for salt. A peculiar custom obtains when mithan, ivory armlets and boar's tushes are bought and sold. These articles are particularly liable to be infected with evil fortune, certain marks being regarded as unlucky, and so on. An old man is therefore always employed as an intermediary (*lantse* or *thantsowe*) between the parties, and he finally settles the price when the bargaining has gone on long enough. Any ill luck is believed to attach itself to him as nominal buyer, rather than to the real buyer, who pays him a commission of Re. 1 for a mithan, eight annas for an ivory armlet and four annas for a pair of boar's tushes. If anything intimately connected with the person, such as a cloth or a dao, be sold the seller retains a thread from the cloth or scrapes a tiny shaving off the handle of the dao, for were he to sell the whole of something which was almost part of himself the buyer might be able to exercise some magical influence over him.[1]

[1] It is with the same idea, perhaps, that an Angami selling an ancestral field retains as his own a sod or two which remain nominally his.—J. H. H.

Loans.

The rate of interest on loans varies according to the nature of the thing lent. That on money is usually 50 per cent. simple interest, running for two years only. The interest on rice is four baskets a year for every six baskets borrowed. The interest has to be paid year by year till the principal has been returned. A debt of seed paddy must be paid before all other debts. The highest rate of interest is demanded for salt, for which 100 per cent. per annum compound interest has to be paid. The result is that loans of salt are promptly repaid.

Agriculture.

Method of cultivation.

The Lhota is above all an agriculturist. Rarely does his ambition extend beyond a bumper crop. Service under Government has few attractions for him. Even if he takes a post he often throws it up after a year or two and says he would rather go back and live in his village and cultivate his land. Rice is the staple food of the tribe and is far and away the most important crop grown. The method of cultivation is that known as "jhuming." A piece of jungle is cut and burnt, and the land cultivated for two years and then allowed to go back to jungle, under which it remains for a period varying from four to fifteen years. If a man is short of land he obviously has to cultivate each piece at shorter intervals. If he is the lord of wide acres the intervals are longer. The bigger the jungle is allowed to grow the more will mould accumulate and the thicker will be the deposit of ash when it is burnt. On an average among the Lhotas a piece of land is cultivated once in ten years. The whole village cultivates in one block, each man having his own piece of land. Isolated patches of cultivation would merely provide food for wild pig, monkeys and other pests. The jungle is cut about December.[1] (The times

[1] The process described below is that employed in the case of ordinary land. On the very poor soil the jungle is often cut in July and burnt at the beginning of December. The soil then gets a longer exposure to the air.

of agricultural operations vary a good deal according to the height and climate of the village concerned.) When the time comes to begin operations each man goes to his land and clears a little piece of jungle. Should he see a snake while so occupied he probably runs home as fast as his legs will carry him, for he would die were he to cultivate that piece of land. If no such evil omen occurs he cuts a stake, sets it up, cuts a notch in the side, puts a little earth from a worm-cast in the notch and goes home. This is regarded as a sort of oath that the owner proposes to clear that piece of jungle. He carefully notes what dreams he has that night. Sometimes he puts a twig from the jungle in question under his head. A bad dream would be enough to make him select another piece of land for that year. On the day when he puts up the stake he must not eat meat from a tiger's kill or the flesh of dog, goat or cattle. His wife may cook his food for him, but he must eat separately from her in the morning, having remained chaste the night before. In clearing the jungle everyone takes part—men, women and children. A man helps his friends and they help him. The jungle is cleared from the bottom of the slope upwards. Bushes and saplings are cut close to the ground. Big trees are left standing, but thin branches are trimmed so that they shall not shade the crop. Usually a bunch of leaves is left growing at the top of big trees of which the other branches are pruned away. Lhotas attach no particular significance to this practice; but among the Aos it appears to be followed only by rich men.[1]

The jungle is left till March to dry, when it is all burnt on the same day. The man who is to start the fire is selected by cutting little chips from a piece of stick and watching how they fall—the ordinary Lhota way of taking omens. The man chosen first makes fire with a fire-stick and sets

[1] The Kayans of Borneo, who have several cultural affinities with Nagas, follow the same practice. They give as their reason the necessity of providing abiding places for the spirits (*toh*) of the locality. (Hose and McDougall, *The Pagan Tribes of Borneo*, II. 23, quoted Sir J. G. Frazer, *Folk-lore in the Old Testament*, III. 70.) The value of the practice is obvious, as it gives the trees a chance of seeding and so of restocking the cleared ground and making it fit for jhuming again.—J. H. H.

the dry jungle alight. Then everyone joins in and lights a long line of fire which sweeps uphill till it dies out in the green, uncut jungle at the top. Next day is *emung*. After that work begins in earnest. Stones and half-burnt logs are collected and little barriers (*oliecho*) are built along the hillsides to prevent the earth being washed away. Sometimes, as at Mangya, rough stone terrace walls are built. The fields are then dug over with a single-handed digger (*chukchü*), a small triangular iron blade fitted like an adze onto a bamboo handle. This preliminary hoeing is omitted by most Northern Lhota villages, who merely clear the land of rubbish before sowing. The fields which have already carried a crop the year before are now weeded, and the weeds gathered into heaps with a small bambo rake (*keya*) and burnt.

Sowing and the ceremonies connected with it.

Before anyone can sow his land certain ceremonies have to be performed. The first of these is *Thruven*, which is performed first by the *Puthi*, and after him in the course of the next few days by anyone who has dragged a stone or done the *Etha* ceremony. The procedure is as follows. The *Puthi* goes with his wife to the spot (*Thruvenphen*) just outside the village where tradition says this ceremony must be performed, generally near the *opya*—the post set up and speared at the *Oyantsoa* ceremony. He takes with him a twig of bamboo (a shoot growing up directly from the ground will not do), some chicken meat, boiled rice, "pita madhu," ginger, a little seed-rice, and some seeds of a plant with a variegated leaf called *orho*. After pouring a little "madhu" on the ground, he arranges four pieces of the bamboo twig in the form of a square and puts a large leaf on the ground to his right and another on his left. On the right-hand leaf he puts ten little pieces, and on the left-hand leaf nine little pieces each of thatching grass, ginger, and chicken meat, and sprinkles a little seed-rice over each heap. The heaps are then tied up in the leaves and put in the square of bamboo twigs. Then close by he sows the *orho* seeds, making a miniature fence round them, the sticks of which are tied together at the top. This is a purely formal act, and it does not seem to matter in the least whether the *orho* seeds ever come up or not. Next morning the *Puthi* sows six seeds of rice in his garden plot. This formal sowing of rice is omitted by the other men who do the *Thruven* ceremony. Sexual intercourse is forbidden the night after this ceremony. When the last man has finished the village keeps one day's *emung*. Anyone who has been married the previous winter, and everyone who has done all social " gennas " and dragged a stone performs a further ceremony before sowing his fields. Among the Northern Lhotas it is done as follows. In the morning one of the old women who acted as *Ponyiratsen* [1] at his wedding, or failing her any old man of his clan who has done no social " gennas," comes to his house, and there ties eight *nungyung* leaves into two bundles of four. She then goes alone down the path leading to his fields, taking with her the *nungyung* leaves, two bamboo " chungas," some rice, and a smouldering brand—for fire is a great protection against evil spirits. She faces towards the fields and lays a bundle of *nungyung* leaves on each side of the path, with a " chunga " on each bundle, and a little bit of smoking brand behind it. She then goes straight to her own home, taking with her the rice, which is her fee. Next day the owner goes down to the field with his friends and sows a little patch first, praying that his crop may be as close as elephant grass, as spreading as a rubber tree and free from weeds. He must refrain from sexual intercourse the night before he does this, and must neither take food nor speak to anyone in the morning till he has sown the first patch. Among the Southern Lhotas the old man or woman who does the ceremony on the first day puts on each side of the path a little heap of rice husks, a smouldering stick and two crossed *yutso* leaves, on which are put six pieces of burnt wood, six pieces of pork, a little boiled rice and a sprinkling of " madhu." The owner of the field must not eat any of the pig which provides the pork used here. The formal act of sowing takes place next day as among the Northern Lhotas. Both on the night preceding and the night after the formal sowing sexual intercourse is forbidden among the Southern Lhotas, and

[1] Cf. pp. 151 *sqq.*

in the morning before going to his fields the man must eat separately from his wife, though she may cook his food. Unlike his neighbours the Aos, the Lhota does not sow broadcast. With the digger (*chukchü*) held in his right hand he scratches a little hole. His left hand is full of seed-rice, of which he allows four or five grains to drop between the middle and index finger into the hole, which is filled in with a stroke of the digger. Both men and women sow. The day's supply of seed-rice is carried in a basket on the left hip, the sowers working their way in a line from the bottom of the hill upwards. From the time the crop is sown till it ripens everyone is busy keeping his fields as free from weeds as possible. The weeder (*ehe*) is a strip of iron about nine inches long and one inch broad, bent into a semicircle and fixed to a short bamboo handle.[1] Every field is weeded at least twice, and often as many as six times—the oftener the better. The weeds are collected into heaps along the edges of the fields, or on stony patches where nothing will grow.

The *Motharatsen* ceremony.

Among the Southern Lhotas a yearly ceremony called *Motharatsen* is performed by the *Puthi* and *Yenga* only when the crop is about half grown to prevent it being damaged by a small white grub (*ora*). On a certain day of which he has given previous notice the *Puthi* collects unhusked rice from the whole village and with some of it buys a pig. This he kills on the day of the ceremony, and going outside the village lays ten pieces of meat and ten pieces of ginger (*osing*) on crossed *yutso* leaves to his right, and nine pieces of meat and ginger on crossed *yutso* leaves to his left. The next day is *emung*. Though the Northern Lhotas still keep the *emung* the ceremony has fallen into abeyance among them. But the Southern Lhotas firmly believe in its efficacy. In 1918 the people of Yanthămo attributed the failure of their crops to the fact that a stranger from another village had entered the house of their *Puthi* after he had collected the subscription of rice and before he had performed the ceremony.

[1] See *Man*, July 1917, "Some Types of Native Hoes, Naga Hills," by H. Balfour, M.A.—J. H. H.

The *Amungkam* ceremony.

When the rice comes into the ear ceremonies are again performed to ensure a good crop. The first ceremony is called *Amungkam*, and is performed by the *Puthi* and *Yenga* at the spot (*amungkampen*) a little way outside the village at which it was performed when the village was founded. The *Puthi* kills and cooks a little boar at his own house and goes with his *Yenga* to the *amungkampen*, taking with him a new cooking-pot, some of the boar's meat, a small live pig, a hen, an egg, a fire-stick and some *yutso* leaves. The *Puthi's* wife may accompany him, but the *Yenga's* wife must stay behind. The *Puthi* makes a fire with the fire-stick, and near it lays out four bamboo twigs in the form of a square, in the middle of which he sets up the egg on end, flanked on either side with forty-two small pieces of meat on crossed *yutso* leaves. He then spears the live pig, praying to *Rangsi*, the deity of the crops, that they may be good. The pig is singed over the fire and cut up, the stomach and entrails being cooked in the new pot and eaten by the *Puthi*. The rest of the meat is divided up, one piece for every man in the village who has dragged a stone. The *Puthi* then strangles the chicken between the finger and thumb of his right hand and watches how the excreta fall as it struggles. If they are dry there will not be much rain and the crops will ripen well. If they are watery, storms will cause the crops to rot. The entrails are next taken out and examined. If they are full the crop will be good; if they are empty it will be poor. These are pushed back into the chicken, which is placed on the ground by the egg. The *Puthi* builds a little fence round the offering and hangs up the fire-stick on it, the pot being turned upside down and left on the ground. He then goes home and calls his friends to his house to drink "madhu" and partake of the pig he killed before leaving home. To each guest he offers a piece of pork and asks if he intends to do the *Rangsikam* ceremony, which is voluntary. To accept the pork means that the answer is in the affirmative. To refuse it means that the answer is in the negative. Early on the morning of the next day, which is *emung*, the villagers go and see if a wild cat or other animal has taken away the chicken which had been left at *amungkampen*. For it to be taken away forbodes ill for the village.

The *Rangsikam* ceremony.

In Akuk no one may do the *Rangsikam* ceremony till after the *Lanvung* "genna," but in other villages it may be done either before or after. The ceremony, which is also known as *Likam*, is performed as follows. The master of the house having slept apart from his wife the night before and eaten apart from her in the morning, though she may cook his food, kills a pig, and taking the cooked meat, "madhu," boiled rice, a live hen and a new pot, goes down to his field-house—a shed built by each man in his fields where he can shelter from the rain or eat his mid-day meal with his wife and family. Having made a fire with a fire-stick inside the house he holds the hen by the wings with his right hand and walks round the outside of the house, swinging the hen and calling out the names of all the different varieties of rice he knows, whether he has sown them or not, and asking *Rangsi* to give him a good crop of them. He then strangles the chicken and takes the omens exactly as the *Puthi* does in the *Amungkam* ceremony. It is worth noting that this is the only occasion on which anything is killed in the field-house. Otherwise it is forbidden to bring raw meat of any kind into a field-house, or kill anything or have sexual intercourse in it. This is why the approaches to field-houses near paths are often "panjied" as a gentle reminder to passers-by that they must not run in to shelter from the rain if they are carrying raw meat. To resume, the hen is plucked, and cooked in the new pot. It is not eaten by the sacrificer, but is taken back to the village and given to an old man of his clan. The entrails are put in the pot, which is covered with a leaf and buried up to the rim behind the field house. The little bamboo basket in which the hen was brought is stuck all over with its feathers and put, together with the fire-stick, beside the pot. All then wash their hands and the proceedings end with a meal from the provisions brought down. From the time when the preparation of the "madhu" for this ceremony is begun till the ceremony is over, sexual intercourse is forbidden and no member of the household must touch a corpse, meat from a tiger's kill or the flesh of cattle, dogs or goats. On the day of the ceremony no man from another village may enter the house before the family go down to the field-house.

The *Lanvung* ceremony.

In the damp climate of Assam jungle grows with extraordinary speed. The seventh day after the *Amungkam emung* is set aside for a united path-clearing (*Lanvung*) [1] by the whole village. During the six days preceding the *Lanvung* day nothing may be sold or killed in the village, and no one may touch a tiger's kill, or perform any "genna" such as *Potsokam* or *Etchhienya*. On the seventh day the working companies each kill a big pig, every man subscribing his share of the price. The next day is a general picnic and the whole village turns out to clear the jungle from the paths. There is much feasting and drinking, and the bucks have jumping competitions and perform feats of strength. Among the Northern Lhotas as each branch path is cleared roof-shaped bamboo erections (*vangkoseng*), like double pen racks with bamboos laid on them in the place of pens, are set up at each fork, to the accompaniment of much ho-hoing.[2] The next day is *emung*.

Protection of crops.

While the crop is ripening the owner is kept busy protecting it from the ravages of beasts and birds. Little look-outs (*zengki*) are built in the trees, well out of the reach of an elephant's trunk. Wild animals are driven away by shouting or clapping two pieces of bamboo together, or blowing a bamboo trumpet (*phupphu*), or by building a big fire and feeding it with bamboos, which go off with a loud bang as each section is burst by the expanding hot air inside it. There is no hedge between field and field, but a rough fence is built round the whole block of village cultivation in order to keep out deer and cattle. In the old days low gaps were left in the fence here and there. Any deer which gave way to temptation and jumped through one of these gaps found

[1] Corresponds to the Angami *Chadangi*, which is performed about the same time of year.—J. H. H.

[2] Most Naga tribes erect some white sign by a path when clearing it. Aos, for instance, set up rows of saplings cut obliquely at the top to show the white heart. Some tribes put up peeled stakes, or stakes split down the middle.—J. H. H.

itself impaled on "panjis." Monkeys are most destructive and difficult to get rid of. One plan is to catch a small monkey, pierce its ears and ornament them with large lumps of cotton-wool. It is then let go and tries to rejoin the troop, who promptly turn tail at the sight of this strange apparition. The more the troop runs away the harder the little monkey tries to catch them, and the harder it tries to catch them, the faster they go. To drive away birds pieces of bamboo leaf-sheaf, sometimes cut into the rough outline of a hovering hawk, are tied from the end of a string to a pole and put to flutter in the breeze.

The eating of first-fruits.

Just before the crop begins to ripen the ceremony of eating the first-fruits (*Mshe etak*) is performed, by the *Puthi* first, and after him by the other households in the village. From the day on which the *Puthi* announces that he is preparing his "madhu" to that on which the last man does the ceremony, no stranger may enter the *Puthi's* house, and selling and killing of fowls and animals and the bringing of meat into the village are prohibited as they are before the *Lanvung* ceremony. On the day of the ceremony the *Puthi* kills a little boar outside his house. He does not eat this meat but distributes it to all the houses in the village in which there has been a death during the year. These portions are offered to the dead in the *Etchhienya* ceremony. After killing the pig he goes into his house accompanied by his *Yenga* and the second *Puthi* if there be one, and in the presence of his family strangles a hen, with a prayer to the *Rangsi* that there may be good crops, no accidents, no raids by enemies, and no prowling tigers. He then takes the omens from the excreta and entrails in the ordinary way. The *Puthi's* wife,[1] or the *Puthi* himself if he be a widower, now goes and cuts the rice sown in the garden plot at the *Thruven* ceremony, no matter how unripe it may be. This the *Puthi* husks in silence. He may be helped by the assistant *Puthi* but by no one else. He puts a little of the grain on the sickle, on both his feet, against his forehead and finally on the hearth-stones. What is left he wraps up in a leaf and half boils. This he pretends, to eat, praying that squirrels, rats

[1] In many Angami villages the First Reaper *must* be a woman.—J. H. H.

and birds may find the rice of the village crops bitter. It is then thrown away, but the hen is eaten. During the next day or two everyone goes down to his fields and brings up a little rice, with which he performs the same ceremony, except that no hen or pig is killed. A little of this rice is preserved and kept wrapped in a leaf at the bottom of the "chunga" or other receptacle in which the day's supply of grain is put every morning. Such is the custom among the Northern Lhotas. Among the Southern Lhotas no rice is put on the sickle, feet, hearth, etc., but the rice is eaten by the whole family with crabs as a relish.

Reaping ceremonies.

The crops ripen about August, those in the old fields being ready first, and as soon as *Mshe etak* is over everyone may cut his rice as soon as it is ready. On the day when he first goes down to cut his crop each man performs at his field-house a ceremony called *Liritang* in honour of the *Rangsi*.[1] He takes down with him "*Rangsi's* load" (*Rangsi'ha*) containing a cooked pig's head, a gourd of "madhu," an egg, a little salt, some cooked rice and the leaves of *sangsu* (a long thin leaf), *lhetyak* (a hairy leaf), and *orungu* (a small leaf, white on the underside). Having arrived at his field-house and seen that all who are to help him that day have come, for no one may come once he has begun the ceremony—he lights a fire with a fire-stick, takes four blades of thatching grass from the roof and bends them double, and places six grains of rice on the threshold (*likingko*) of the field-house. He then cracks the egg over the six grains of rice and pours the contents into the leaf in which he wrapped it when he left his house. This leaf he ties to the post of the field-house, taking it home when he goes in the evening and either giving the contents to his children or eating them himself. He then lights the thatching grass at the fire, and holding the *orungu*, *sangsu* and *lhetyak* leaves with the thatching grass in his right hand, goes outside the house and waves them with a sweeping motion from left to right, the smoke from the thatching grass thus driving evil spirits away. He then says the following[2] traditional words :—

[1] *See* p. 115.

[2] The charms recorded for this ceremony are those used in Akuk. The formulæ used in ceremonies vary considerably in different villages.

Orung-na ranga ranga phang (*orungu*, asking, asking remain). *Lhetyak-na tyaka tyaka phang* (*lehtyak*, sweeping, sweeping remain). *Sangsu-na sangsu lithana, sangsu lithana oro tamtam chudechia* (*sangsu, sangsu*, changing, changing with *sangsu*, coming in a stream pour out).

This is said to mean—for the words are not clearly understood by the Lhotas themselves: "*Orungu* leaves pray the *Rangsi* continually to give me a good crop; *lhetyak* leaves sweep the grain into my field-house, and *sangsu* leaves come one after the other and pour rice in a stream from your loads into my field-house." The man then re-enters the house and sprinkles the floor with "madhu" from his gourd while he repeats the following words:—

"*Satung* *rampeng* *Rangsi* *tchhüchi*
Fish-trap hunter's deity, water-side

rhempi *Rangsi,* *lipphu* *liteng* *Rangsi,*
wanderer's deity, hillside company's deity,

tsatso *rüku* *mpito* *Rangsi* *rencheli*
hurt wounded men's all deities come out of hiding."

In other words he prays to all *Rangsis* belonging to men who are busy fishing or snaring birds by the pools or are hurt (*i. e.* all men who do no cultivation and so have no need of *Rangsis*), together will all the *Rangsis* of the hillside to come and help him. The "madhu" is then sprinkled along the threshold from end to end and the ceremony is at an end and reaping begins. At midday the owner and his helpers come back to the field house for a meal. The owner first undoes the pig's head and puts salt on it. This can be eaten only by him and old people. If he happens to have an *oha* (luck-stone) in his house, no one but he can eat the pig's head, or they will have a bad cough.

The crop is reaped with a small iron sickle (*vekhuo*) with a saw edge. Several stalks are grasped together with the left hand and cut a few inches below the ears. The unthreshed rice is stored in the field-house till everyone in the village has reaped his crop. Each man on the day when he first goes down to thresh again performs the

Liritang ceremony as before, except that a fowl—either cock or hen—takes the place of the pig's head. To thresh the grain the ears are heaped on mats outside the field-house, and after being well trampled are flicked against the right shin.[1] To winnow the grain one man pours it slowly from a basket held with both hands above his head while another fans it vigorously with a winnowing fan (*saveng*)—a bamboo mat with the two corners of one end drawn together, resulting in a thing rather like a sugar scoop in shape.

All that remains now is to carry up the grain as fast as possible. If the fields are a long way from the village, small temporary granaries (*echengrangki*) are built half-way in which the crop can be stored till the field-house, where wild pig and elephants are likely to do most damage, has been emptied. The grain is carried up in baskets (*otyak*), and every man, woman and child in the village helps, going down to the fields with torches in their hands long before dawn and coming up with the last load long after sunset. When the harvest is safely in each man goes down and rolls up the mats in his field-house, and takes them home, uttering as he does so a prayer to *Phuri Rangsi* (Mister Rangsi) to be favourable to him next year. Ahead of him lie a few weeks of well-earned rest till the time comes to cut the jungle for the next year's crop.

Varieties of rice.

Many varieties of rice, both white and red-grained, are sown by the Lhotas. For example, the principal kinds in Okotso are as follows:—White, *amorü* (very coarse), *otsi emhuho* (coarse), *laza* (medium), *motiro* (fine), *wochio* (with black husk), *tambaktsok* (with red husk): Red, *oriepyo* (coarse), *kamtiya* (fine), *santungo* (fine), *moyo* (fine), *changkiu* (fine), and *mhumyandhro* (very fine). No variety is used exclusively either for eating or for "madhu," but the best kinds for "madhu" are *santungo, otsi emhuho, oriepyo, kamtiya* and *moyo*.

Other crops.

Besides rice there are a number of subsidiary crops, generally sown along the edges of the fields or in patches among the rice. Maize (*tsunghundhro*) is sown along the boundaries

[1] Persons of another village are on no account allowed to help in threshing.—J. H. H.

of the fields, or among the chilies, never in large patches, which would only attract bears. Millet (*Setaria italica*, Lhota *teni*) is not an important crop as it is among the Semas and Changs, though a good deal is grown by some of the villages high up on the slopes of Wokha Hill. It is sown about February and cut about July. Giant millet (*Sorghum vulgare*, Lhota *lichophuk*) is sown mostly along the boundaries of fields, the time being about the same as that of millet. Job's tears (*omung*) is also sown along the edges of fields at the same time as the rice and ripens about ten days or a fortnight later. Of taro (*Colocasia antiquorum*, Lhota *mani*) there are several varieties, the principal being *tsampang* (large, reddish root), *vakhundro* (small root) and *loro* (a very large root). This is generally planted along the little soil-barriers (*oliecho*) and scattered among the rice, but sometimes a patch of ground is devoted exclusively to it. Chilies (*machi*) are sown both in the garden patches and on low rich land at the bottom of the fields. The sowing takes place in March, and the plants begin to bear in July. It is a biennial, and in the second year begins to produce pods in May. If left for a third year there will be a few pods, but they are small and shrivelled. Cotton (*khungko*), after rice, is the most important Lhota crop. Sufficient is grown for home consumption and for a considerable export trade. It is sown in March on sunny slopes from which light jungle has been cleared, preferably with a rather gritty soil, and is ready for plucking in October. Whole fields are devoted exclusively to it, but it is an annual and is never sown twice running on the same ground. Several varieties of lentil (*orho*) are grown, all climbers. It is sown in March at the base of the trees left standing about the fields and plucked in October. "Stinking dal" (*limcham* or *nyingtyingsing*) only grows to the height of French beans. Whole fields are often given up to it, and it is often sown in rotation after cotton in February or March, and is ready about November. When the rice is sown, lufas (*longchungo*) are sown at the foot of trees in the field. The green gourd-like fruit is eaten in October, and in January the dry fruit is plucked, the stiff fibrous interior being used to clean pots, etc. Big and small gourds (*shammo* and *zükhe*) are grown for their hard shells, which are used as bottles. They are sown along the edges of fields in March and are ripe in October. A very insipid variety of water-melon (*hmeliti*) is sown scattered about among the rice and is ready from July on. Several varieties of thick, short cucumber (*lishakti*) are sown at the same time as the rice and ripen from July to November. Black sesame (*Sesamum indicum*, Lhota *penching*) and white oil seed (*Perilla ocimoides*, Lhota *pentsü*) are sown in March along the boundaries of the fields, the crop being ready in October or November. In cold villages whole fields of *pentsü* are grown. Tobacco (*mukuyo*) is extensively grown both in garden plots and in corners of fields set apart for it, as well as along the boundaries and scattered about among the rice. It is sown in March, and gives a continual crop of leaves from August on. Indigo (*Strobilanthes flaccidifolius*, Lhota *tchemo*) is grown to a certain extent in garden plots, but chiefly in damp, shady places in the jungle. Cuttings are put in in May and June, and are full grown by August of the next year. It is forbidden for men to touch this plant. The only garden vegetable grown is mustard (*hangi*), the leaves of which are eaten. A kind of giant taro (*taktsü*) is grown in gardens occasionally for its leaves, which are used to line the baskets in which "madhu" rice is set to stand. No part of the plant is ever eaten.

Flowers. The Lhota likes to have flowers handy to put in his ears, and grows a few varieties in his little garden. The chief kinds are wild canna (*lentala*), wild cock's-comb (*thropentera*), marigold (*yantantera*), a small purple flower (*kambentera*), a pale yellow flower (*narisen*), and a red flower (*echamtera*).

Fruit, etc. A large number of oranges [1] (*tsampen* or *khongkeng*) and bitter oranges (*tsampenyimo*—"foolish orange") are grown in

[1] The wild orange is found in the forests along the foot of the Naga Hills on the Assam side, while the culture of limes and pomelos, though apparently not of oranges themselves, was brought up from the Chindwin valley by the Southern Sangtams, who carried the seeds with them on their wanderings. Cf. also Gurdon, *The Khasis*, p. 41.—J. H. H.

the hot villages, a considerable trade in the former being carried on with the plains. The trees are grown from pips and are never manured or pruned or looked after in any way. Other fruit trees are the pomegranate (*tsaramtiven*), which is propagated by cuttings, and a huge plantain (*echamyuti*), which is horriby wooden and astringent and has to be cooked before it can be eaten even by a Lhota. The Christians of Okotso now grow a few tea bushes (*cha*). A very small number of betel nut palms (*mma*) are to be found in villages on the range nearest the plains. These villages do a big trade in " pan " leaves (*lamo*) with the plains, where hill " pan " fetches a good price. The " pan " vines are grown up trees in the jungle wherever the soil is suitable. They are not cultivated in any way, but every vine belongs to some individual though it is growing in unreclaimed jungle. The vines are propagated by means of cuttings.

Live-stock.

Mithan (*Bos frontalis*, Lhota *tsiro*) are regarded as a sign of wealth, but are no longer kept in large numbers by the Lhotas. They do a lot of damage to the crops, and as an investment are too risky to suit the taste of the careful Lhota, being very liable to rinderpest, an outbreak of which may kill off a whole herd. Further, they are practically only used for sacrificial purposes, for which cattle will do almost as well. Bulls which are marked in such a way that it would be unlucky to sacrifice them are sometimes killed for food, but cows are only eaten when they die of old age or disease. A pure-bred mithan is black, with white stockings and grey forehead, but many individuals are found marked with white or brown on the body. This appears to be due to the fact that the strain of mithan in the Naga Hills has become hopelessly contaminated by allowing them to interbreed with cattle.[1] An ordinary

[1] I have heard of one case of a mithan interbreeding with a gaur (*Bos gaurus*), a few of which are still to be found in the foot-hills of the Lhota country. The calf died, however. Such crosses are said to be not uncommon in the North Cachar Hills.

cow mated with a mithan bull produces a hybrid, which in turn is fertile when mated with a mithan. The result of this cross when again mated with a mithan produces an animal which in size and shape resembles a mithan, but which often shows its humble origin in its colouring. Animals of this unpure strain have contaminated the whole breed and any pair of mithan is liable to produce a throw-back. Though mithan calves are sometimes tied up outside the owner's house till their legs get strong, the animals are generally allowed to run more or less wild in the jungle, the owner merely calling them and giving them salt occasionally. Beasts are occasionally marked by having their ears split. No bells are worn and no herdsman is kept to look after mithan or any kind of cattle. When a mithan calf is born the owner observes six days' "genna" if it is a bull and five days' if it is a cow. During those days no stranger from another village can enter his house and he must not eat meat from a tiger's kill. This "genna" is observed for the calves of all cattle. In the case of mithan a necklace of six seeds of the sword-bean (*khuro*) is put on the neck of a bull calf, and one of five seeds on the neck of a cow calf, and after being worn for a few hours is taken off and hung up in the owner's house.[1] A curious custom which appears to be common to all Nagas and applies to cattle of all kinds and often to pigs, is that by which a man will own half or one leg of an animal. Often a man prefers to distribute his risk by investing in a share in a number of mithan rather than own the whole of two or three beasts. The hybrid (*tyangtso*) of a mithan bull and ordinary cow is a black or very dark brown animal midway between its parents in size. They are allowed to run wild, but generally come and sleep in the village. Large numbers of ordinary cattle (*mangsü*) are bought in the plains. They are of the common Assamese breed, and miserable creatures as a rule. Some are kept for food and breeding, but usually they are taken straight through into the Ao and Sema country and sold.

[1] The Semas have a similar custom. The intention apparently is to keep a certain amount of control over this semi-feral animal by retaining something which has been in close contact with it.—J. H. H.

The Lhota never milks his cattle, simply because it is not the custom to do so, but he will drink milk if it is offered to him. There is a black and black-and-white breed of cattle known as *süpi* which the Lhotas regard as indigenous to their country. These carry a good deal more meat than the Assamese cattle. All cattle are allowed to run loose in the jungle, the owner only going to have a look at them every two or three days. Buffalo (*juzü*) which are past work are sometimes bought in the plains and brought up for food, but they are never bred by Lhotas and are useless for sacrificial purpose, as they are regarded as "stupid" beasts. Pigs (*woko*) swarm in Lhota villages and a man must be very poor indeed not to keep one or two. They are closely akin to the wild pig, with which they occasionally interbreed. When a sow farrows the owner observes five days' "genna." Every boar is castrated when it is only about two months old. This operation is generally performed with a sharp piece of bamboo by a man who is known to be skilled at it. Ashes having been put on the wound it is sewn up, and the little pig runs off apparently none the worse. The ears of all boars are clipped at the time when they are castrated. Little pigs are generally shut up in the *mpongki* at night, but when they get big they are allowed to roam about the village at will, only coming home for a meal of rice husks, "madhu" waste and taro once a day. A pig which is a bad wanderer and does not come home as it should is punished by having its ears pierced and a piece of string run through them and tied to the wall of the house.[1] Ordinarily dogs are the only animals to which names are given, but in some villages pigs are called after the person from whom they are bought, a custom which is generally viewed with no great favour by the seller if he gets to hear of it. Sometimes little pigs become household pets. I knew one in

[1] Lhotas give to newly acquired pigs the bulbous root of a small ground orchid which they call *wokoloha* (pigs' luck-stone). This is believed to have the effect of inducing them to take to their new surroundings without running away (as we put butter on a cat's paws) and prevents their fighting with the other pigs in the house. It also seems to promote the prosperity of the pig generally.—J. H. H.

Seleku which spent most of its time playing with the children. It had its own special cloth spread for it by the fire and would sleep nowhere else. It was sold by its callous owner when it began to get big, and no doubt became pork shortly afterwards. Goats (*nyanya*) are kept in large numbers, white goats with long hair being particularly valuable. This hair is sold to be dyed red and used for all kinds of ornaments. The wretched animals used to be plucked alive, one goat giving several crops. But this has now been stopped and the hair is cut off. Goats being particularly attractive to leopards, they are kept at night in little houses (*nyanyarangki*) placed high up on poles in the village, a couple of notched posts forming a ladder up which they can scramble.

Except in the villages near the plains, where they are supplanted by Assamese curs, Lhota dogs are of the ordinary Naga type, black, with white chest and often one or more white paws. There are often brown and white markings on the body, and one type is entirely white with long hair.[1] The latter used to be plucked alive as white goats were and their hair used for ornaments. All dogs have names. Examples are *Keri* ("white paws," lit. gauntlets), *Pangri* ("piebald"), *Humthe* ("soft-haired"), *Phunyung* ("red dog"), *Taphuno* ("stay-at-home," lit. "hearth dog"), *Mhakuk* ("ditch-on-face," *i. e.* with a depression over the nose), *Kimung* ("stay-in-the-house"), *Yimo* ("fool"), *Okharo* ("little one," a pet name for the last-born child). The tails of all dogs are cut short, and the ears of male dogs are also clipped. The severed bits of tail are put in a cleft stick and stuck up in the house out of the way of rats, for were a rat to eat a tail the puppy to which it lately belonged would die. A Lhota feeds and treats all his dogs well, but is especially careful of his hunting dogs. They

[1] There are two distinct types of Naga dog—one with a short and hard coat, sometimes red, but usually black with white chest and often with white paws and collar or a white splash on the back of the neck; the other long-haired and either black or red, though sometimes all white or white with a few black blotches. The long-haired type, like the other, has a good nose, but its coat is too thick for it to be able to hunt game for long.—J. H. H.

are never punished as other dogs are, the result being that they are hopelessly disobedient. It is quite common for the dogs to spoil a whole day's hunting by going off on the wrong line and remaining deaf to their masters' shouts. Hunting dogs are never eaten, and when one dies it is wrapped in a cloth and given decent burial outside the village. A Lhota strokes but never pats his dog. When he wants to make much of it he holds its head between his hands and allows it to lick his face, returning the compliment by dribbling onto its nose. When a bitch has puppies her owner observes five days' "genna," with the same restrictions as in the case of cattle and pigs. Cats (*onyiro*) are never kept, though they are occasionally bought in the plains and eaten.

The Lhota fowl (*hono*) much resembles the red jungle fowl (*Gallus ferrugineus*), with which it often interbreeds. Crosses with the kalij pheasant (*Gennœus horsfieldi*) too are by no means unknown. Fowls live on what they can pick up, but never seem to wander far from home. Old baskets are put up on shelves in the *mpongki* for hens to lay in and hatch their chickens out of the reach of rats. The owner must take the chickens down from the basket either after sunset or before sunrise. Before doing so he puts a piece of burnt wood (or in some villages five pieces of burnt wood) into the basket and says: "When you wander may you not be lost or fall a prey to wild cat or hawk." The egg-shells are strung on a bit of bamboo and hung up in the house, it is said in order to keep a reckoning of the number of eggs hatched in the year.[1] Nowadays pigeons (*vephu*) are kept by a few people. Ducks are never kept, though large numbers are brought up from the plains for food.

Hunting.

Guns being comparatively scarce, the Lhota still hunts deer with dogs and spear as his forefathers did before him. Sambhur (*sepu*) are chiefly found in the flat river valleys,

[1] It is probably also thought that the preservation of the shell aids the preservation of the chicken during its infancy.—J. H. H.

and when hunted invariably make for the water, which they cross and recross repeatedly. Tracks having shown that a sambhur is in a certain piece of jungle, the dogs are worked through it by their owner, who encourages them with a shout like a loud laugh. With him goes a thin line of spearmen to guard against a break back, while other spears wait at places where the quarry is likely to cross the stream. The dogs give tongue lustily enough as soon as they pick up the scent, so that the waiting spearmen can change their position according to the line which the deer seems to be taking. This goes on till the deer is either killed or gets clean away. The method of hunting serow (*tsiyo*) and barking deer (*sanu*) is the same, except that these animals are found in the little valleys running down the hills and are ambushed at the points where they try to get through into the next valley. The Lhota is a wonderful judge of the line a deer is going to take and can generally be relied upon to get his spear into a running target at twenty yards, so that these hunts are more often successful than unsuccessful. No hunting takes place on the day on which anyone has died in the village, not apparently from any idea of showing respect to the dead, but because it is regarded as a foregone conclusion that luck will be bad that day. If an animal killed is found to have died with its tongue hanging out of the left side of its mouth, hunting is probably stopped for the day, as it is believed that no more game will be killed; but to find the tongue hanging out of the right side of the mouth means that if the hunters go on they will rouse and kill another deer. *Sityingo*[1] is the jungle deity who owns all wild animals as a man owns domestic animals. If a hunting party kills a deer with a torn ear they will hunt no more that day, for have they not killed a deer whose ear *Sityingo* has snicked as a sign of ownership. The deer, however, can be eaten. Furthermore, the dogs must be purified before they can hunt again. Their owner orders his wife to prepare a little "madhu." This she must do in silence. Next day no stranger from another village may enter his house, nor anyone who is doing

[1] Corresponds to the Angami *Tsikeo*.—J. H. H.

a "genna" of any kind. The following day water is added to the "madhu" and the "madhu" rice given to the dogs to eat. The owner, taking them with him, goes with an old man to a spot outside the village, where the latter makes a fire with a fire-stick, and lifting the dogs in his hands passes them through the smoke, uttering as he does so the following prayer to *Sityingo*: "We have made new 'madhu' and new fire, and have purified the dogs. May all the deer wherever they be come to our village and be hunted by these dogs." He then watches to see what insects come near the fire. If big insects come the dogs will get sambhur. If small insects come they will get barking deer.

Much though he enjoys the sport, the Lhota hunts primarily to get meat. The division of the spoil is therefore carefully regulated by custom, which is strictly adhered to. In the case of deer the first spear gets a hind-leg, second spear a fore-leg, and the owner of the dogs a hind-leg, the head, liver and heart,[1] the remaining fore-leg going to the oldest man of the hunting party. The rest of the meat is divided among the remaining spearmen, the older men getting slightly bigger shares than the younger. A spear which only hits the animal in the face or on the hock does not count. Were the thrower to claim a share of the meat on the strength of such a hit it is believed that either he or one of his family would die. From every deer killed *Sityingo* is given his share. This consists of six little bits of liver wrapped in one leaf and five little bits in another. These are eaten by the oldest man in the village of the clan of the owner of the dogs. Wild pig (*oni* or *lipung*) are occasionally hunted with dogs, but generally are only speared if a man happens to meet one. The same applies to bears (*sivan*). A wounded bear is not generally followed up till next day. It is then relentlessly tracked, alike over soft ground where every footprint is plain and over rocky slopes where nothing but a few bent leaves show which

[1] By the Semas, at any rate, something, if only a scrap, must be given by the owner of the dogs to the dogs themselves. Cf. S. C. Roy, *The Oraons of Nagpur*, p. 157.—J. H. H.

way it has gone, for a Lhota will pick up what, to European eyes, is a hardly perceptible trail as easily and quickly as he will follow an ordinary path. In the case of animals such as pig and bear killed without the aid of dogs, the first spear gets the head, hind-leg, fore-leg, liver and heart, and the second spear the other fore-leg and hind-leg. Remaining members of the party take the rest of the meat. There are no chiefs as there are among the Semas and Changs to get a share of the meat whether they join in the hunt or not. Dogs are also used to hunt porcupines (*liso*), an animal much sought after for its flesh, the skin of the back being especially esteemed. For a tiger (*mharr*) or leopard (*mharrtero*) hunt the whole male population of the village turns out with daos and shields and spears, and, in Moilang and its neighbours, wearing cane helmets. A rough circle is cleared round the piece of jungle in which the beast has been marked down, and a V-shaped palisade is built at the bottom. Outside this the old men wait with their spears ready poised, while the young men drive the animal downhill, cutting the jungle as they go. Any man who is charged falls with his shield over him, while a shower of spears distracts the tiger's attention. Eventually if all goes well the tiger is driven into the palisading and speared by the old men waiting there. If a tiger happens to break a spear the shaft must either be left in the jungle or stuck in the ground under the head of the quarry when it is hung up after a successful hunt. If this is not done the owner will some day be killed by a tiger. The tiger's head is cut off by a man who has done all social "gennas" and is a warrior of repute, and the paws by a man who belongs to a family a member of which has been killed by a tiger. This in a sense removes the curse from the family.[1] The head and paws are hung on a tree by the side of the path up to the village, and *tsombhondhro* leaves are stuffed in its mouth, some say to prevent it eating people in the Land of the Dead, and some say so that it may not be able to tell the dead what clan killed it. Under the head the hunters

[1] In some villages of the Northern Lhotas the curse is removed by cutting off the head, not the paws.

jab the ground with their spear butts till it is thickly covered with little marks. If the spirit (*omon*) of the tiger comes wandering round it will see these marks and refrain from troubling a village which possesses such a mighty army of warriors. The man who cut off the tiger's head must not eat beef, pork, goat's flesh, jungle birds, taro or any boiled relish, or have intercourse with his wife for twelve days. A similar prohibition for one day applies to the other men of the village.

Monkeys such as *Pithecus brahma* (*otham*) and *Macacus assamensis* (*kirango*) are shot with the crossbow (*olo*) and arrows, but a tailless ground-monkey (*Macacus arctoides*, Lhota *mitham*) is driven with great success, the day's bag sometimes totalling thirty or forty. A troop which takes up its abode in a jungly gully flanked by cultivated fields is doomed. All the men of the village surround the jungle, and a tunnel (*vaksap*) is built of interlaced jungle and brushwood at the lower end, like a duck-decoy tunnel on a small scale. The monkeys are driven from the upper end, and keeping to the ground enter the tunnel. Finding no exit at the lower end they completely lose their heads and cling to one another and whimper till they are killed.

Before the making of pitfalls (*soku*) was forbidden by Government large numbers of elephants, deer and wild pig were killed by means of them. Elephant-pits were huge affairs, but the ordinary pitfall was about ten feet deep, with the bottom covered with big jagged rocks and "panjis," so that any animal which fell in was likely both to have its legs broken and to be impaled. Many kinds of snares are used, mostly for small animals and birds, though a running noose (*putha* or *ozo*) used to be used by the Southern Lhotas for deer. The commonest trap is the triangular trap (*tsiri*), which is also used by Aos, Changs, Semas and Angamis. It is set in runs or at holes in fences and is most effective. It consists of a triangle of bamboo, the base of which is extended to form a bow. The side nearest the bow is double. Through this is passed a noose which is set in such a way that any animal or bird trying to get through the triangle releases the bow and is caught by the noose against the double side. Birds and small animals are also caught by running nooses (*khükcha*), platforms which release nooses when trodden on (*chambo*), and fall-traps (*otyo*). Are Yanthamo appears to be the only village which possesses a box-trap for leopards, though these contrivances are common among the Aos, from whom Are Yanthamo probably copied the one in question. It consists of a small low shed made of stout saplings securely tied in place and is divided into two compartments, in the hinder of which is put the bait, a live goat. The leopard enters, and in making for the goat treads on a little platform which releases a catch and drops a heavy wooden door behind it. Only once did a leopard enter the Are Yanthamo trap, and then it raged and roared in such an alarming way that the local Nimrods sat in the village and quaked, till it eventually managed to break its way out. A monkey is not an easy beast to snare, but a genius in Changbang invented a booby trap for monkeys which is said to have been very successful. He watched the line which monkeys took when chased off his fields. In their path he dug a pitfall, and over it at some height arranged a dry branch in such a way that monkeys would be sure to run along it in their flight. He cut this branch nearly through, so that the first monkey which used it snapped it off and came to an untimely end in the pitfall. Kabuis use a similar trap for monkeys.[1] Bird-lime (*onyi*) made of a mixture of the sap of the rubber tree (*nitsütung*) and *Ficus religiosa* (*nitsotung*) is extensively used. The two kinds of sap are boiled down in separate "chungas," which are then split and the resulting rubber-like cakes extracted and cut into small pieces. The bits of thickened *nitso* sap are chewed to soften them and put in a broken potsherd. Then the pieces of *nitsü* juice are toasted over the fire on the end of an old umbrella stay and mixed with the *nitso* sap in the potsherd while they are hot. The resulting bird-lime is sometimes put on twigs stuck up by the side of pools at which birds come to drink, and sometimes put on twigs fixed on bushes and baited with a live cockroach impaled on a thorn. The use of decoy birds is

[1] Cf. T. C. Hodson, *Naga Tribes of Manipur*, p. 57.

unknown. An accurate knowledge of its habits enables a snarer to catch even the Great Indian Hornbill (*rücheng*) with bird-lime. This bird never flies straight to the berries on which it is going to feed, but always first perches on the thick part of the branch and then hops out towards the end, raising its wings slightly at each hop. Limed twigs are therefore put along the side of the branch at such an angle that they will touch the bird's body as it raises its wings. At such a touch it shuts its wing down on the limed twig and is helpless.

A word on the taking of bees' and hornets' nests may find a place under this section. There are men who for some curious reason appear to be immune from stings, but the ordinary Lhota either smokes out the nest he wishes to take, or else kills all the occupants by taking a handful of the pounded skin of the chalmăgra fruit (*hmhmti*) and blowing the fumes into the hole.[1] Honey or the juice of the pounded leaves and bark of a certain tree (*tsungnung*) is often rubbed on the body as a protection against bee stings. A man who intends to take a bees' or hornets' nest must remain chaste the night before. Both the honey and grubs are eaten, and a species of large bee (*tsakmen*) which builds under overhanging rocks and branches makes good wax. The other principal species are a medium-sized bee (*takrhi*), a small bee with a negligible sting (*ndhrontso*) and a very small bee with a severe sting (*lungtsak*). Hornets' nests, which are sought for for the fat, juicy grubs they contain, are not so easily taken. The nest of one species (*tsaktsü*) is underground and the tiny hole by which it is entered is hard to find. Anyone, therefore, who has a craving for *tsaktsü* grubs puts out a bit of bad meat as a bait and catches the first hornet which settles on it. He carefully extracts its sting and ties a bit of cotton-wool or a white feather to its legs and lets it go. Hampered by the feather, which can be seen from a good distance, it flies slowly towards home and can generally be followed if the jungle is not too

[1] This fruit, thrice cooked, is used as food by the Konyaks and pronounced very good—"like *ghi*." Cooked once only, it is used by them as a rat poison.—J. H. H.

thick. The nest once found a big fire is lighted over it at night when all the hornets have gone in and it is dug out. Another kind of hornet (*chengkuku*) with a red head and a fearful sting builds huge nests in the branches of trees. At night a fire is lighted underneath and burning straw held to the nest at the end of a bamboo. Any hornets which escape the burning straw drop into the fire and the nest can be safely taken.

Though Lhotas possess a wonderful sense of direction, it sometimes happens that a man out hunting loses his way in the jungle. Should this happen he cuts a stick and makes a few cuts in the bark to represent the pattern on a python's skin. This stick he leaves on the ground and is then sure to be able to find his way without difficulty. The custom is connected with the belief that the python has a habit of leaving its saliva on leaves, and that anyone who touches one of these leaves by accident will go mad and lose his way.[1]

Fishing.

Lhotas are keen fishermen and expert swimmers. Fishing rights over any particular stretch of water are governed by custom, being held by the village or villages who exercised them in the past. The rights to "poison" in any particular pool are generally held jointly by two or more villages, while each village has the right to erect weirs in particular stretches of water. "Poisoning" is by far the most important method of fishing. Formerly the root of a small plant called *notsü* was much used. The juice of this kills every fish with which it comes in contact and its use has been prohibited by Government. The other so-called "poisons" only stupefy the fish. The commonest is the juice of a creeper (*niro*), which for some reason affects cat-fish (*zyümo*) even when it is too weak to stupefy other fish. On one occasion when the writer watched the fishing

[1] A Chang who loses his way cuts off a bit of his hair and sticks it in a cleft stick or the fork of a tree, no doubt as a substitute for his own person. After which the python lets him go and he finds his way home. A Sema under similar circumstances offers a bit of the fringe of his cloth.—J. H. H.

FISHING
Pounding the " poison " creeper on the bank.

FISHING
Pounding the " poison " into the water.

[*To face p.* 71.

of a pool insufficient poison was used. Yet thirty-six huge cat-fish were caught, while the rest of the bag consisted of only about a dozen small fish.[1] Other "poisons" used are *cheti* (the berries of a tree with leaves rather like mahogany leaves: this poison is much used by the Aos, who call it *arr*), *pitsü* (a creeper with small leaves), *opyak* and *achak* (the bark of two species of trees), *mwemti* (little berries, chiefly used in small streams), and *mozi* (a creeper, weak and not much used). All the villages who have the right to "poison" in a certain pool agree to combine to do so on a certain day. On the night before the fishing is to take place sexual intercourse is forbidden, nor may anything be killed in the morning before going down to the water. The presence of women is absolutely forbidden when fishing is going on. Every man brings with him a bundle of creeper (assuming *niro* is being used). This is first thoroughly pounded on the bank to ensure that all the cells are broken. Trees are felled and placed on rough stone supports across the stream to serve as pounding benches for the final pounding, each village making its own line or lines of benches one above the other. As each bench is finished the men lay their half-pounded bundles of creeper on it. The braves then line up on the shore facing up stream, and all ho-ho together and brandish their daos. Then a rush is made for the benches and everyone pounds his bunch of creeper, dipping it in the water at intervals. All chant as they work, and the men on each line of benches pound more or less in time. Meanwhile old men are watching the

[1] My experience of fish "poisoning" by Lhotas is that the discipline of the leaders over the younger men beating the "poison" into the river is so poor that the invariable result is that almost the only fish taken are a few labeo, a bottom-feeding fish more susceptible to poison than mahseer, and any cat-fish (*Bagarius yarrellii* or *Silundia gangetica* or some similar Siluroid) that there may be in the river. Ultimately I came to the conclusion that, as far as game-fish at any rate were concerned, poisoning by *niro* did more good than harm, as it cleared out the predatory fish while scarcely affecting the mahseer and its kin. I found later that Mr. Soppitt's experiences among the Kacharis in the North Cachar Hills had led him to precisely the same conclusion (see C. A. Soppitt, *Historical and Descriptive Account of the Kachari Tribes in the North Cachar Hills*, Shillong, 1885. Reprinted with an introduction by E. C. Stuart Baker, 1901, pp. 51, 52).—J. H. H.

pool below and a shout goes up when the first fish is seen to come floundering to the top. This is the signal for all to throw their bundles of creeper into the water and rush down to the pool. Some wait round the edge with long-handled landing nets, while others put a heavy stone into their "lengta" band and chase the fish at the bottom of the pool, slipping the stone out when they want to come to the top. The young bucks are like otters, and it is a common sight to see a man come up with a fish in his teeth and one in each hand. Cat-fish are great prizes. They are often heavier than a man and require all a man's strength to drag to the top. Indeed it is by no means uncommon for a Lhota to struggle with one of these enormous fish at the bottom till he is exhausted and drowned. When anyone has landed a cat-fish he cuts it with his dao in such a way that he will be able to recognize it and claim his share when the catch is divided up. Small fish he strings on a slip of bamboo at his waist. Every man who lands a cat-fish gets a specially big cut from it, but the fish found in their stomachs are only eaten by old people. Otherwise the whole catch of a village is divided up among the members who came down to fish according to their age and importance. Whether they came down or not a share is given to the *Puthi* and anyone whose house has ever been "apotia."[1]

Fish-traps are of various kinds. The most elaborate is that called *osa*, which is used on the Doyang and consists of a V-shaped bamboo weir pointing down-stream, with a long spout-like outlet, closed with stakes set closely together, and roofed at the end so that fish cannot jump out. The floor of the outlet is covered with bamboos laid lengthways, so that a fish once caught in the rush of water can get no grip to work up-stream, but is held by the current against the stakes at the bottom. Another type, also called *osa*, is used on smaller streams and consists of a semicircular weir of bamboo or piled-up stones, with gaps at intervals, each gap being blocked with a strong bamboo basket from which, if a fish is once swept in, it cannot escape against the stream. This kind of trap is particularly successful if

[1] See p. 160.

otters fishing in the pool above drive the fish down, a curious parallel to the way in which Biscayan sardine fishers used to depend on porpoises to drive the shoals of sardines into their nets. A third type used on moderate-sized streams is called *eyinga.* This consists of a bamboo weir right across the river and another weir with a big opening in the middle about twenty yards lower down. Fish feeding their way up-stream in the evening pass through the gap, which is closed at night, shutting the fish in. A rough inner fence of bamboo is built along the lower weir, and the fish trying to jump over on their return down-stream are caught between the two fences. Fish weirs are in operation throughout the cold weather, till they are swept away by the first big flood. The task of building a weir is not one which can be entered upon without due precautions. For three days beforehand the builder must not speak to strangers and must refrain from sexual intercourse. On the last morning neither he nor any of the men who are to help him may kill anything, and the working party while engaged on their task may speak to each other but to no one else at all, whether of their own village or not. A man begins by helping his father, or one of his father's friends, when he is a boy, and gradually grows up to be the owner or joint owner of a weir himself. Were a man who had never done so before to take it into his head to go down and build a fish-trap he would surely die. When he was sleeping near his trap at night the deity of the stream, the Water Master (*Tchhüpfuo*), would come along and look at the soles of his feet and see that they were not white like the soles of men who spend much time in the water. Then he would cause illness to come upon him so that he would die. In a few villages a small hand-trap (*naching*) is set in swampy pools for mud-fish. It consists of a small bamboo basket entered by an inverted funnel, so that a fish once in cannot find the way out. When the rivers are high fishing-rods (*ngoko*) made of bamboo are used, with a line made of twisted *chütsung* bark, the bark used for bow-strings. Hooks (*mukhu*) are either bought at a shop or made out of umbrella wire. It is unlucky to catch a kind of fish called *süwo* with the rod and line. Anyone who does so splits the fish in half lengthways and lays the two halves on the ground. He then goes home by a road other than the road by which he came. Were he to go home by the road he came he would meet and be killed by a tiger or leopard. This fish can be eaten without any precautions if it is caught in any other way. Where a stream is divided into two channels with an island in the middle, one channel is often blocked with a temporary weir and all the water diverted down the other. The fish in the blocked channel can then be caught by hand. When a stream is both cold and highly coloured the fish appear to lose their vitality and large numbers are caught by hand in holes and cracks.[1]

Food.

Rice is the staple food, but some relish, even if it be only jungle leaves boiled with chilies and salt, is always eaten with it. Meat is preferred if obtainable, but the Lhota will eat most things at a pinch. His diet includes the meat of all domestic animals and most wild animals and birds, fish, both fresh and dried, bee and hornet grubs, large spiders, a kind of beetle, white ants, cultivated plants and innumerable jungle leaves and berries. Certain things are forbidden, but villages near the plains are much less particular in this respect than those on the inner ranges. The general reason why certain animals and birds are not eaten is either that they are obviously unclean or because they are thought likely to impart their properties to the eater or to his children. Generally speaking old people can eat things which young people cannot, because it does not much matter what happens to them and in any case they will have no more children. Tigers and leopards are absolutely forbidden to all because they eat men. Leopard cats can be eaten by old people who no longer cultivate. Were a young man to eat it he would get poor crops. Wild dog

[1] I have known Lhotas diving in the Doyang in the rains, when that river was muddy and in spate, catch fish by hand without any sort of aid, apparently picking them up stupid from the river bed.—J. H. H.

if eaten causes a raging thirst. Phiyosao of Akuk ate only a little of the skin of one, but he had to leave the village school because he could never sit through a lesson without going out for a drink. Whoever eats or even kills an otter will never be able to get his fields to burn properly.[1] None but very old people may touch, much less eat, either the big or little flying squirrel (*Petaurista yunnanensis* and *Pteromys aboniger*). Anyone who does so will frequently be guilty of indecent behaviour with the opposite sex of his own clan. Several kinds of birds are forbidden. The Large Streaked Spiderhunter (*Arachnothera magna*) is only eaten by very old people " because it is such a very funny-looking bird, and has such a very long beak." The local species of minivet (*Pericrocotus brevirostris*) is forbidden to all because the cocks are supposed to have got their scarlet markings from being splashed with human blood. The Velvet-fronted Blue Nuthatch (*Sitta frontalis*) goes about in little flocks and is such a confiding little bird that if one is killed the rest of the flock will wait near till they are killed too. Therefore if a man were to eat one, one death in his household would be followed by a series of deaths. A solitary old man or woman can, of course, eat this bird with impunity. The Whitecapped Redstart (*Chimarrhornis leucocephalus*) and Whiteheaded Babbler (*Gampsorhynchus rufulus*) are not eaten because they would cause the eater to become grey-headed. Parrots and crow-tits (*Paradoxornis*) are not eaten because of the shape of their beaks. The eater's children would be everlastingly pinching their friends. Scimitar babblers (*Pomatorhinus*) if eaten would make the eater unable to remember his dreams and so deprive him of an important guide in life. The clan of anyone who ate a sun-bird (*Æthopyga*) would dwindle in numbers, for sun-birds used to be as big as fowls, but are now the smallest of all birds. Swiftlets and swallows are

[1] On the other hand, the Aos and Changs place a high value on otter flesh. They believe that fish-bones will never stick in the throat of anyone who has eaten it. If a particularly large fish-bone does by any chance stick in the throat of a Chang who has ever eaten otter meat he has only to murmur " I am an otter," and down it goes.

never still. The children of anyone who ate the flesh of these birds would be idle and always wanting to run about and play. The flesh of the Tree or House Sparrow is said to cause the itch. The Red-headed Trogon (*Harpactes erythrocephalus*) is not eaten because it is supposed to have got its brilliant colouring from human blood. Owlets (*Scops*) are not eaten owing to the extraordinary belief that they hatch their eggs by lying on their backs on them. The nightjar when disturbed only flies a short way and then settles on the ground again as if inviting one to follow. In this way it used to lead men on and on like a will-o'-the-wisp till they found themselves in an ambush and were killed. Therefore nightjars are not eaten. The Green Magpie (*Cissa chinensis*) is not eaten owing to a supposed habit of sitting on the bamboo erections built over graves. The loud laughing cry of the Himalayan White-crested Laughing Thrush (*Garrulax leucolophas*) is particularly sudden and startling. Were a man to eat its flesh he would become nervous in the jungle and would jump whenever a twig or a leaf dropped near him. The cry of the Long-tailed Broadbill (*Psarisomus dalhousiæ*) is a sign of rain, and whoever eats its flesh will always have bad weather when he goes to work in his fields. The hoopoe is such a curious bird that to eat it might mean disaster to the clan. Hawks are continually dropping excreta. Whoever ate one would spit continually.[1] The Rufous-bellied Hawk Eagle (*Lophotriorchis kieneri*) is forbidden to all but old people who expect to have no more children, for sores appear on the heads of the eater's children. The two species of Racket-tailed Drongo (*Dissemurus paradiseus* and *Bhringa remifer*) are only eaten by old people, for as they have two very long conspicuous tail-feathers, so whoever ate their flesh would only have two children. The Indian Roller, commonly called the Blue Jay, is only eaten by old people, for the children of the eater would be as noisy as the bird itself. Ashy Swallow-Shrikes (*Artamus fuscus*) have a habit of sitting on branches in rows, each bird touching its neigh-

[1] Most Nagas, including Lhotas, eat hawks with avidity. Possibly this accounts for it.—J. H. H.

bour. It is therefore eaten by none but very old people, for were any young man or woman to eat it he or she would never be able to sit alone, but would always want to go and sit cuddled up against one of the other sex, a habit full of possibilities of trouble. The flesh of the Great Indian Hornbill (*Dichoceros bicornis*) is absolutely forbidden to members of the Tompyaktserre phratry, and is very rarely eaten by members of other phratries. The bird has a croaking note, and were a man to whom its flesh is forbidden to eat it he would die of violent hiccoughs. Of reptiles the python is eaten by all in the villages near the plains, but elsewhere it is only eaten by old people. (Even villages near the plains never speak of it as "python" (*ongam*) when talking of it as an article of diet, but always call it by the politer name of *sosiyo*, "long meat.") It is believed that black marks are liable to appear on the back of the eater, who will be semi-paralysed and only able to move his body slowly like a python. A Rephyim man called Lobenthang is supposed to have been affected in this way. Snakes other than the python are forbidden to all. Old women may eat the same things as old men, but there are a few kinds of meat which men may eat, but young and middle-aged women may not. These include serow, wild mithan, buffalo, bear, elephant, monkey, white-browed gibbon ("huluk") and pangolin. Most of these are forbidden for no reason which is known now,[1] but gibbon is prohibited because these animals are supposed to have no more than a single young one once in nine years, and this peculiarity would assuredly pass to the eater. In some villages these prohibitions are only observed at the time of pregnancy.

[1] Probably the reason, in some cases at any rate, is the fear that the propensity of the animal for destroying and wasting paddy will pass to the woman, who is responsible for regulating the household consumption, and thereby cause the household store of grain to be unduly depleted. This is almost certainly the reason in the case of the monkey and might apply equally to the wild mithan and buffalo, to the bear and to the elephant. It could hardly be applied to the serow or to the pangolin. The former of these two is a roaming animal and rarely sleeps long in the same spot, which offers an obvious reason for the prohibition. The pangolin is such a curious beast that anyone might shy at eating him. The Sema forbids gibbon meat lest the children inherit the cry.—J. H. H.

Rice is invariably cooked separately from the meat or whatever is to be eaten with it. Meat and vegetables are boiled together with a lavish allowance of chilies and salt. Practically all food is boiled, though maize is roasted and eaten cold and plantains are roasted in their skins. A very favourite relish is bamboo pickle (*dhrüchong*) made of the hearts of young bamboo shoots pounded up with water and then dried, and boiled again when required. Though the Lhota prefers his food fresh he will eat both meat and fish which is pretty far gone. The flesh, entrails, blood and skin of an animal are eaten—in fact, practically everything except the hair. The men who went to France with the Naga Labour Corps thought our method of cleaning an animal and throwing away the offal most wasteful. Meat is stored by cutting it into small pieces and smoking it over the fire. In this way it will keep for a year.

Drink.

To deprive a Lhota of his " madhu " (*soko*) would be like depriving a British workman of both his beer and tea. The Lhota only drinks water if he can get nothing else. He drinks " madhu " both at meals and between meals. It is made as follows. Rice is boiled in the ordinary way and spread on a mat to cool. A cake of yeast (*vamhe*) is then broken up and well mixed with it, and the rice put to ferment in a basket lined with leaves. Next day the liquor begins to run off and is collected in a bamboo " chunga." This is *zutsü* (Assamese " rohi "), the most potent form of " madhu." When new it is the colour of rather greenish water. If kept it will remain good for five or six months, gradually increasng in strength and turning a pale sherry colour. It is this form of " madhu " which is always offered to guests of importance. In some villages of the Northern Lhotas the rice is not put into a basket to ferment, but into a vat, a hollow section of bamboo being placed upright in it to collect the *zutsü*, which is allowed to drain off for three days. The fermented rice from which the *zutsü* has been drained off is put into a " madhu-sieve " (*cham*) and hot or sometimes cold water is poured on to it. It is well kneaded, and the resulting brew is *chemcho* (Assamese " saka madhu "), the usual Lhota drink, and is of about the potency of light beer. Sometimes, especially among the Southern Lhotas, millet, giant millet or Job's tears, or a mixture of maize and rice, is used instead of rice for making " madhu." The yeast is made as follows. Rice is ground into flour and wetted and kneaded into dough. To this a little old yeast is added, and either the water from crushed *phyushako* bark, or from the crushed leaves of *yimerhe* or *shingwo*. The dough with this added is again well kneaded and divided into cakes about the size of penny buns. These dry of themselves and remain good for six or seven months.

The mild form of rice beer called in Assamese " pita madhu," which is so popular among the Angamis, is hardly made by the Lhotas except at harvest. A little unhusked rice is kept damp until it sprouts, and is then dried. Husked rice is ground into flour and put into a vat with hot water. Next day when it has become cold the dried sprouted rice is ground up and mixed with a little yeast and added to the water. This ferments and is ready for drinking next day. It is drunk diluted with water and is called *etha soko*.

Medicine.

Illness is generally ascribed to evil spirits (*tsandhramo*) or the wandering of the patient's soul (*omon*), who accordingly calls in a medicine man (*ratsen*) to extract from his body the bit of earth or wood or hair which the evil spirit put there, or causes a ceremony to be performed to call back his soul. A few medicines are, however, known. Fat pork is eaten as an aperient. For an emetic, chicken dung and rat dung are whipped up with water and the mixture is drunk —probably as effective an emetic as any known to science. For diarrhœa the remedies are roasted goat's hoof or the gall of either cow or pig. For stomach-ache and intestinal worms an infusion of the bark of *nshitong* (*Stereospernum chelonoides*) is drunk. For indigestion and stomach troubles in general a little of the dried upper stomach of the porcupine is ground up and taken mixed with water, or a poultice of wild lemon leaves (*tsoshü*) or the crushed leaves of *Maesa indica* (*tsandhrammozü*, lit. " devil's medicine ") is put over the affected part. For a cough the green pentagonal-shaped berries of the *yenkuti* tree are chewed, or a berry called *riko* is ground up and taken with " rohi madhu." The *yenkuti* berry is also used as a tonic for weak children. Bat's flesh is another tonic for children whose mothers cannot suckle them properly. For headache the leaf of the *kizu* tree (*Bischoffia javanica*) is laid on the forehead. For wounds the commonest remedy is a poultice of the ground-up bark of young shoots of the *nungnung* tree (*Callicarpa arborea roxb.*, fam. *Verbenaceæ*). This has the effect of stopping bleeding. The mashed-up leaves of the *pontengcho* tree have the same effect. A bush called *temphak* (*Rhus semialata*) provides two medicines. The juice of the berries is a cure for stomach-ache, and a cooling lotion for use in cases of chicken pox and smallpox is prepared from the pounded leaves. The gall of the python is said to cure fever and intestinal troubles. A lotion made from *Taraktogenos kurzii* (*hmhmti*) bark is used to disinfect wounds. If maggots get into a wound in an animal a mash of pounded giant woodlouse (*sharhi*) is applied. Soot (*live*) is applied for skin diseases. For burns the ash of the leaves of the *woropentung* tree is applied. For dog-bite a whisker of the dog which bit the man is singed and put on the wound. Another example of the " hair of the dog " is the practice of drinking very hot " rohi madhu " as a remedy for drunkenness. To bring a boil to a head a little yeast (*vamhe*) is damped and rubbed over it. When ready it is lanced with a sharp splinter of bamboo. To get rid of warts a black-and-yellow beetle called *potso tsiro* (" god's mithan ") is crushed on them. This causes them to fester and disappear. Goître is not common except in Are. When it occurs it is regarded as being due to drinking water from a spring near which plants with bulbous roots grow. The only known remedy is to run a red-hot umbrella wire through the goître, but this heroic measure is rarely employed. Most sufferers prefer the disease to the cure. For soreness of the eyes the leaves of the *mongsentung* are crushed up and held to the face so that the fumes reach the eye. For a sprain of any kind the great remedy is to draw blood. In the case of slight sprains the affected place is scratched and made to bleed and a leech put on to suck. For more serious sprains or contusions the swelling is cupped. The instrument used is a serow horn. The base is smoothed down so that it will lie closely against the skin, and a small hole is bored near the tip of the horn, round which a thin, slightly withered leaf is wrapped. The skin is pricked with a splinter of bamboo and the horn being placed in position the blood is sucked up into it by the hole near the top. The thin leaf allows the air to be sucked from the interior of the horn, but acts as an efficient valve when the operator stops to take breath. This method of cupping is used for sprains, bruises and dropsy, in fact in any case where it is desired to reduce a swelling. In cases of snake-bite the limb affected is first tightly bound above the bite. An infusion of the bark of a tree called *nungatsung* is rubbed on the legs as a protection against leech-bites.

Drugs.

Home-grown tobacco is cured by drying the leaves in the sun for three or four days. They are then stamped and rolled with the feet and again dried. The result is a coarse-smoking tobacco, very hot to the tongue and difficult to keep alight. Hence the popularity of cheap cigarettes among boys nowadays. The short pipe (*tsintsanmukukhu*) is simply a short section of bamboo with a small bamboo tube stuck in the side of it, a few lines being sometimes scratched on the bowl by way of ornamentation. The big pipe (*murimukukhu*) is a more elaborate affair, with a bowl cut out of soft black stone and set in a wooden base forming one piece with the stem, which is bored with a hot iron and ends in a small bamboo mouth-piece. From the bowl a small bamboo tube some four inches long runs down through the wooden base into a section of bamboo about five inches long. This is detachable and is kept full of water when the pipe is in action. All the smoke is drawn through the water, which becomes nothing but very dirty diluted nicotine. This foul liquid is carefully kept and sipped now and again as a pick-me-up. If he does not take his big pipe with him when he goes down to his fields a man will often take a little gourd of this stuff. Though they are in such close touch with the plains, opium eating is unknown in Lhota villages, a great contrast with the Aos and Konyaks. Betel nut is chewed with "pan" and lime in the villages near the plains. Lime used to be made locally from the ground-up shells of freshwater snails, but is now bought in the plains.

A remarkable number of suicides by poisoning take place among the Lhotas. For this the root of a common flowering plant called *rhisa* is used. This poison has a very strong taste and cannot be given to another man without his knowledge. Mixed with boiled rice it is used as rat poison. Tradition has it that men of standing used to be poisoned by their enemies through the agency of old women and children, and a man once told the writer that he was nearly poisoned in that way. But no authentic case of murder by poisoning appears ever to have been known.[1]

Games.

Wrestling and running are not much indulged in, but both high jump (*untsongeyen*) and long jump (*eyenda*) are popular. For the former the competitors run straight at the jump and clear it with their feet together, the "scissor" style of jumping being unknown. A good jumper can clear a reed the height of his own chin. For the long jump a flat stone is put in position to take off from, and the mark which counts is that made by the jumper's feet in landing, whether he falls backwards or not. For the "jump-and-kick"

[1] A Lhota woman was accused in my court of having poisoned her husband under circumstances which left little doubt as to her guilt in my mind, though the charge could not be proved in court. It is generally believed that women have knowledge of poisons which are unknown to men, and I am inclined to think that the belief is not without foundation. —J. H. H.

(*nshü*) the jumper makes a standing jump and while in the air kicks with both feet together at some mark such as a leaf stuck on the end of an upright spear. It is quite common for a man to be able to kick a mark as high above his head as he can reach with his hand. A variety of this (*choa-nshü*) is one in which the jumper takes a standing jump from one leg and kicks the mark with the foot from which he jumped—a most difficult feat. Putting the weight (*olungeyen*) is done either with one hand in the English manner or with both hands from above the head.

A game called *khurocho* in which sides are taken is played with seeds like big flat chestnuts obtained from the large bean-like pods of the sword bean (*khuro*). These seeds are also the Lhota substitute for soap. The game is played at sowing time on coming back to the village in the evening. There are generally three or four players a side, though there may be as many as seven or eight. A number of seeds equal to the number of players on each side are set up on edge in a row with their edges touching. About three yards from them and parallel to them a line called *epfu* [1] is scratched on the ground. A yard behind *epfu* another line called *esi* is marked, and behind that at intervals of a yard two more lines called *sichemo* and *sikao*. Each side has an innings in turn, while the other side puts back the seeds which are knocked out of place. Each member of the side which is in throws at the line in turn with another seed and tries to knock away every seed in the line. The first throws from *epfu*, and if some member succeeds in knocking away all the seeds in the line, the side moves back to *esi* and throws from there, and so on to *sikao*, from which it works back to *sichemo*, *esi* and *epfu* and begins again, till it happens that no one in the side succeeds in knocking away all the seeds, when the side is out and the other side comes in. A seed is not counted as knocked out unless it is knocked at least a cubit from the line of seeds. The thrower may stride forward as far as he likes provided his back foot is on the line from which his side is throwing. This

[1] The names of the lines given here are those current in Akuk. The names vary considerably in different villages.

game appears to resemble that known among the Manipuris as *kang*.[1]

A game also called *khurocho*, but entirely different though the same seeds are used, is played in Yimpang and seems to be peculiar to that village.[2] The players are usually two a side. The seeds are laid in pairs one on the top of another in two converging lines meeting in an apex about two yards from the mark at which the spinner squats. The player holds a seed in the palm of his left hand and with a flick of his right forefinger spins it at the lines of seeds. The object is to knock as many of the top seeds off as possible. If a bottom seed of a pair is knocked out of place it counts as a miss. One side uses one line and the other the other for scoring their points, which is done with a bit of wood laid between the pairs to mark the number of top seeds knocked off by that side. It does not matter from which line they are knocked off, though the spinner must hit one or both of the two pairs nearest him, and not break the line in the middle. Whichever side is able to move its mark up from the bottom to the top of a line first wins.

Tops (*phiro*) shaped like double cones are made of hard wood. The string is wound round one cone and the end held in the fingers. The top is then thrown either underhand or overhand and the string jerked back while it is still in the air. The object is to knock over someone else's top which is already spinning. Tops are spun at and just after sowing time. The Changs attach some special significance to top-spinning. All indulge in the sport at and just after sowing, but a man who spins a top at any other time is fined by his fellow-villagers. Lhotas inflict no fine, but the custom is that tops should be spun only at the time mentioned. Another game, if game it can be called, is a competition to see who can eat most fat pork and salt. Toys are unknown, though little boys carry miniature bamboo spears in imitation of their fathers, and little girls

[1] Cf. T. C. Hodson, *Naga Tribes of Manipur*, p. 62. Cf. also Lt.-Col. J. Shakespear, *Kuki-Lushei Clans*, for its prevalence throughout the hills.

[2] This variety is, I think, identical with the Bean game as played by the Angamis, while the other variety probably bears more resemblance to the Sema game.—J. H. H.

carry sticks or stones wrapped in a cloth on their backs as mother carries the baby. Notches are often cut on the edges of the beds in the *champo*, and little boys play a game (*ekhirandhapen*) in which they say, " bom, bom," as they touch each notch, beginning at the end of the line, the object being to see how far you can get without taking a fresh breath.

Music.

Besides songs, of which some account has been given in the section on language, the operations of reaping, threshing and carrying up the crop are accompanied by simple wordless chants. Only the proper chant which tradition sanctions may be sung. Were a man to use the wrong one, the reaping chant while threshing, for instance, the listening spirits of the fields (*Rangsi*) would be displeased and refuse him their blessings.

Three varieties of musical instrument are used. Of these the simplest is the trumpet (*phupphu*), consisting merely of a bamboo tube about sixteen inches long, from which a bellowing noise can be produced. A more elaborate type of *phupphu* has a tube about four and a half feet long of light wood from which the pith has been removed, terminating in a trumpet-shaped piece of gourd. The Lhota has an accurate ear for music, and with this he can give wonderful imitations of bugle calls. But the instrument upon which he is most expert is the flute (*philili* or *phiphili*). This consists of a thin bamboo tube about forty inches long, open at both ends, with a small square mouthpiece cut about two inches from the thick end.[1] The player either sits down or lies on his back, with his right wrist resting on the ground. With the palm or one of the fingers of his left hand he stops up the broad end, and using the mouthpiece like that of a flute, produces a rather pleasing tootling tune by opening or closing the small end with the middle finger of his right hand. This instrument is a favourite one with young bucks, who lie on their backs in the " morung " and tootle the names of their lady-loves in simple tunes. In

[1] The Sema, like the Angami, flute has two round holes, burnt.—J. H. H.

every village a particular combination of notes represents the name of each fair one, and strange though it may seem, no one listening ever seems to have any doubt as to what lady's fame is being celebrated.

Daily Life.

The family get up before dawn, the wife being the first to blow up the fire, set the pot on to boil and open the door. After a meal all go down to the fields, taking with them "madhu," cold rice and some cooked meat or vegetables. This the family eat while they take a short rest in the middle of the day in the field-house. The evening meal is eaten when they come back from the fields. After that it is soon time for bed. When the harvest is in there is less work, and men go away on short trading tours, or make up hunting parties, while the women stay at home and weave and gossip.

PART III

LAWS AND CUSTOMS

Exogamy—Polity and Village Organization—Property—Inheritance—Adoption—Settlement of Disputes—Oaths—Friendships—War and Head-hunting—Slavery—Position of Women.

THE Lhota tribe may fairly be said to have an exogamous system which is in the process of breaking down. There are three phratries divided into clans (*chibo*) which are in some cases further split up into kindreds (*mhitso*, lit. " tail "). Strictly speaking a man ought to take his wife from a phratry other than his own. On this Lhota opinion is quite clear. On the other hand, marriage between members of different clans is allowed everywhere and is especially common among the Southern Lhotas, though it is viewed with a certain amount of disapproval by the conservative members of the tribe. In some villages, again, chiefly among the Southern Lhotas, marriage between members of different kindreds of the same clan is permitted. The reason for these innovations—for innovations of the last three or four generations they are believed to be—is that a man's choice of a wife is limited, for he is almost forced by circumstances to take one from his own village, or at any rate from a neighbouring village. A man in search of a bride naturally thinks first of marriageable girls whom he knows of near home. The parents of a girl, too, usually much prefer that she should marry a man in their own village, sometimes because they are fond of her, but more often because they want her to come in and give a helping hand in the house or look after them when they are ill. The Lhota marriage-price system is another potent factor in reducing a man's field of choice. The bridegroom naturally does not want to go and work for a father-in-law in a distant village where he will have to live among strangers, with no chance of keeping an eye on his own fields and those of his parents. The money part of the marriage price too is always paid in instalments and never in a lump sum, for a father fears that were he to take a lump sum he would be regarded as selling his daughter, as indeed he is to all intents and purposes. It is therefore convenient to have a son-in-law close at hand, where his memory can be conveniently jogged when instalments get overdue.

The following are the phratries and clans of the tribe, the clans which are regarded by Lhotas as having an extraneous origin being marked with an asterisk :—

PHRATRY.	CLAN.
Tompyaktserre	Kikung. Ovung.* Tsangsükikung.* Pathong. Chami. Worore.* Chongyichami.* Tsoboi. Kuwang.
Izumontserre	Nguli. Sempinguli.* Sityingonguli.* Mozoi.* Rangpang.* Shetri. Humtsoi. Kithang.
Mipongsandre	Muri. Othui. Eni.* Thangwe Eni.* Lapung. Chorothui.* Ezong. Tsangle. Yanthang.* Moyoyanthang.*

The three phratries, Tompyaktserre, Izumontserre and Mipongsandre, are said to be descended from three brothers, Limhachan, Izumontse, and Rhankhantang, or Rankhanda,[1]

[1] The order given is that in which the first ancestors are said to have emerged from the earth. The three phratries are regarded as being of equal status. *Tom-pyak-tserre* is said to mean "forehead-scraping-clean-men," *Izumon-tserre* "scattered-men," and *Mi-pong-san-dre* "with fire-smoke-conquering-men."

who were the first men to come out of the earth. The origins of the different clans, so far as tradition relates, are as follows. In the Tompyaktserre phratry, Pathong, Chami and Tsoboi are said to have been the three sons of Kikung. Pathong is said to have taken his father's head at the instigation of a friend whose name is not recorded. The Kikung clan claim a vague headship over the phratry, and say that in the good old days they alone had the right to wear ivory armlets and keep mithan. The Ovung and Tsangsükikung clans, the latter of which is found chiefly at Yimbang, are said to be descended from "jungle men" caught by members of the Kikung clan long, long ago. Chongyichami and Worore are regarded as closely related to the Chami clan, the former being descended from Aos absorbed when the Lhotas invaded the Ao country. The Worore or "bird clan" are particularly interesting. They are found only in Pangti, the last Ao village taken over by the Lhotas, where tradition says that the two tribes lived together for some time. The story of the origin of the clan is identical with that told about the Ao "bird clan," Wozakumrr, and there can be little doubt that the Worore are really Aos who have been absorbed into the Lhota tribe. The story is that a Chami woman was sitting weaving outside her house one day when a hornbill flew over her head and dropped one of its tail feathers in her lap. She tucked the feather into her waist, and by it became pregnant and bore a son who was the ancestor of the Worore clan. Among the Aos no member of the Wozakumrr clan may kill a hornbill or even see the dead body of one that has been killed. Nor may he eat its flesh or wear its feathers till they are thoroughly dry. In common with the rest of the Tompyaktserre phratry the Worore clan do not eat the flesh of the hornbill, but otherwise they are under no special prohibition with regard to it. There appears to be no tradition relating to the Kuwang clan, which is regarded as closely related to the Tsoboi clan, and is often called Tsoboi-kuwang. The names of the two kindreds of the Ovung clan—Worosaeromo and Worosanromo—mean respectively "those who make bird platforms" and "those who do not make bird platforms."

One kindred makes a little platform on which the cooking-pot and remains of the chicken are left behind after a "genna" in the fields, and one does not. No reason is known for this divergence of custom.

The original clans of the Izumontserre phratry are Nguli, Shetri and Humtsoi, descended from and named after three brothers. The Sempinguli clan is only found in a few villages such as Pangti, Lungla, Yemkha and Lungithang. and is said to be descended from Sema fugitives who attached themselves to the Nguli clan. The Sityingongnuli form another small clan reputed to be descended from a "jungle man" caught in a snare. They have the reputation of being expert snarers. The Mozoi clan is said to be descended from another "jungle man" caught by some members of the Nguli clan who were "poisoning" a river for fish. The Rangpang clan in turn is believed to be descended from a slave or orphan brought up by one of the Mozoi clan, and is often called Mozoirangpang. The origin of the Kithang clan is obscure. One tradition classes them as Izumontserre and another as Tompyaktserre. They take wives from all clans but their own nowadays, and have no tradition that any phratry was ever forbidden to them.

In the Mipongsandre phratry the Muri and Othui clans are regarded as descendants of two cousins named Muri and Othui who lived when the Lhotas were settled near Lazemi,[1] and were the great-great-great-great-grandsons of Longchethang, the first man to dig himself out of the earth according to one tradition. The Eni clan is believed to be descended from a slave or "jungle man" brought up by Othui. Thangwe in turn are descended from a "jungle man" caught by Eni when he was in the jungle cutting a species of bamboo called *ticho*. It is believed that in the year when these bamboos seed and die a large number of the Thangwe clan die. Members of the Thangwe clan are not prohibited from using these bamboos in any way. The Lapung clan, which is practically confined to

[1] A big Sema village of the Asimi clan in the Doyang valley, south-east of the present Lhota country.

Lotsü village, is regarded as closely akin to the Thangwe clan. The small Chorothui clan originated as follows. An old man of the Othui clan [1] was in the act of sacrificing a pig, when on drawing back his spear for the thrust the butt came in contact with someone behind. The old man looked round and found a stranger standing watching. He took the stranger to his house and fed him, but the only reply he could get to his questions as to whence he had come was the one word "Chorocho"—"I came down," *i. e.* from the sky. From this the name of the clan is derived. Ezong and Tsangle are regarded as original clans, sprung from cousins or brothers of Muri and Othui. Yanthang means "Rengma," and the clan is descended from Rengmas who rejoined the Lhotas after the two tribes had split up. The Moyoyanthang clan is only found in Lakhuti. Their ancestors are said to have been a wandering band of Rengmas who were only allowed to settle there on condition they never claimed any rights in the village. To this day they can never provide a *Puthi* and may not take any part in the dance at the building of a new "morung." This is a unique example among the Lhotas of a particular clan being regarded as of inferior status. With this exception all clans have equal rights, whether they spring from a supposed extraneous origin or not.

The number of clans which tradition says sprang from "jungle men" (*orakyon*) is remarkable. These "jungle men," as the Lhota word literally means, are said to have been like Nagas to look at. They are generally heard of in stories as being found hiding in trees or stealing from traps. Possibly they represent aboriginal inhabitants encountered by Nagas at some period of their migrations.

Some clans are still undivided. Others have split up into two kindreds which intermarry and call themselves "big" and "little," *e. g.* Ezongterowe and Ezongtsopowe. Others, again, are divided into many kindreds, each called after some ancestor. The following are among the kindreds

[1] Another tradition says that the old man was of the Nguli clan. The Chorothui clan only numbers nine households all told. They do not know to what phratry they belong.

of the Nguli clan—Yemkhashandre, Yemphuhore, Ritsenshandre, Monglema, Pyakore, Yemtsore, Shungentsore, Yamphentangre. Besides this arrangement of phratries, clans and kindreds within the tribe there is a system of intertribal corresponding clans existing in all the Naga tribes with which the writer is acquainted. A Lhota will say, for instance, that his clan is "the same" as some particular Ao clan. That Ao clan in turn will say that they are "one clan" with some particular Konyak clan, which in turn has a corresponding Phom clan, and so on. For instance, Lhota Chami corresponds to Ao Chamirr and Sema Yepothomi; Lhota Kikung corresponds to Ao Longchacharr, Sema Shohemi and Rengma Apungza; Lhota Muri corresponds to Ao Pongrr and Sema Chishilimi; Lhoti Nguli corresponds to Ao Alangcharr, Sema Wotsami [1] and Rengma Ketenini, and so on. A Sema who comes and settles in Are becomes a Lhota and incorporates himself into the clan corresponding to his old clan. If he or his children go back they slip into their old clan again. In cases where a Lhota marries a woman of another tribe he may, however, take a wife from a corresponding clan. For the clans being of different tribes they are regarded as being so widely separated, though corresponding, that there is no harm in intermarriage. But it is quite possible that intermarriage was once forbidden,

[1] I have always heard the relationship stated as between the Sema Wotsami and the Lhota Shetri. In any case I am inclined to think the relationship between respective clans of different tribes an artificial growth no doubt derived from the considerable diffusion of common blood among the Naga tribes. If it were genuine the Wotsami clan of Semas should be associated with the Othui rather than the Nguli or Shetri clans. *Vide infra*, Part V.: Story of "How men were turned into Gibbons." Up to a certain point there is no doubt a real connection, as the Ao Pongen or Pongrr, like the Sema Chishilimi, claim a patrician descent distinct from that of other clans, while the corresponding Ang clan among the Konyaks still retains its distinct patrician position. I believe the Changs' refusal to intermarry with a corresponding Ao clan is probably no older than the absorption by the Changs of a number of Ao villages at a comparatively recent date, when they also adopted the practice of exposure of the dead. At the present time they expose or bury as they feel inclined, but Colonel Woods, who toured in their country in 1900, states specifically that they bury their dead and makes no mention at all of exposure, though this was certainly practised at that time by the neighbouring Ao, Phom and Konyak villages also visited by Colonel Woods.—J. H. H.

for Changs who keep old customs very strictly will not intermarry with a corresponding Ao clan.

The Lhota table of relationships is given herewith in the form suggested by Professor Rivers.

Relationships.

Father.	*opo.*	Son.	*otsotyungo.*
Mother.	*oyo.*	Daughter.	*otsoloro.*
Elder brother (M.S.) (W.S.).	*ota.*	Younger brother (M.S.).	*onyuro.*
Elder sister (M.S.) (W.S.).	*ota.*	Younger sister (M.S.) (W.S.).	*oyilo.* *onyiro.*
Father's elder brother.	*oporamo.*	Younger brother (W.S.).	*opye.*
Father's younger brother.	*oporo* (all Lhotas) or *oponunghowo* (Northern Lhotas).	Brother's son (M.S.).	*otsotyungo.*
Father's elder brother's wife.	*oyo* or *oyoramo.*	Brother's daughter (M.S.).	*otsoloro.*
Father's younger brother's wife.	*oyo* or *oyonunghowo,* or *oyoramo* (if she be older than speaker's mother).	Husband's brother's son.	*otsotyungo.*
Father's brother's son.	*ota* (if older than speaker). *onyuro* (if younger than speaker).	Husband's brother's daughter. Brother's son (W.S.).	*otsolovo.* *ongo.*
Father's brother's daughter.	*ota* (if older than speaker). *oyilo* (if younger than speaker).	Brother's daughter (W.S.).	*oka.*
Father's elder sister.	*onnoramo* (Northern Lhotas). *onno* (Southern Lhotas).		
Father's younger sister.	*onnoro* or *onnonunghowo* (Northern Lhotas). *onno* (Southern Lhotas).		
Father's elder sister's husband.	*omoramo* (if of clan of speaker's mother). *onung* (if not of clan of speaker's mother).	Wife's brother's son.	*orrho* (if brother's wife of same clan as speaker). *onung* (if brother's wife not of speaker's clan).
Father's younger sister's husband.	*omonunghowo* (if of clan of speaker's mother). *onung* (if not of clan of speaker's mother).	Wife's brother's daughter.	*orrhovo* (if brother's wife of same clan as speaker). *orrham* (if brother's wife not of speaker's clan).
Father's sister's son.	*orrho.*		
Father's sister's daughter.	*orrhovo.*	Sister's son (M.S.).	*orrho.*
Mother's brother.	*omo.*	Sister's daughter (M.S.).	*orrhovo.*
Mother's brother's wife.	*ongi* (unless of same clan as speaker, when whatever term blood relationship required would be used. Northern Lhotas). *onno* (Southern Lhotas).	Husband's sister's child.	*ongo* (m.) and *oka* (f.).
Mother's brother's son.	*omo.*		
Mother's brother's daughter.	*oyonunghowo.*		

Mother's elder sister.	*oyoramo.*
Mother's younger sister.	*oyonunghowo.*
Mother's sister's husband.	*oporamo* (if older than speaker's father). *oporo* (if younger than speaker's father).
Mother's sister's son.	*ota* (if older than speaker). *ongo* (if younger than speaker).
Mother's sister's daughter.	*ota* (if older than speaker). *oka* (if younger than speaker).
Father's father.	*omotsü.*
Father's mother.	*otyo* (Northern Lhotas). *otsü* (Southern (Lhotas).
Mother's father.	*omotsü.*
Mother's mother.	*otyo* (Northern Lhotas). *otsü* (Southern Lhotas).
Husband.	*orapfu.*
Wife's father.	*omo.*
Wife's mother.	*ongi* (Northern Lhotas). *onno* (Southern Lhotas).
Husband's father.	*omo.*
Husband's mother.	*ongi* (Northern Lhotas). *onno* (Southern Lhotas).
Wife's elder brother.	*onung.*
Wife's younger brother.	*onung nunghowo.*
Wife's elder sister.	*orrhamm eramo.*
Wife's younger sister.	*orrhamm nunghowo.*
Husband's brother.	*orrhang.*
Husband's sister.	*onung.*
Wife's sister's husband.	*ozi* (if not of speaker's clan). *oporo* or *ota* (if of speaker's clan).
Husband's brother's wife.	*ota* (if older than speaker). *oka* (if younger than speaker) *oyeni* (if of same age age as speaker).
Son's wife's parents (M.S.).	*omo* (m.) and *ota* or *oka* (f.).
Son's wife's parents (W.S.).	*oporo, oporamo, ota* or *ongo* (m.), according to age, and *onung* (f.).
Sister's daughter's husband (M.S.).	*ota* or *ongo* according to age.
Sister's daughter's husband (W.S.).	*omyako.*

Sister's son (W.S.).	*otsotyungo.*
Sister's daughter (W.S.).	*otsolovo.*
Wife's sister's son.	*otsotyungo.*
Wife's sister's daughter.	*otsolovo.*
Son's son (M.S.). (W.S.).	*orrhe.*
Son's daughter (M.S.). (W.S.).	*orrhevo.*
Daughter's son (M.S.). (W.S.).	*orrhe.*
Daughter's daughter (M.S.). (W.S.).	*orrhevo.*
Wife.	
Daughter's husband (M.S.).	*eng.*
Daughter's husband (W.S.).	*omyako.*
Son's wife (M.S.).	*omi* (Northern Lhotas). *orrkoro* (Southern Lhotas).
Son's wife (W.S.).	*oka.*
Sister's husband (M.S.).	*onung.*
Sister's husband (W.S.).	*orrhang.*
Brother's wife (M.S.).	*omi.*
Brother's wife (W.S.).	*onung.*

NOTE.—For the sake of clearness only one word for mother (*oyo*) has been given in the above list. But in speaking of women born in certain clans the terms *opfu, opfuramo,* and *opfunughowo* are invariably used instead of *oyo, oyoramo,* and *oyonunghowo,* irrespective of what clan their husbands may belong to. These clans are all the clans of the Tompyaktserre phratry, and the Ezong clan of the Mipongsandre phratry. In speaking of women of the Nguli, Kithang, Sempinguli, Sityingonguli, Shetri and Humtsoi clans the Northern Lhotas use *oyo* and its derivatives, while the Southern Lhotas use *opfu* and its derivatives. The custom with regard to women of the Yanthang, Moyoyanthang and Tsangle clans varies in different villages. The Lhotas cannot account for the existence of two terms for 'mother,' nor can they say why a particular term is used in speaking of women born in a particular clan.[1]

In ordinary conversation the general *ongo*, boy, and *oka*, lass, are used instead of the formal terms *otsotyungo* and *otsolovo*. In the case of a woman speaking of her brother's child *ongo* and *oka* are invariably used instead of *otsotyungo* and *otsolovo* in order to avoid any suggestion of marital relations with her brother. The terms *orapfu* and *eng* are rarely used in address, or when a man or woman is speaking of his or her own wife or husband. Instead, *okikhamo* (m.) and *okikhamm* (f.), meaning "house-mate," are substituted.

Though they may be of a different phratry there are certain women whom a man may not marry. (1) His mother's sister's daughter, even if his mother's sister has married into another clan, for he calls his mother's sister *oyoramo* ("big mother") or *oyonunghowo* ("little mother"); (2) his own sister's daughter (*orrhovo*); (3) his father's sister's daughter (*orrhovo*); but he can marry his mother's brother's daughter (*oyonunghowo*). A man is rather expected to take his wife from his mother's clan There is no fine for not doing so, but his mother's clan are likely to take offence. He is fined if, having taken one wife from his mother's clan, he takes a new one from another clan. The fine amounts to about Rs. 5, and is called *lolang 'ntyakma* (the price of not taking from the mother's clan). A man is not bound to marry his deceased brother's wife, but he may do so if he wishes without paying any marriage price. He may also marry his father's widow provided that she is not his own mother, but such marriages, though pretty common, are viewed with a certain amount of disfavour.[2]

[1] Cf. *The Angami Nagas*, Part III., "The Exogamous System," and Appendix III. under "Lhota."—J. H. H.

[2] The Semas, who do the same, regard such marriages with favour rather than disfavour, I think.—J. H. H.

Polity and Village Organization.

Every village is an independent unit in the tribe. Leagues of villages were formed for purposes of war, and in these cases the advice of the most powerful village would naturally carry most weight. Thus Pangti and Tsingaki respectively were the informal heads of leagues against the Aos and Semas. But except for war no village ever acknowledged the authority of any other village. There are very rarely definite boundaries between the lands of different villages. In the case of villages situated close to one another the lands of individuals of either village are inextricably mixed up. The writer once asked a Lhota why they had no village boundary disputes like Semas and Angamis, to which he replied, "It would be a shameful thing. Every man knows where his own land is, so how could there be a quarrel?" The fact that the Lhotas do not suffer from shortage of land as the Semas and Angamis do also helps to produce this peaceful state of affairs. In the days when villages were constantly at war each village was ruled by a chief (*ekyung*) assisted by an informal council of elders. The chieftainship was hereditary in the family of the man who originally founded the village, but did not at all necessarily pass from father to son. The most suitable man became chief by force of character. His main function was that of a leader in war, and his perquisite all the spoils brought home from raids In some villages he is said to have had the privilege of the free labour of the village for his field two or three times a year, but this right has not been exercised anywhere within living memory and apparently lapsed before the Hills were taken over, if indeed it ever existed. The Pax Britannica having put an end to his *raison d'être* and its sole concomitant privilege, the post of *ekyung* has virtually ceased to exist and the word even is rarely heard. Villages are now managed by an informal council of old men and men of influence, with headmen selected by Government through whom the village is dealt with. The old men are appropriately called *sotsoi* (meat-eaters), for they inflict fines of pork in petty cases and eat the fine. *Sotsoi* are divided into two classes called *tonnti*, the upper division, and *chochang*,[1] the lower division. Under them is a council of vague dimensions called *pangi*. Usually the village is run as an undivided whole, but where the "khels" are big the tendency is for the leading men of each "khel" to manage their affairs independently. Among the Aos every village is divided up by an ancient and elaborate system into working companies. The Lhota system is far simpler. Working companies (*yengaten*) are composed of the children of neighbours. Boys and girls work together and help in the fields of the parents of the various members of the company when there is a pressure of work. Anyone who is short of labour may hire a company for the day, giving them their midday meal and a small wage.

Property.

Cattle, houses and so on are the property of the individual, but land can be held either by the village, a "morung," a clan, or an individual. The land close to a village is usually waste land and common property, as are the rights of "poisoning" in certain pools. Every "morung" owns land which is the property of the "morung" as a whole and not of any individuals in it. It is worked by the boys of the "morung" and the produce used to buy meat for ceremonies such as the rebuilding of the "morung." Boys when they get married and leave the "morung" have to pay a small fine of meat to their late companions as compensation for the loss of labour. A very large proportion of the land in the Lhota country is clan land, which is held in common by all members of that particular clan in the village. A man who leaves a village loses all right to clan land in the village, a far better system than the Sema system by which a man claims, though usually in vain, ancestral rights in clan land in a village in which his great-great-grandfather was the last member of the family to live Every year the members of the clan in a Lhota village meet and

[1] Cf. Sema *chochomi*.—J. H. H.

apportion out the land which each is to cut that year, the senior men getting the bigger share. Strangely enough this delicate operation never seems to result in a quarrel. Strictly speaking a man may not sell land which he has inherited. When direct heirs fail the land becomes clan land. Were this to go on indefinitely the whole of the land in a village would in time become clan land, and no one would ever be able to buy or sell land. To prevent this from time to time, when the amount of common land becomes unwieldy, the clan meets and divides it up among the members, who thus each become private owners of a portion of it. The process then begins again. Heirlooms such as the ancient daos and spears which the Lhota so prizes are held in trust by the senior member of the clan in the village, provided he has done all the social "gennas." To alienate them would bring disaster on the whole clan.

Inheritance.

Property is inherited exclusively by the male heirs. Failing sons or grandsons, brothers, brother's sons, first cousins in the male line, and so on, inherit in that order. The need of the heirs is the primary consideration, a system which in theory is almost ideal and in practice works excellently. An actual example taken at random will make the details more easily understood. A died, leaving a widow and three sons B, C and D, of whom B was the oldest and D the youngest. Of the rice, which was by far the most valuable part of the property, B got half a granary, C one granary and D three granaries. What cash there was was divided in the same proportions. D also got the house. In this case B got least because he was married and independent and had done all his social "gennas." C got rather more than B because, though he was married and independent, he had not finished his "gennas." D got most of all because he still had his marriage price to pay and all his "gennas" to do, and had to live with and support his mother in his father's old house. The widow inherited nothing in her own right. Had there been a married daughter she would have got nothing. An unmarried daughter, however, would have lived with her mother and been supported by D, who would have had his share increased accordingly. Had all the sons been married either the widow would have been given enough to live on and the rest shared by the sons, B getting slightly the largest share, or supposing the widow were too old and feeble to work for herself, she would either have been supported by all the brothers jointly, or by one of them who would have been given a proportionately larger share. In short, where one or more brothers have had their marriage prices paid and have been launched into the world by their father, they get less than a younger brother who has not had so much spent on him. Had there been no widow the younger brother would have gone to live with one of his elder brothers, who would have taken both his share and his younger brother's share of the property, and paid his younger brother's marriage price and launched him into the world as his father would have done had he lived.[1] All land inherited from the father would have been held in common, as described above. Debts are inherited just as property is, and many a man inherits nothing else. Where the assets exceed the debts the heirs pay the debts in proportion to their shares of the assets.

Adoption.

Though so common among Changs and Semas, adoption is practically unknown among the Lhotas. One reason is that there are very few people poor enough to be willing to be adopted, and another that while among the Semas and Changs an adopted man and his descendants become practically the serfs of their adopter, among the Lhotas the chances of material gain for the adopter are few. Adoption of a girl seems to be unknown. There are generally relations of some kind ready to bring her up and get her marriage price. But boys are very occasionally adopted. Supposing A adopts B, he becomes to all intents and purposes A's son,

[1] This is what is normally done by the Semas.—J. H. H.

and enters A's clan, though he can never marry a woman from the clan out of which he was adopted. A has to find a wife for B and pay his marriage price, yet if B has a son, the son inherits B's property, A only inheriting if B has no sons. There is no ceremony of adoption.

Settlement of Disputes.

When a quarrel arises between two villages, messengers are sent to fix a day, and if both sides so agree the elders of the respective villages meet on the path half-way between the two villages and settle the matter, exchanging drinks of "madhu" and eating together. If the responsibility for the quarrel can be fixed on any individual he is fined, and the fine either divided among the elders of both villages, or given to the village against which the wrong was done. In the old days villages such as Okotso and the Ao village of Nankam were in a chronic state of war. It would occasionally happen that Okotso decided to cut their fields which lay towards Nankam in the same year as Nankam decided to cut their fields towards Okotso. Obviously cultivation would be impossible for either side unless a peace of some kind were patched up. The elders of both villages would feast together on the boundary, and an armistice would be agreed upon to remain in force till those fields were finally reaped, when the game of war would go on as before. All preliminary negotiations between villages actually at war were carried on by ambassadors (*lantsalanpeng*), of which there were two in each village. These had a permanent safe-conduct, and it was believed that to kill one would bring dire misfortune on the slayer and his village. The same custom exists among Aos, Changs and Phoms.

In the case of disputes within the village both sides are summoned before the elders, and what sounds like the prelude to a free fight takes place. Both the parties, all the witnesses, and most of the spectators talk at once at the top of their voices. However, after much shaking of fists and stamping, and solemn affirmations from the one side that they will never pay such a big fine, and from the other that they will never accept such a small one, a settlement is arrived at. Each side goes in company with the elders to the other's house and drinks " madhu " and promises not to quarrel again. This is regarded as binding. In the old days if one party would not pay the fine agreed on, the other party simply went and looted his property and took it. Nowadays cases which cannot be settled in the village are dealt with in court. Before the Hills were administered, murder was punished either by turning the murderer out of the village or by taking the whole of his property and dividing it among the rest of the village other than the clan of the murdered man, who could not touch any of it. In no case could any relations of the murdered man ever eat with the murderer. If they did their teeth would fall out. Nor would the descendants of either side eat together. This breach can never be healed, and there are still families who cannot eat together.[1] For adultery the guilty man had to hand over to the husband's and woman's families all his clothes and personal ornaments and a cow or a large pig. The husband could not himself take any of this fine, for it was the price of his wife's immorality. A clear distinction is drawn between adultery by a man of the husband's clan and adultery by a man of another clan. The former offence is often condoned on the guilty party promising not to repeat it, but a fine is invariably demanded for the latter offence. A thief had to return the goods in full, or their equivalent, to the owner, and pay a large pig or a cow to his clan. If he could not pay up he was sold as a slave. No punishments other than fining or selling into slavery or expulsion from the village were inflicted on fellow-villagers. But a man of another village who broke a village *emung* was put in the

[1] A serious quarrel between villages resulting in bloodshed entails a similar prohibition. For instance, Pungkitung once killed a number of Lungsa men, and Lungsa retaliated in kind. To this day members of the two villages cannot eat together, and a Lhota of another village who has accepted hospitality in either Lungsa or Pungkitung cannot on the same day take food from the hands of a man of the other village. This bar does not, however, prevent the inhabitants of the two villages from intermarrying freely.

stocks and had to be ransomed by his friends. Naga justice was decidedly crude. The elders accepted "presents" freely from both sides and then favoured the most influential party. There once lived a famous judge in the Ao village of Ungma who openly amassed a considerable fortune from "presents." Yet people came to him from all over the Ao country, and he died universally respected and is still regarded by the Aos as a model judge. His reputation chiefly rests on the fact that none of his decisions were ever questioned! Hardly believing that this could be due to their justice, the writer inquired the reason, and found that Ungma had sworn that whosoever questioned the decisions of their beloved judge, his village should be raided. Ungma being the biggest Ao village, this threat effectively stifled criticism. Troublesome children are sometimes punished by being whipped across the stomach with nettles, or by having a nettle put in their ears instead of a flower.

Oaths.

The oath is held in high regard among the Lhotas as it is among the Angamis. A man who is accused of an offence on suspicion may clear himself by taking an oath. The commonest form is for a man to bite a tiger or leopard's tooth and to swear that if he did such and such a thing may a tiger or leopard kill him. The formula used is the same in all cases, excepting, of course, that whatever offence the man is accused of is inserted. For instance a man accused of adultery would swear—

Ana	*itsongi*	*nsopi*:	*osi ana*
I	your wife with	have not committed adultery;	but I
itsongi	*sopi*	*lina*	
your wife with	committing adultery	if am in the habit of,	
mharrki	*a-rhamtoksi*	*yantaroki*	
by a tiger	me allowing to be bitten	all the village men	
sena	*mi-hm*	*penphia*	*a-mungitokle.*
bamboo shavings	fire-stick	using	for me let them keep *emung*.

In other words, may he be killed "apotia" by a tiger and the whole village purify themselves with fire and keep *emung* for him. A few hairs from the swearer's head, with a little earth, are often bitten instead of the tooth. In cases where the accusation is of stealing thread or some such thing, a skein of thread being said by one side to be stolen, and by the other side to be his own, a little of the thread is put with the hair and the earth. A very solemn oath which entails a day's *emung* for the village is that on a leaf of the *mingetung*. The heaviest of all is on a *bonne bouche* consisting of a little earth from the place used by the boys of the "morung" as a latrine, a piece of wood from the house of a man who has died "apotia," a little earth from a grave and a few hairs from the swearer's head. This oath is very rarely taken, and is thought to involve certain death for the swearer if taken falsely. Land disputes are occasionally decided on oath, which is invariably sworn on a little soil from the land in dispute. Whichever side will take the oath gets the land. It is probably never knowingly taken falsely, as all Lhotas firmly believe that whoever swears this oath falsely will die before he can reap a harvest from the land he has dishonestly gained. An ancient oath, which is only remembered by old men, was taken on the huge boulder known as Deolung. Each side in turn held an egg and swore by Deolung that their story was true. Whoever went mad first lost! The custom was abandoned, it is said, "because it was such a terrible oath." The idea of making both sides swear and then awaiting results resembles the Ao custom, by which both sides take the same oath, and the decision goes to the party which suffers no loss of any kind within thirty days, a system by which the party who is in all probability guilty does, curiously enough, generally lose. A curious instance came to my notice. The oath was taken in Ungma on the spot specially associated with the deity of the wind. When the ceremony began a gale blew up, so suddenly as to attract my attention in my garden three miles away. Out of a village of six hundred houses thatch was only blown from the roof of the houses of two men, and those were the two principals on one side in the case. The blowing of thatch from a man's roof if he has taken an oath is looked upon by Aos as a sure sign of false swearing. This story is true and other equally remarkable instances are known to the writer.

Friendships.

Formal friendships are of great importance. Two men become friends (*okam*) by exchanging gifts, consisting of half a pig, and a spear or dao or some such present, a piece of iron invariably forming part of the gift. It is usual for the sons of "friends" to become friends in turn. A man will often possess friends of this kind belonging to different villages, and frequently to a different tribe. When travelling a man will stay in his *okam's* house in each village he reaches. He in turn will entertain any of his *okams* who come to his village. A man may not kill his *okam* even if he belongs to a hostile village. Should he happen to kill him in battle with a spear thrown at a venture he will not take his head. Even if no gifts be exchanged, two men of the same name regard one another as *okams*. I have known a man go out of his way to entertain a stranger whom he had never met before because he bore the same name as his dead son.

War and Head-hunting.

By putting a stop to head-hunting the British Government has profoundly changed the mode of life of all the tribes in the administered area of the Naga Hilla. In the old days war was the normal and peace the exceptional state of affairs. War between Lhota villages was rare, and it was absolutely forbidden for one Lhota to take another Lhota's head.[1] But unless peace had been definitely arranged, any village of another tribe was regarded as hostile and fair game. This never-ending state of war affected every man, woman and child in their daily lives. In the morning a band of young men fully armed scouted round the village and had to

[1] One "khel" of Rephyim is supposed to have died out because the head-taking ceremony was once performed there with a Lhota head.

report no enemy lying in wait near before any women and children were allowed to leave the protection of the village fence. All went down to the fields for the day's work in a compact body, the men fully armed, leaving behind the small children and old men and women in the village with a guard. Careful watch, too, had to be kept while work was going on in the fields, for a favourite method of attack was to rush isolated family parties while they were weeding or cutting the jungle. Like all Nagas the Lhota was very keen to take heads, but preferred to do so with the minimum of risk to himself. A strong, forewarned enemy was rarely attacked. Usually a party of raiders would either lie in ambush by the village spring, and kill a woman as she came down to take water, or rush an unsuspecting party working in their fields, or cut off a straggler on some path. If a whole village turned out to destroy another village a surprise attack at dawn was generally attempted. Once the defenders had a few casualties or found the enemy were through their fence they generally turned tail and fled in a wild rout out at the other end of the village, leaving the wounded and aged to the tender mercies of the raiders. Similarly, an attack was rarely pressed home against a stout defence, and once the attackers began to make for home the defenders followed them, cutting off stragglers. Though heads were not taken, prisoners were captured in affrays between Lhota villages, and were kept in the "morung" in a sort of stocks consisting of a heavy log cut to receive a man's ankle, with a bar of "nahor" wood to keep the foot from being withdrawn.[1] These prisoners had to be well fed and looked after till they were ransomed by their friends. Akuk once, having captured a rich man from Pangti, had to send a message to his relations asking that he might be ransomed without further delay, as he drank so much that the village was beginning to run short of "madhu." Lhotas took the heads of men, women and children indiscriminately, except those of infants who had not yet cut their teeth. These were merely killed, for a head without teeth did not

[1] So too the Kachins (*Gazetteer of Upper Burma and the Shan States*, I. i. p. 432) and the Northern Brè (*ibid.* p. 533).—J. H. H.

count in a warrior's toll of heads, and so was not worth cutting off. A woman's head, however, was regarded as a finer trophy than a man's, for women were likely to be carefully guarded. Ordinarily, from each of the slain, the head, toes and fingers were taken. But if the enemy were pressing close and there was no time to take the head, an ear only would do as well. A Lhota[1] who died recently much desired when he was young to marry a certain Phiro girl. The minx said she would only accept him if he would take the head of a Rengma girl and show it to her as a proof of his valour. This put the ardent lover in a quandary, for, with the British established at Kohima and Wokha, it appeared that he must either lose his well-beloved or take a head and get into serious trouble. But a brilliant idea struck him. He caught an unfortunate Rengma girl, cut off her ears without killing her, and after giving this proof of his valour and devotion, triumphantly married the Phiro girl.

When a raid had been decided upon, those who were to take part in it, having slept apart from their wives the night before, assembled in the morning at the *ekyung's* house. There a cock and a pig were killed and a meal eaten. If the cock squawked when its throat was being cut it was regarded as a bad omen and the expedition was usually put off. Similarly, anyone who hiccoughed when he was eating the pork stayed behind, for if he went misfortune would befall him. The credit for every head taken was shared equally by the men who got in first, second and third spear, called respectively *Lingta*, *Ethung* and *Kiwen*. It did not matter who actually cut off the head. The head, fingers and toes were brought home wrapped in a cloth. When the party got within earshot of their own village they began to chant "O Shamashari!" ("O we have killed an enemy!"). The hearing of this in the distance was the signal for wild excitement and uproar in the village. All streamed out to meet the returning heroes and see the trophies, replying to each

[1] Yampongo of Phiro, a man of great note in his time. He died of a burst blood-vessel when leading home a mithan captured in the operations against the Kukis in 1918, and he over sixty at the time.—J. H. H.

chant of "O Shamashari!" with "O Imaiyali!" ("O we are glad [1]"). From each head a few hairs were taken and put in a cleft stick which was set up outside the village gate. The meaning of this is obscure. Lhotas call it *orrülama*, deriving the word from *orrü* ("enemy") and *lama* ("warm"), and say that it means "warming the earth with an enemy's head," so that the crops will grow and the village increase and multiply. The term may be compared with *humtse-lama* (post-warmer), the piece of the scalp which used to be nailed to the post of a new "morung." [2] The writer has made careful inquiries and can find no trace of any definite belief that the spirits of dead enemies were in this way made to act as guards of the village gate, though in some vague way they were believed to help the village. When the heads were being brought in, anyone who wished to do so and proposed to perform the proper ceremonies afterwards could touch them with his spear and thereby share in the credit of the raid. The procession of warriors went round the village, and halting in front of the house of each man who had taken part in the expedition sang for a few minutes. Then all the men went to the "morung," where the old men brought them food and "madhu," and sat and listened to their account of their exploits. Every man who had taken a head or jabbed his spear into one had to pour a little "madhu" on the ground and throw away a little rice before he could eat or drink anything. This was an offering to the spirits of the slain enemies. It was believed that if this was not done the "madhu chunga" and food would be knocked

[1] Compare the Sema song sung by returning warriors, "O Yemusali, O Yemali," the meaning of which is not known to the Semas. The words are obviously the same as those in the Lhota song; and if, as seems possible, there has been a more intimate connection between the Lhotas and the Southern Sangtams than now appears, then the Semas may have acquired the phrase from the numerous Sangtams whom they have absorbed during the comparatively recent growth and extension of their (the Sema) tribe.—J. H. H.

[2] See p. 25. One Lhota from Pangti told me that *orrülama* were left by the returning warriors at each cross-roads they came to on their way home, the object being to guide the spirit of the slain enemy as it followed the head. The Changs believe that the spirits of dead enemies follow their heads some hours later, whimpering as they go.

out of his hand by a blow from an invisible spirit. One man assured the writer that this did actually happen to him once when he forgot to make the necessary small offering. If there was time that day the heads were hung up at once on the *mingetung*. If not they were left in the "morung" till morning. Preparatory to hanging them up the man who had taken most heads in the village pushed a sharp piece of wood through each head from one ear to the other, so that a piece of wood about six inches long stuck out on each side of it. A man's head was ornamented with the big cotton wool ear pads which are worn with full dancing dress. A long bamboo with a cane string ornamented with cane leaves on the end was leant against the branches of *mingetung*, and the head tied by the piece of wood running through it to the string, so that it hung about six feet from the ground. Anyone could assist at this. The fingers and toes were enclosed in bamboo basket balls and hung up like heads.[1] Everyone who had jabbed the head or any part of the corpse could have a basket ball hung up as if he had taken a head. That day all who had taken heads or jabbed a corpse killed a cock. They had to sleep apart from their wives for six nights, and were forbidden to eat meat from a tiger's kill. Further, a woman had to remain chaste while her husband was away on a raid.[2] Any breach of this rule, it was believed, would cause her husband to be killed by the enemy. She was also forbidden to weave lest her husband's foot should become entangled in jungle creepers and he should be caught and killed. The blood was not wiped off daos and spears till the day after the warriors had returned.

On the sixth day after the heads had been hung up the *Ramo* "genna" took place. On the fifth day everyone who had taken a head or jabbed a corpse killed a small chicken and hung it up with some boiled rice and "madhu" rice wrapped in a leaf from the roof of his house in the *mpongki* on the left side as you go in. He then cleaned his dao and

[1] The Southern Sangtams put them into gourds and place them on the top of bamboo poles outside the "morung," the head or gourd being transfixed vertically with a bit of wood like a spear.—J. H. H.

[2] So too the Sea Dyaks of Sarawak and some African tribes.—J. H. H.

Mingetung

Showing bamboo balls containing pieces of enemies' heads and fence set up at the *oyantsoa* "genna."

Village *Oha* at the foot of *Mingetung*

They have just been lifted and counted at the *oyantsoa* "genna."

[*To face p.* 108.

took the omens by pouring the contents of a small "chunga" of "madhu" on the ground and splitting the "chunga." Then he wrapped the two halves in a leaf, and opening the leaf suddenly let them fall to the ground. If one side fell one way up and the other the other, it meant that the omen was good and it would not be long before he did the head-taking ceremony again. If both halves fell the same way up no successful raid would be made in the near future. He then hid the pieces of split "chunga" in the roof of his house. Next day all the men in the village put on full dress and went round in procession singing from the *Puthi's* house to that of every man who had taken or jabbed a head six days before. Vats of "madhu" and great wooden dishes of pork were standing ready outside each house, and everyone ate and drank as much as they could, which was doubtless a good deal. In the evening the little chickens and the bundles of "madhu" and rice were taken down and left in the *Puthi's* house. He did not eat them himself, but gave them to old people.

It was most important that every Lhota should either take a head or at least touch an enemy's corpse, for unless he had done so he could not put on the ornaments of a warrior: hornbill tail feathers in his bearskin wig, boar's tush necklace, red-fringed gauntlets, red dao-belt, and dark blue lengta with red lines. One hornbill tail feather could be worn for each head-taking ceremony, but a man rarely wore more than six or eight at the outside, however many times he had performed the ceremony.

Whatever may have been the case in the past, at the time when Government first took over the Lhota country the aspect of a head as a trophy of war and proof of bravery had become subordinated to a view of it as something which would bring fortune to the village and enable those who took it or touched it to put on the ornaments of a warrior, no matter how it had been obtained. The result was that Lhotas were ready to descend to what was practically human sacrifice. The last head taken by Akuk, some time in the 'seventies, is a case in point. No heads having been taken for a long time, they arranged to buy a slave from Nankam.

On an agreed date a party of Nankam men set out towards Akuk, taking with them the unsuspecting slave, who was carrying a load. Half-way between Akuk and Nankam they were met by some men from the former village. All sat down and drank and talked. The slave was given a drink of "madhu," and at a prearranged signal an Akuk man killed him with a blow of his dao from behind. The head was cut off, and pieces of the body sent as presents to various villages. Many men touched the head and these blossomed out as "warriors." This horrible practice of buying and murdering slaves was, however, comparatively rare among the Lhotas, who were no worse than many other Nagas in this respect. Among the Phoms in unadministered territory it is by no means uncommon at the present day to sell slaves, or in some cases even troublesome freemen of a village. I have heard of a well-authenticated case in which a Phom sold his own brother.[1]

An interesting relic of war was the practice of mock fights which existed up to about fifteen years ago. A Lhota village such as Pangti would challenge an Ao or Sema village to battle on a certain day. Both sides used to turn up at the appointed place in full dress and feast together. They then separated and fought for say half an hour. Sticks and stones would fly, and then the two sides would close and attempt to tear off each other's ornaments. Daos and spears were barred, but sticks and shields were carried.[2] At a signal the fight would cease and the late enemies would settle down to quench their thirst in amicable groups. Looted ornaments were not returned, however. Men were pretty badly hurt and occasionally even killed, but I believe

[1] The practice of buying slaves or orphans for this purpose is perhaps worst among the unadministered Konyak villages, where it is a matter of common occurrence, and is probably normal when a chief's son wishes to put on warrior's dress and marry. His father buys a slave, who is tied up in the village, where the boy kills him in public.—J. H. H.

[2] In some Lhota villages—*e. g.* Lungithang—specially made wooden clubs were kept for use in village rows, and no doubt also fights of this sort, to avoid recourse to edged tools. The Yachungrr tribe does the same, clubs being made for women as well as men in this tribe, and I have known Kacha Nagas (Maruongmai) also to use made clubs, long and flat, for village riots.—J.H. H.

no report was ever made to the officials of the district; to have done so would have been considered unsporting. Men who took part in these battles were allowed to put on the ornaments of a warrior, provided, of course, they gave the necessary feast to the old men.

Slavery.

In common with their neighbours, Lhotas used to keep slaves (*'ndri*). A thief could be sold by the man whose property he had stolen if he could not return it, or a debtor could be sold by his creditors. The Aos were great slave-holders and were always ready to trade in slaves with the Lhotas. There is an old freed slave woman now in Nankam who was sold by Okotso. The usual price was two or three cows. Masters had the power of life and death, but slaves seem generally to have been treated more or less as members of the family, and for the purposes of marriage were regarded as members of their master's clan. It was thus forbidden for a man to have immoral relations with his female slave. He would find a husband for her and take her marriage price. Her children were then free and regarded as ordinary Lhotas. If, however, a Lhota girl was arranged as a wife for a slave-man the children of the marriage were in turn slaves and had no right of inheritance whatever.

The Position of Women.

Were it to be suggested to a Lhota that he should go and consult his wife about something he would reply with a look of utter scorn: "What does a woman know about such things?" Nevertheless he would very likely not only ask his wife's advice when he got home, but take it into the bargain. A Lhota's wife is by no means a slave or chattel, but a very real companion. Her duties are nevertheless sharply defined. She must cook for her husband, look after the children, make the clothes for the family, and carry up firewood and water. Her husband will help her with a load if need be, and in the fields they work side by side. You never see, as you do in Konyak country, the young men idling all day in the shade in the village while their wives are toiling and digging in the sun. When guests are present it is the wife who sees that all have enough "madhu," but as a rule she takes little part in the conversation. Girls are often married when young, and almost invariably without being consulted in the matter. The result is that divorces, in which it is the wife who refuses to stay with her husband, are pretty frequent. Often for the slightest of causes, or even for no ascertainable reason at all, a woman simply refuses to live with her husband. She will shed floods of tears over her own supposed grievances and pay not the slightest attention to his earnest entreaties. It is comparatively rare for a man to divorce his wife without very good cause, partly because he will not get his marriage price back if he does. Among the Aos, on the other hand, where there is no marriage price, a man will divorce his wife in the most heartless manner when he gets tired of her. One much-respected Ao acquaintance of the writer's has up to date divorced nine successive wives because they presented him either with no children at all or with daughters instead of sons. Very rarely indeed does a case occur of a Lhota treating his wife cruelly. Were a husband to beat her in the traditional Whitechapel style she would leave him at once, and her relations would extract a fine.

PART IV

RELIGION

Religion—Deities and Spirits—The Soul and Life after Death—Magic—Religious Officials—Public Ceremonies—Individual Ceremonies—Ceremonies for Illness—Social "gennas"—Birth—Marriage—Divorce—Death—Miscellaneous Beliefs.

THE religion of the Lhota is of that type which is vaguely termed Animism. He believes in no Supreme Being who rewards the good and punishes the evil. The deities to whom he sacrifices are some of them neutral, if kept in a good temper with the proper offerings, and some of them definitely malicious. Yet he is very far indeed from being devil-ridden and haunted with ghostly fears. He cheerfully carries out what he conceives to be his religions duties and meets his end like a man when the time comes.

The nearest equivalent to gods is an order of beings called *Potso*,[1] who live in a world like ours, of the earthy floor of which our sky is the underside. The world of the *Potsos* in turn has a sky which supports yet another *Potso* world, and so on for an unknown number of layers. The only *Potsos* who affect us are those in the world immediately above our sky. They resemble men in appearance and have hosts of attendants who are sometimes regarded as their servants and sometimes as their relations. It is believed that just as the Lhotas have their *Potsos*, so the Semas, Aos and other tribes have theirs. The language of *Potsos* is different from that of men, Some members of the Tsoboi clan are said to claim to know it. *Potsos* are believed to visit earth from time to time and hold converse with the village seer (*ratsen*), coming in pairs with a train of attendants Deities and Spirits.

[1] = Sema *Kungumi*, and Chang *Müghka*.—J. H. H.

and bringing articles symbolical of the fortune the village is going to enjoy during the year. They send a servant ahead who appears to the *ratsen* in a dream and tells him that his masters will come on such and such a day. From the time when the warning is received till the *Potsos* come nothing must be killed in the *ratsen's* house, and between these dates he must not go outside the village land, or indulge in sexual intercourse, or eat the flesh of anything killed after he received the warning, though he may eat meat dried before. For their visit he makes ready "pita madhu" (*etha soko*) and some small fish and rice, and has plantain leaves brought up from the fields for use as cups. On the night when the *Potsos* are expected all in the village must go to bed early and shut their doors. The *ratsen* himself sleeps in a room separate from the rest of his family. The *Potsos* then come and speak to him in a voice which no one else can hear, and show him symbolical articles from which the future can be foretold. In the morning the marks of the spear butts of the *Potsos* and their servants can be seen outside the *ratsen's* door. They are easily distinguishable, it is said, from the ordinary marks of spear butts, for they are much smaller and deeper. This belief seems to show that the *Potsos* are regarded as coming in material form. The objects brought by the *Potsos* are generally believed to be taken back by them, but Niroyo village claim that some of their rice is from seed rice given to a *ratsen* by a *Potso*. A typical instance of this curious belief that these beings from another world sometimes visit the earth is the supposed visit of *Potsos* to the *ratsen* 'Nchemo of Illimyo in April 1919. 'Nchemo reported that two *Potsos* came with fourteen attendants and brought with them reeds, meaning sunny weather, part of a railway carriage (!), meaning elephants would give trouble, two loads of dark blue thread, meaning that someone would die "apotia," and a broom, meaning that wind would damage the crops. The day after a village is visited by *Potsos* is kept as an *emung* both by the village to which they came and by its neighbours. Formerly if any village was visited in this way all Lhota villages, however distant, kept one day's *emung* when they heard the news. Apart from special ceremonies performed to appease or gain the favour of the *Rangsis*, *Sityingo* and such-like godlings, it is to the *Potsos* that prayers are offered in sacrifices. Just as in England huge circular depressions in the hills are often called Devil's Punchbowls, so the Lhota tends to assign big or curious things to the *Potsos*. For instance, the polished stone celts which are sometimes found in the fields are regarded as thunderbolts and are called "*Potso's* axes" (*Potsophü*). The long flat seed-case, too, of a certain tree is called "*Potso's* weaving-sword" (*Potsotsitam*).[1]

Sityingo is regarded as the lord of wild animals, which he keeps just as men keep pigs and cattle. Sometimes he can be heard calling the wild pig, but to hear him is very unlucky. He lives in the jungle and is like a small man, with his head twisted to one side. By his favour men have luck in hunting. *Okisityingo* ("house-*sityingo*") is the good genius of the house. He is like a man, but has enormously long fingers and is spotted all over. He is only seen by men in delirium. So long as he is in a good temper his influence is good, but he can be harmful if due respect is not shown him. It is very unlucky if he leaves the house. *Ngazo* is another jungle spirit, practically identical with *Sityingo*. To every village and every man is attached a *Rangsi*, by whose favour the crops are good. No one has ever seen one or knows what one is like to look at. Just as crops and wild game have their genii, so have the rivers and streams in *Tchhüpfu* ("water-master"[2]), a being like a man with hair of enormous length, who lives at the bottom of deep pools and uses human skulls as hearth-stones. Small offerings are made to him by some villages after doing the *oyantsoa* ceremony. One is believed to inhabit a pool called Tchhüpfu izzü in the Doyang below Morakcho. In the days when men first came out of the earth they were persecuted by a fiend called

[1] *Potso* is commonly used as a form of address to highly respected persons such as sahibs, like the Assamese *Deota*, which is, or at one time was, employed in the same way, and means a godling of some kind.—J. H. H.

[2] This is the translation given me by Lhotas. The word may really mean "water-mother," *opfu* being one of the Lhota words for mother.

Khyuham, who ate their children and carried the skulls of his victims about in a basket on his back. Rankhanda, one of the ancestors of the Lhota tribe, managed to shut him up in a hole in the earth, the entrance of which he blocked, some say with a stone, others with a mithan horn. Yet even now a yearly ceremony called *Epuetha* is performed by every family in order to ward off the evil influence of *Khyuham*. Almost every illness is put down to the unhallowed attentions of *Tsandhramo*, invisible fiends who out of sheer malice make men sick by detaining their souls or by introducing hair or bits of wood or small stones into their bodies, making it necessary to call in a *ratsen* to extract them. The bright rust-coloured mud which is often seen oozing out of cliffs is regarded as the excreta of *Tsandhramo*. If these patches are sprinkled with dogs' teeth the fiends will abandon the place. In Lakhuti the custom obtains of leaving a spear sticking through the roof of a house from inside when an inmate is ill. This is supposed to ward off further attacks of evil spirits. During the influenza outbreak of 1918 the village simply bristled with spears. The jungle is believed to be haunted by wailing fiends called *Nangkamo*. A famous haunt is below the village of Akuk on the northern slope of the range. Men are tempted to follow the wailing. If they do they will be affected with such madness that they will think level ground is steep ground, and steep ground level ground.[1] Ramphan, the great Lhota hero, once speared one of these fiends with a red-hot spear, and buried it. In the morning he dug it up and found that though when speared it had the appearance of a man it was now a lizard.[2]

Respect rather than worship is paid to a huge boulder

[1] The Sema belief as to *Muzamuza*, the corresponding Sema deity, is stated in the same terms, but *Muzamuza* is Echo.—J. H. H.

[2] The lizard, in particular the sand-lizard with a very shiny skin, is the subject of some superstitious belief among most Nagas. Thus it is engraved by Tobu (a ? Konyak village east of the Chang country) on the long daos they make, tattooed by Chang warriors on their breasts, painted in black gum on the central white band of the Rengma head-taking cloth, and sometimes, I think, painted or carved in Konyak "morungs." The Semas seem to associate it somehow with the distinction between the sexes (v. *The Sema Nagas*), like some Australian tribes.—J. H. H.

called Deolung on the north-west side of the path between Lakhuti and Akuk. Everyone who passes it lays a leaf on a stone in front of it. Lakhuti once sacrificed a chicken to it, but the experiment was followed by many deaths in the village and was not repeated. Formerly very solemn oaths were taken on this stone. The story goes that long, long ago Deolung was attacked by another huge boulder called Tarrlung, who cut his head off. But Deolung's friend Matishi, another boulder, was near, to whom Deolung cried out, "Matishi, Matishi, Tarrlung has cut off my head. Go and waylay him." So Matishi took a sharpened bamboo as a spear and waylaid Tarrlung and wounded him so seriously that he only had strength to stagger away and toppled into the Doyang near Morakcho. Deolung's leg is supposed to be somewhere in the plains, but the wound where his head was cut off, and his head itself, now a rough piece of stone, are still pointed out. Close to Deolung and a little to the south is a flat slab of stone known as the grave of Orhendhromo, Deolung's son, sometimes called Orhendhreni, his daughter. The little escarpment on which Deolung stands is called "Deolung's wall" (*Deolung piku*). Matishi is now a big boulder a little distance below the Naga path and to the south-east of it between Deolung and Akuk. It is regarded both as Deolung's friend still standing guard near him, and as his mithan. A lowing sound heard coming from it forebodes some great disaster. A mark in the sandstone in Akuk village is shown as the mithan's track, and a natural hole through a rock there as the place where the mithan was tied up. Another rock called Napa is believed once to have been endowed with life and to have walked up from the bed of the Doyang to the place where it now stands on Pyopsü land.[1]

[1] Cf. *The Angami Nagas*, Appendix VII., *The Meitheis* (Hodson), p. 99; *The Khasis* (Gurdon), p. 170. Mr. W. S. Furness (*Journal of the Anthropological Institute*, XXXII., 1902, "Ethnography of the Nagas of Eastern Assam") states that a stone called Puzzi, near the Sema village of Champhimi, which used to be erect but is now laid flat, was killed by the Angami god Tukko, who knocked him down and cut off his head. This god "Tukko" is clearly Tŭkăhŭ, which is the Sema name for Japvo mountain.—J. H. H.

Beliefs concerning the Soul and the Life after Death.

The Lhota usually regards himself as having two distinct souls called respectively *omon* and *mongyi*. The *omon*, which is visible in the form of the man's shadow and shows its good sense by disappearing into him when the sky is cloudy and rain threatens, leaves the man some time before death in cases of serious illness. It may just wander about, in which case it can often be induced by the proper ceremonies to return, or it may go straight along the Road of the Dead to the next world, in which case the man dies.

As an example of this belief the following story, told to the writer by a Rephyim man, may be related. The man said: "The Road of the Dead in our village runs past the *champo* in which I used to sleep. One night when I was lying awake I heard someone go stumbling past towards Wokha Hill, groaning as he went. Then I heard him say, 'Oh, oh, I cannot walk,' and recognized the voice of my brother-in-law, who was very ill. I was frightened and shouted and woke all in the *champo*. My brother-in-law died next day, for his soul (*omon*) had already gone ahead." The *mongyi* leaves a man at the moment of death and goes straight to the World of the Dead, where it joins the *omon* which has already gone on ahead except in cases of very sudden death. Some men do not distinguish *omon* and *mongyi* (lit. "stupid soul"). The fact is that the Lhota does not analyse the details of such an unpleasant certainty as death. The Lhotas also believe in a sort of personal evil destiny called *nyok*, and when looking at the corpse of a man who has died a violent death will hold bunches of leaves before their faces to prevent his *nyok* affecting them. It appears to correspond to the Angami *temi* or *rhopfü* (cf. Hutton, *The Angami Nagas*, pp. 98 and 183). A curious belief, apparently at variance with all their beliefs as to dead men walking to the Land of the Dead, is held by Lhotas in common with Semas and Aos. It is that if a man kills a flying squirrel during his life, at his death his soul will fly to the Land of the Dead under the shelter of the wings of the soul of the squirrel. Col. Shakespear records that the Lushais hold a similar belief with regard to a bird called *vahluk*.[1] There are also traces of a belief in the reincarnation of the soul in some lower form of life. No member of a household in which a death has occurred may take the life of any creature, whether animal, bird, or insect, till the days of "genna" are accomplished and the soul has finally left for the Land of the Dead, in case the creature killed should be the dead man in another form. The Aos have a similar belief.[2] The Land of the Dead (*etchhili*) lies under our world and has the bottom of our world for a sky, just as our world lies under the world of the *Potsos*. There the dead live exactly as men live here, those who have done good deeds here being rich and happy, and those who have done evil deeds being poor and miserable.[3] As the sun passes under the earth every evening their day is our night. The entrance to it is a cave (*etchhiku*) on the precipitous eastern face of Wokha Hill. It is inaccessible and no living man has ever been into the cave, though the story goes that once a man desperate with grief at the death of his nine children from smallpox managed to scramble down to it. There on the floor he found spittle and on the side of the cave he found the smallpox scabs which had been rubbed off against the rock as his children passed in. He could not enter, for he was still alive, but he went away comforted, for he knew that his wife and children had really gone to the Land of the Dead, where he would meet them some day. The cave, which a telescope seems to show does really exist, lies at one end of a narrow, conspicuous stratum of white rock which looks exactly like a path and is known as the Road of the Dead (*etchhililan*).[4] Below it is another

[1] Shakespear, *The Lushai Kuki Clans*, p. 64.

[2] All Naga tribes that I know hold these two conflicting beliefs as to the life after death, regarding the soul as inhabiting a butterfly or other insect, and also as continuing an anthropomorphic existence. The discrepancy does not seem to occur to them till pointed out, and not to worry them much then. "Who knows?" is all they say.—J. H. H.

[3] The Angami differs in sending the souls of the "good" to the sky and the rest only to the underworld.—J. H. H.

[4] On this road the spirit, *Etchhilivanthamo*, lies in wait for passers-by to catch and destroy them if he can. To appease him every dead Lhota has a bead tied to his wrist when buried, so that he can give it to this spirit and get by.—J. H. H.

similar stratum, also apparently terminating in a cave, which is believed to be the road used by the spirits of dead animals, for animals, too, go to the Land of the Dead. In Yemkha, from whence the roads are clearly seen, it is believed that sometimes at night lights can be observed moving on the upper road when the dead come out with torches to meet new-comers and light them on their way. Some say that the spirits of those who die "apotia," or at the hands of enemies or by witchcraft, are earthbound and cannot go to the world of the dead. Others say that they go, but by some different road. The dead have knowledge of what goes on in this world and jealously watch the disposal of their property! They can even at times punish the living with sickness. They appear in dreams, sending their *omon* to the dreamer, for the dead man himself cannot leave the place where he is. As a sign that he has really been, the *omon* sometimes leaves a present of dead men's rice (*etchhitsok*). Zambomo of Pangti still uses rice descended from such a present. It is occasionally necessary to appease the dead. A pig is killed and a share given to a dreamer (*hahang*), who offers it to the dead man in his dreams. This ceremony is called *etchhienya*, and is done by anyone who is heir to the whole of a dead man's property, and when there have been many deaths in a family, or if children die one after the other. Though the dead themselves cannot leave their habitation, the deer they hunt, if hard pressed by dogs, sometimes come right through the earth and appear on the surface of the ground in the form of moles. That is why to find a mole above ground forebodes ill luck, and perhaps even death. Hence the consternation when the writer's fox-terrier one day laid a dead mole at a Lhota's feet.[1] Similarly, the male of the Little Pied Flycatcher (*Cyornis melanoleucus*) is regarded as the hornbill of the dead.

Life in the Land of the Dead is certainly not regarded as everlasting, but the Lhota is very vague as to what the next stage is—the truth being that he does not worry

[1] The Angamis regard the shrew mouse as the wild boar of the dead.—J. H. H.

himself about the matter. One theory is that men die again and become flies. Another theory is that every man passes through nine successive lives [1] and then ceases to exist.

Religion and Magic.

The religion of the Lhota teaches no moral code. The blessings it offers him are material, not spiritual. Yet many, many Lhotas lead clean, straight, honest lives and are ever ready to help a lame dog over a stile. It is true that virtue in this world is vaguely believed to be rewarded with happiness in the next, but this belief weighs little with a Naga, who rarely turns his thoughts to what is in store for him after he dies. Whatever it be which causes so many Lhotas to lead virtuous lives it is not their religion. His religion presents itself to a Lhota as a series of ceremonies and observances laid down by custom, any one of which it would be dangerous to omit. Mingled with this idea is the belief in the to the Lhota self-evident maxim that like produces like. If children squirt water from their mouths rain will fall. To pretend that you are carrying a heavy load of rice up to the village will ensure good crops! And so on in every department of life.

Religious Officials.

The *Puthi*.

The priest of the village and takes the leading part in all ceremonies concerned with the welfare of the whole communi and called by the Northern Lhotas *Puthi* and by the Southern *Puki*. Formerly every village had two *Puthis*, the one first elected performing the ceremonial acts, while his partner acted as his assistant and repeated the prayers after him. Nowadays in many places there is only one *Puthi*, the chief reason being that few men are eager to accept the post, which is a risky one, for verbal mistakes in the ceremonies may call down divine displeasure on the officiant. Where there are two *Puthis* the junior automatically succeeds the senior one on the death of the latter. An

[1] Probably in the under-world or as insects; cf. the Angami belief (*The Angami Nagas*, Part IV.).

awkward interregnum is thus avoided, for in the absence of a *Puthi* public ceremonies cannot be performed.[1]

Five days after the death of a *Puthi* the old men of the village meet at the late priest's house and discuss the question of his successor. Ordinarily the man in the village who has done must social "gennas" is chosen, provided he is otherwise qualified. That is to say, he must belong to one of the clans who have provided *Puthis* for that village in the past, and he must never have been wounded by an enemy or wild animal, or have hurt himself by falling from a tree or rock, or have burnt himself. In other words, a man who has only just escaped an "apotia" death is not eligible. Nor must he be deformed or mutilated in any way Once installed he holds office for life. The sole charge on which he can be dismissed is that of deliberately uttering curses instead of blessings at ceremonies. But even in this case the village must make good the expenses he has incurred during his time of office. He is forbidden to go outside the boundaries of the village, lest he should fall into the hands of enemies and be killed, for in some mysterious way the life of the village is regarded as bound up with that of its *Puthi*. On his death his successor must perform the ceremony of "making the village" (*oyantsoa*).[2] The other occasions on which this ceremony is performed are at the first founding of a village, when a branch of the *mingetung*, or the *mingetung* itself, falls, and at intervals of nine or ten years, when the *Puthi* thinks it is time it was performed in order that the children, cattle and crops of the village may increase. It may take place any time during the cold weather before the rice is sown. The *Puthi* announces that the ceremony is to take place and goes round with his spear (*phui*) in his hand and his *Yenga* walking behind him, and collects a contribution of rice from every male in the village. When all have prepared "madhu" the ceremony begins with the killing

[1] In Phiro and Saki the term *Puki* is used to denote not only the religious officials of the village, but anyone who has performed all the social "gennas," a use closely resembling that of the title *Kemovo* among the Angamis (of the Kohima group only, where *Pitsü* is used = *Puthi* in its usual sense, other Angamis using *Kemovo* = *Puthi*, and *Pitsü* for the oldest male in the village.—J. H. H.

[2] Cf. *The Oraons of Nagpur*, p. 111, note.—J. H. H.

AN *OPYA* BRISTLING WITH BAMBOO SPEARS THROWN AT IT AT THE *OYANTSOA* "GENNA"

Photo by J. H. Hutton.]

MORUNG (*CHAMPO*) AT PANGTI

[*To face p. 123*

of a dog outside the *Puthi's* house. The formalities are the same as at the building of a new " morung," except that the man who decapitates the dog at once cuts off its ears and places them on the roof of the *Puthi's* house, over the door. Next morning the unmarried men and boys of the village, having remained chaste for three days, go into the jungle and cut a log about six feet long and a foot and a half in diameter. This is trimmed flat on one side. One end is left square and the other end is sloped off from about two feet from the top. This they drag up to the village and set up just outside the village fence at the place (*opyachama*) which the tradition of the village ordains, with the flat side facing the village. No woman must see it dragged in, and for the three preceding days the village must keep strict *emung*, even sewing and weaving being forbidden. In front of the post, which is known as *opya*, all the males of the village in full dress assemble and feast. The women may look on from a distance, but may not mix with the men. Then the *Puthi* holds in his right hand a perfectly clean dao lent by an unmarried man who has observed strict chastity during the preceding three days, and in his left hand a cock. After the traditional prayer (*dranda*) for the prosperity of the village he cuts the cock's throat with the dao and proceeds to take the omens from its entrails. A sharp stick is then run into the base of the bird's skull at the back and it is set up at the foot of the *opya*. Then at a signal from the *Puthi* all, shouting as if in battle, throw mock bamboo spears at the *opya*. All then repair to the " morung " chanting *shamashari*, the chant of warriors who are bringing home heads, and *hoiki enyam*, a long-drawn high note followed by two short low notes. From the " morung " they go to the *Puthi's* house, and after chanting there disperse. All men must refrain from sexual intercourse for this night. In some villages (*e. g.* Rephyim) a straw collar is fastened round the *opya* at the point where the flat side is sloped off towards the top. Only warriors and men of importance, who fasten a little tuft of red goat's hair to the butt of their bamboo spears, may spear the *opya* above this collar.[1] The *opya*

[1] In Morakcho I was told that anyone who speared the *opya* in the " head " would die within the year.—J. H. H.

may be compared with the figure put up by the Quoireng and Kabui Nagas, who make a similar distinction between hits on the head and on the body.[1] Whether the *opya* represents a human sacrifice or the killing of an old *Puthi* whose failing powers would involve disaster to the village is perhaps an open question. But it is significant that the *opya* is believed occasionally to groan after being speared. The next day the *oha* (lucky stones) under the *mingetung* are counted. The whole village having assembled at the tree, while the women look on from a respectful distance, the *Puthi* lifts up the *oha* one by one, and on the place where they were lays the two ears of the dog which were put on his roof. He then replaces the stones one by one, counting them as he does so, and announces the total to the village. If the stones have increased since the last counting it is a good omen. If they have decreased it is an evil omen. All then stand round the tree and flourish their spears and chant the *shamashari*. A light fence is next built round the tree, with a door which is, however, carefully kept shut. After much walking round the tree and chanting all go to their own houses. Some days later—in some villages after five days, in others after ten—the young men and the *Puthi* again repair to the *mingetung* to open the door in the fence. Before this can be done the *Puthi* squats in front of the gate in the fence holding a good dao with the unsharpened face [2] of the blade upwards in his right hand and an egg in his left. Addressing the *Potsos*, he says, "I have remained chaste. I have eaten no unclean thing. Now help me and be favourable." He then rolls the egg very slowly down the blade of the dao. It is an evil omen if it falls either over the edge or over the back. He sets the egg on its end on the ground and puts thirty tiny pieces of dog's flesh on each side of it. The gate is then opened and after the usual chanting the ceremony is at an end. A

[1] See Hodson, *Naga Tribes of Manipur*, p. 119.

[2] The blade of a dao is ground on one side of its edge only, giving a plano-convex cutting edge, so that blows can be made to cut only by a downward stroke from the right, or an upward stroke from the left, or, in the case of a dao made on purpose for a left-handed man, *vice versa*.—J. H. H.

village which has done the *oyantsoa* "genna" must not allow any uncooked rice to leave the village till after the next *Tuku* "genna."

After the *oyantsoa* "genna" and before the fields are cut for the next year's cultivation, some villages perform a ceremony called *Pyotsoja* in honour of *Tcchüpfu*, the godling of rivers. On the appointed day the *Puthi* sets out from the village early in the morning, accompanied by all the grown-up men of the community. A bird-hunt is organized, and when one has been caught alive all go down to the Doyang. On the bank the *Puthi* kills a hen and lays out ten scraps of its flesh on his up-stream hand for *Tcchüpfu* and nine scraps on his down-stream hand. A miniature raft of bamboos is made, on which are put an egg, a little cotton wool and the live bird tied by the leg. The raft is then allowed to float down-stream. If it upsets it is a bad omen and it is believed that someone will be drowned during the term of office of the *Puthi*. A little poison is then pounded into the stream and the *Puthi* gets into the water and flounders about like a stupefied fish. His *Yenga* plunges in and seizes him and calls out, "I have caught such and such a fish! No, it is such and such a fish! No it is not; it is such and such a fish," and so on, calling out the names of different kinds of fish. Of the fish killed the first is offered to *Tcchüpfu* as the chicken was, and the rest are divided up among those present.

Oyantsoa is followed by the ceremony of "calling the *Rangsi*" (*Rangsitsa*), which takes place when the rice has begun to sprout, before the season of thunderstorms sets in, for the thunder would prevent the *Rangsis* from hearing the voices of those calling them. The *Puthi* kills a big pig in his house, and taking a bamboo mat, some of the boar's meat, an egg, a fowl and a little rice goes with the whole village a short way down the path up which the first Lhota settlers came to found the village. The chicken is killed and the omens taken and the egg and meat laid out on the ground exactly as in the *Amungkam* and *Rangsikam* ceremonies. The *Puthi* then spreads the mat in the ground and sprinkles a little unhusked rice over it. Then beginning with Honohoyanto,

Kisiyo and Dilungcham he calls out the name of every Lhota village, both extinct and existing, and summons its *Rangsi* to come and give rice to his village. Meanwhile the whole village, every man, woman and child having brought a rice basket, sets the baskets on the ground and beckons to the *Rangsis* who are supposed to be trooping up in obedience to the summons. The baskets are held as if someone were pouring rice into them and then covered quickly with a cloth. All go home in single file with much grunting, as if they were carrying heavy loads, the *Puthi* bringing up the rear. Arrived at the village everyone carefully pours the imaginary rice out of his basket into his rice house. Among the Northern Lhotas the young men of the village on the day before this "genna" make a point of trying to steal water from some other village's supply to put into their own. If they are caught they must submit to a good hiding.

The *Yenga*.

The assistant of the *Puthi*, who accompanies him at all ceremonies and carries his load, is called *Yenga*. He must be an old man who has done no social "gennas" and is appointed for life. In villages where there are two *Puthis* each has his *Yenga*. He receives a share of the meat at all "gennas" and one small basket of rice from every house in the village once a year. In cases where the only or both *Puthis* are ill the *Yenga* may perform ceremonies as if he were *Puthi*.

Minor Religious Officials.

The post next in importance to that of *Puthi* is that of *Wokchung* ("pig-killer"), of which there are usually two in a village, though in big villages such as Tsingaki there are two for each clan. A *Wokchung* may carry a *phui* spear as the *Puthi* does. His duty is to kill animals at private sacrifices. Below the *Wokchungs* are two *'Nchuko* ("hearth-bringers"), who bring the small stones with which miniature hearths are made at social "gennas." Next below are two *Sorhung* ("meat-dividers"), who divide up the meat at all sacrifices and settle all disputes as to the respective shares. No one may act as *Wokchung*, *'Nchuko*, or *Sorhung* unless he has performed all social "gennas" and dragged a stone. There is nothing to prevent the offices of *Puthi*, *Wokchung*, *'Nchuko* and *Sorhung* being combined in the same person.

Public Ceremonies.

Besides the ceremonies intimately connected with agriculture which have already been described, there are certain other public ceremonies of a more general character. The year officially opens with the *Pikuchak* "genna," but before that is performed the omens for the whole village are taken at a ceremony called *Sirosi*.

The *Sirosi* ceremony.

The procedure at Pangti, to take an instance, is as follows. The men of the village all assemble in front of the senior *Puthi's* house, the boys of each *champo* bringing meat in new baskets and "chungas" of "madhu." The two *Puthis* in full dress lead the way a short distance down the path to Okotso, each holding a "chunga" of "madhu" in his right hand. A short distance beyond the village fence they sit down and together say the *dranda*, praying that their enemies may make peace and come and eat with them, that tigers may not kill their cattle nor hawks their chickens, and that the village may flourish and grow big. This prayer is offered facing away from the village, and at the end of it each *Puthi* pours a little "madhu" on the ground. Some meat and "madhu" are distributed, and all go up to the village again and a short way down the path to Are, where the same ritual takes place. On the Are path, just below the place where the prayers are said, is a small clump of big trees growing close together. Between their stems is the traditional spot at which omens are taken at *Sirosi*. The prayer ended all the boys rush down the hill shouting, and hurl bamboo spears at the trees. Then all go down and scrape the earth clean at the proper spot. Here each *Puthi* sets up an egg on end, asking that the good or evil fortune of the coming year may be revealed, and takes the omens by cutting chips from a green twig and watching how they fall. The future is really believed to be revealed by the kinds of insects which are caught near the egg, and all sit and watch while the boys hunt industriously in the grass. Locusts mean that sambhur hunting will be good (for they have big legs). Stick insects are interpreted as showing that many men will take new wives, but will have no children by them. Small white insects show that the crops will be poor, and so on. When a few insects have been caught, and their significance has been expounded by the *Puthis* and old men, all go home.

The *Pikuchak* ceremony.

The *Pikuchak* "genna" marks the beginning of the agricultural year. The Northern Lhotas do it before clearing the jungle on their fields, and the Southern Lhotas after. In any case it must be done before the rice is sown. The *Puthi* announces the day on which the ceremony is to be, and every *champo* buys meat, and each *champo* in turn the cock which is to be sacrificed. On the night before the "genna" sexual intercourse is forbidden. On the day all the men of the village assemble at the place where the *opya* is set up. In front of the *opya* the *Puthi* sets up a miniature *opya*, and in front of that again puts an egg on the ground with a leaf on each side. Ou the leaf to his right he puts ten little bits of pork and ten little bits of ginger, and on that to his left nine little bits of each. He then recites the *dranda*, holding the cock in his left hand, and a dao in his right. This dao belongs to the youth who caught the cock the night before, the *champo* whose turn it is to provide the cock having selected some days before a youth whose duty it is to go to the house of the seller of the cock and catch it on the evening before it is sacrificed. This youth must abstain from all intercourse with the opposite sex from the time he is chosen to the end of the ceremony. The *dranda* being ended the *Puthi* cuts the cock's throat, takes the omens from its entrails and ties it on to the miniature *opya*. The old men sit down and eat some of the meat which the boys from the *champos* have bought and all go back to the village with much chanting. Parties of boys walk singing six times round each *champo*. The rest of the day is given up to feasting. Next day is kept as an *emung* and no one goes to the fields, but a party, consisting of boys and one or two old men, go out on a mock head-taking raid. First they go to the *opya*, where one of the old men sets up a miniature *opya* and makes the same offerings of an egg, meat and ginger as were made the day before. Then the party goes into the jungle and throws spears at trees and shouts as if engaged with the enemy. Then all return to their *champos*, in some villages openly, in other villages by roundabout paths and in dead silence. Finally after sitting in the *champo* for a little, as they would after a raid, all go to their houses. It is believed that this mock raid ensures good crops and hunting and a high birth-rate for the village.

The *Rangendri* ceremony.

After *Pikuchak*, but before the crops are sown, a " genna " called *Rangendri* is performed, at which imitation heads are hung on the *mingetung*. The *Puthi* collects rice and with it buys a pig which he kills outside his house. Going outside the village fence he lays thirty tiny pieces of the flesh on each of two leaves and prays that inasmuch as the warriors of the village are following the customs of their forefathers, good fortune may come to all. Then a few men of standing make globular bamboo baskets, such as are used for fingers, ears, bits of scalp and other trophies of Naga warfare, and hang them up on the *mingetung*. These are spoken of as " heads," and each man who hangs one up sacrifices a fowl and feasts the village as if he had really taken and hung up an enemy's head. The performance of this " genna " does not permit a man to wear any of the ornaments of a warrior, but entitles him to have one representation of a head put on his grave for each time he does it.

The *Tuku* ceremony.

The agricultural year closes with the *Tuku* ceremony. Five days after he has given notice of the " genna " the *Puthi* goes round with his *Yenga* and collects unhusked rice from every house. Men married in the course of the year have to make an extra large contribution, and receive in return a special blessing from the *Puthi* when he visits them on his round. Two days later he collects husked rice in the same manner. With some of the unhusked rice he makes " pita madhu," and with part of the rest buys a pig. The eighth day from that on which the unhusked rice was collected is known as *kichan*. On it the *Puthi* spears the pig at the *opya*, or among the Northern Lhotas just outside the village fence. The stomach is eaten there by the *Puthi* and the old men, and the rest of the meat divided up and distributed, those who gave most rice naturally getting most pork. The pig must not be singed to get the hair off or the crops will fail. From the day when the unhusked rice is collected to *kichan* nothing must be killed or sold in the village, and no meat from a tiger's kill must be brought in. The day after *kichan* is called *remphi* or *tuku inshuk*. On it animals and fowls may be killed and the day is given up to feasting, the working companies especially who have worked together during the year holding little feasts to which they have all subscribed, or visiting the houses of the different members. Next day *emung* is observed. On it the ornaments and all erections on graves are thrown away.[1] No rice may be cut after this "genna." *Tuku emung* being intimately connected with the dead, it is chosen as a time for taking omens which will show who is to die in the course of the year. The night before the boys of the *champo* sprinkle ashes carefully round the entrance to their sleeping-rooms. These are examined for tracks very early in the morning before anyone has gone out. Should a track be found fitting the foot of any of the boys it is believed that that boy's *omon* has gone to the Land of the Dead, and that he will assuredly follow it before the next *Tuku emung* comes round.

Ceremonies for Rain.

The rainfall in the Naga Hills is usually adequate. Nevertheless various rain-compelling ceremonies are practised, most of them of a very simple nature. The usual one resembles that in vogue among the Semạs. A gibbon's head and a small dead *tserü* fish, with its mouth kept open by a piece of stick, are pegged down to the bottom of the nearest stream. When enough rain has fallen the gibbon's head is taken out, the fish being left in the water to rot. Another common method is to dig a little tunnel and pour in water at

[1] The Kalyo-Kengyu preserve the bodies of the dead in coffins in their houses during the year, and on a fixed day at the "genna" for sowing throw away all the bodies collected during the year, together with their coffins, belongings, etc. The bodies, however, are broken up first and the bones collected out of them and put in an earthen pot and kept at the back of the granary, where they are left to decompose of themselves. —J. H. H.

one end and let it run out at the other. In Akuk a stick is rattled about to imitate the sound of rain in the hole to which Deolung tied up his mithan, water being poured in meanwhile. Sometimes children go about with " chungas " of water and spray it from their mouths over passers-by and each other. Niroyo, Wokha and their neighbours fell a tree across the path leading from the village to the Road of the Dead. All then go home holding leaves over their heads and saying that it is raining. To increase the flow of the village spring in times of drought someone goes down at night to the Doyang, and leaving an offering of four little bundles of meat and an egg on the bank, brings up a little water in a " chunga " and pours it into the village supply.

Individual Ceremonies.

The *Potsokam* ceremony.

Many of the ceremonies performed by individuals, such as those connected with agriculture, have been described under their respective headings. Three main classes may, however, be considered here, namely, those performed regularly for the general welfare of the household, those which are connected with illness, and those social " gennas " on which the status of the individual Lhota depends.

A " genna " called *Potsokam* (" present to the *Potsos* ") is performed every year, or oftener in case of sickness. The regular time for it is just before the new " jhums " are cut. The master of the house kills a small pig of either sex inside the house. He then mixes " madhu " and a few blades of rice which have sprung up in his granary among the damp grain, and ties them in a leaf which he affixes to one of the centre-posts of the house. Then of the pig which has been killed he cooks sixty small pieces, which he wraps up in a *yutso* leaf and holds up near the centre-post, with the prayer that there may be no sickness or misfortune in the house. The bundle is then put in the basket or " chunga " in which the day's supply of rice is kept. Then two leaves containing six pieces of meat each and two leaves containing four pieces of meat each are prepared for the dreamer (*hahang*) whom the performer of the rite patronizes. The dreamer must come and fetch them himself in the evening. When he goes out the door is shut hurriedly after him lest the good genius of the house (*okisityingo*) should escape. None of the flesh of the pig may be eaten that night, during which the husband must sleep apart from his wife. In the morning the dreamer comes to report what visions he has had and counts the pieces of meat in the rice bin. If the full number is found and the leaf is wet with congealed moisture all is well. A reduction in the number of pieces foretells evil. It is regarded as particularly fortunate if a little rice is found mixed with the meat. This is regarded as a gift from the dead and ensures good crops. Anyone may see the sacrifice of the pig, but were anyone to steal and eat a piece of meat his mouth would become deformed.

The *Epuetha* ceremony.

The story goes that the evil spirit *Khyuham*, when shut up in a hole in the earth by Rankhanda, exacted a promise that he should be appeased by a yearly sacrifice. In fulfilment of this the Lhota householder, year by year just before the *Thruven* "genna," kills a small boar in his house and puts into a carrying basket twenty-three little pieces of the meat, a handful of rice husks, an egg, a handful of boiled rice and a "chunga" of "pita madhu." The ceremony is performed in the *lhurhui* room, by an old man who has done no "gennas," called in for the purpose. Holding a "chunga" of "saka madhu" in his hand he prays for the welfare of the household, and after spilling a little on the ground drinks. He then pounds up some ginger, the usual magical disinfectant, in a leaf and pours a little "pita madhu" over it. While he is doing this members of the family scrape all their daos and spears one against the other. Then the old man, addressing *Khyuham*, says, "We have given you all the things in this house. Do not harm anyone," and as he speaks sprinkles a little of the ginger and "pita madhu" about the room, laying what is left in a leaf at the foot of the main post of the house, that is to say the post between the *lhurhui* and the *mpongki*. This done he takes up a brand from the hearth and the carrying basket containing the twenty-three pieces of pork and other things, and goes out of the house, calling on all evil spirits to follow him. As he goes the household throw after him ashes and burning brands, another powerful type of magical disinfectant, and shutting the door quickly keep it closed for a few minutes. The old man goes into the jungle just outside the village fence and there lights a small fire and spills a little "pita madhu" on the ground. Setting the egg up on end he puts on each side of it a little heap of rice husks on a leaf, six little sticks, six little pieces of ginger, and six scraps of meat. The "chunga" which held the "pita madhu" is by this time empty. This he splits with his dao and watches how the two halves fall. If both fall inside up or outside up the omen is good, but if one falls one way and one the other it is bad. The two halves are then laid on either side of the egg, and the old man having eaten the rest of the rice and meat goes straight to his house. He must not enter the house where the ceremony was performed again that evening. In the morning he goes back to return the carrying basket and receives a small handful of rice as his fee.

Ceremonies for Illness.

A Lhota when sick usually attributes his illness to the malice of an evil spirit (*tsandhramo*), who has either introduced some foreign matter, such as hair or a little stone, into his body or has caused his soul (*omon*) to desert him at a certain place. In any case a *ratsen* has to be called in, who can see and "extract" any foreign body which may be the cause of the trouble, or can say at what spot his soul left him and is likely to be lurking. To enable the man to regain his soul a soul-caller (*montsai*) is required, who must be an old man who has done no social "gennas." If it is on his own land that the man's soul has left him a dog must be sacrificed. The *montsai* and the sick man, if he be well enough, go down to the spot indicated by the *ratsen*. If the sick man be too ill, as is often the case, a near relation goes, who may be either a man or a woman among the Southern Lhotas, but must be a man among the Northern Lhotas. On arrival at the spot the *montsai* lights a fire, and killing the dog by knocking it on the head, singes it and cuts it up. On his right the *montsai* puts ten pieces of meat and ten pieces of ginger on two leaves, and nine pieces of meat and nine pieces of ginger on two leaves on his left. The paws, ears and nose are cooked in a pot which has been specially brought for the purpose, and left there in the pot. The rest of the meat is the *montsai's* perquisite. He goes back to the village, repeatedly calling the sick man's soul by the man's name to follow him.

When the *ratsen* says that it was at some place in the jungle or on the village path that the patient's soul left him and is being kept away by a *tsandhramo*, an interesting ceremony with a scapegoat chicken is performed. The *montsai* and a relation of the patient go to the spot where the soul is said to be, taking with them a carrying basket containing two "chungas" of "madhu," sixty pieces of plantain stem blackened with soot, twelve pieces of burnt wood, sixty little bits of pork, a small chicken, a cowrie, some ginger, some taro, some heads of a species of wild mint called *rarakham*, which is believed to be an infallible antidote against evil spirits, and a burning brand. Throughout the ceremony the patient's relation is a mere spectator. Assuming that the "genna" is being performed on a path, as is usually the case, for the patient was probably travelling along a path when the *tsandhramo* took possession of his soul, the *montsai* places equal portions of the ginger, *rarakham*, meat, plantain stalk, burnt wood and taro on either side of the path. This he does sitting facing away from the village to which the patient belongs. He pours the "madhu" from the smaller of the two "chungas" onto the ground, and lays the empty "chunga" down with its base towards the village. The carrying basket is split in half, and half put on either side of the path. The *montsai* now drinks the contents of the large "chunga," and splitting it with his dao lays his dao on the ground with the blade away from him. Then six times if the patient is a man, or five times if she is a woman, he drops the two halves of the split "chnuga" together onto his dao, asking each time, "Will he live or die?" If both halves come to rest on the same side of the dao the illness will be a long one. If one falls on one side and one on the other the patient will either die or get well soon. Next having tied the chicken's wings together over its back and fastened a cowrie onto its leg, he tosses it up and catches it six times for a man and five times for a woman, and undoing its wings lets it go into the jungle. He then takes his spear and jabs the butt into the ground a number of times, in order that the *tsandhramo* may think that a large number of men have come to call back the sick man's soul and so be more ready to let it go. Finally, he calls out the name of the patient eight times, and says, "O so and so. We have let a chicken go for you. Come back, come back." On his way back to the village he must keep on calling the sick man by name, and on arrival at the patient's house he says, "I have called so and so. Has he come?" and one of the inmates will answer, "He has come." The *montsai's* fee for this ceremony is a small basket of rice. This account is of the ceremony as performed by the Northern Lhotas. The only difference the Southern Lhotas make is that instead of sixty pieces of pork they take down either a crab or a jungle rat or squirrel, which they laboriously divide up into sixty tiny pieces. The reason for this is that they regard it as essential that a whole animal, however small, should be offered. This employment of a scapegoat chicken is common to Lhotas, Aos, Semas, Changs and probably most Naga tribes.

If a man be only slightly indisposed on his return from a journey the *ratsen* will tell him that a *tsandhramo* is detaining his soul at such and such a place on the path along which he came—always a spot conveniently near the village—and that an offering of eggs is all that is required. The sick man will then either go with a *montsai* or alone to the place. There the *montsai*, or the patient if he goes alone, puts on either side of the path a big leaf and an egg, and on the leaf taro, ginger, boiled rice, burnt wood and cotton, chilies, or whatever he may have been carrying when his soul was enticed away. He then goes home, calling his soul in the ordinary way. The cheapness of this method of regaining his soul appeals to the Lhota, who performs the ceremony on the least provocation. In cases of long illness more persuasion is required to induce the soul to return. A meal is prepared in the house, great care being taken that no stranger touches it, and put wrapped up in leaves in a carrying basket with a new cloth and the patient's ornaments. This is taken to the *montsai's* house, who that night meets the patient's soul in his dreams and tries to persuade it to return by pointing out that food and new clothes and ornaments are all ready for it if only it will come back. If it cannot be persuaded to return by these inducements the patient is doomed.

A person suffering from intermittent fever or some similar slight ailment gets rid of it as follows. He gets up from his seat in his house and puts any bits of rubbish, such as sticks or leaves, into an old carrying-basket. Taking up this load he says aloud, "I am going out to get some things." Having reached the outskirts of the village he hangs his load on a bush and says, "Watch this; I am coming back very soon." He then leaves the load with the illness watching it, as he thinks, and returns to his house by another path. Semas practise a similar custom for ophthalmia.

The Social "Gennas."

There remain to be described the social "gennas," which play such an enormously important part in Lhota life. Beginning from the first small "genna" they increase in costliness and importance till the ceremony at which two stones are dragged is reached. Almost every one of them entitles the doer to wear a distinctive cloth. The wealth and consequently the importance of a man is gauged by the number of these social "gennas" he has done, for the Lhota, like all Nagas and members of not a few other races, is a great respecter of wealth. It is therefore the ambition of every man to perform the full series if he possibly can. At the first stone-dragging ceremony one stone is dragged, and at the second, third and so on two stones are dragged. There is a limit to the number of times the stone-dragging ceremony may be done, which varies in different villages, but is so rarely reached that it practically exists only in theory. The only man the writer has ever come across who has reached the limit is Wonchămo of Pangti, who has dragged twenty-five stones. The only course open to him now if he wishes to do any more social "gennas" is to "become a boy again" and sleep in the *champo* and begin the whole series again from *Wozütana*, the first small "genna." This he does not propose to do. Though cases have been known in the past of men reaching the limit, there is no tradition of anyone who began the series again.[1] The "gennas" are public feasts which the whole village attends, but the man who proposes to do one must never announce his intention beforehand except in a whisper to his nearest friend and the necessary religious officials. This custom is strictly adhered to. Even a Lhota in Government employment who wishes to go to his village to perform a social "genna" will never say when he applies for leave what he wants it for. Were a man to announce that he was going to do one of these ceremonies and then not be able to do so it would, it is believed, entail a serious illness or some other misfortune.

For the ceremonies where a mithan is sacrificed a black hybrid or black bull may be substituted, but the substitute is invariably spoken of as a mithan. The following defects[2] make an animal unfit for sacrifice—a hole in the horn, one horn deformed or shorter than the other, one horn missing, teeth missing or broken, white marks on the body, white on the tail or forehead (though an animal with white both on the tail and forehead may be sacrificed), deformed hoof and white on the leg unless all four legs are white. It is

[1] Formerly it was the custom for a man who had performed the whole series to give a final feast, to which even birds and beasts were invited. Rice and food were scattered on the ground for the village pigs and chickens, and a special share of meat and rice was taken down to the performer's fields and left there for the crows. There is no one alive now who has dispensed hospitality on this lavish scale.

[2] Among the defects which disqualify a mithan in the view of Ao Nagas is any defect in the position, etc., of the whorls of hair on the animal's throat and muzzle, about which the Aos are very particular.—J. H. H.

believed that were a man to sacrifice an animal with one of these defects he would almost certainly die. Under no circumstances may the flesh of an animal which has been sacrificed be eaten either by the sacrificer or any of his household. It is believed that anyone who broke this rule would go mad. There is a man in Pangti who is supposed to have become insane for this reason. Whatever may be the real cause he is certainly afflicted with madness, and of a kind particularly obnoxious to the writer, for it takes the form of making interminable complaints about imaginary wrongs. Again in Humtso the writer came across a case in which a woman tried to poison her husband by scraping shavings off the horns of a mithan he had sacrificed and mixing them with his "madhu."

The First Social "Genna."

Like all social "gennas" the first one, *Wozütana*, is usually performed in the cold weather when there is a certain amount of leisure from work in the fields. It is a very simple affair which is often performed by a man before marriage. He invites all the men of his clan in the village who have done *Wozütana*, and kills a bull of any colour behind the house. This is divided up among the guests and much "madhu" handed round. Little presents of meat, too, would ordinarily be sent to fellow-clansmen in neighbouring villages. Next day the man who has done the "genna" must not give a drink of "madhu" to a man of another village. The head of the bull sacrificed on this occasion is not kept. The man who performs this "genna" is entitled to wear the cloth called *phangdrap*.

The Second Social "Genna."

The second social "genna," *Shishang*, or, as the Southern Lhotas call it, *Wozüyua*, is a much more elaborate business and is usually not performed till after marriage. A big pig and a bull of any colour are bought and "madhu" is prepared and kept in the middle room. From the time the "madhu" is made till the end of the "genna" the man doing the "genna" must not eat meat from the kill of a tiger or leopard or other animal. When all is ready he calls a *Wokchung* to his house, gives him a "chunga" of "rohi madhu" and formally announces to him that he proposes to do the *Shishang* "genna." The *Wokchung* thereupon offers a prayer for the performer's welfare, and after pouring a little of the "madhu" on to the floor drinks the rest and departs. Then the husbands of women of the sacrificer's clan go into the jungle and fields and bring *yutso* leaves and plantain leaves for cups for the next day's ceremony. Next day the same men kill the pig and the bull in front of the performer's house, the bull by cutting the skin over the heart and then pushing a sharpened stick home, and the pig with a blow of a stick on the back of the head. In "the good old days" before the Hills were administered the bull was beaten to death as slowly as possible—"great fun," as old men often say with a sigh. The two *Wokchungs* and two *'Nchukos* are in attendance, and the latter lay out six small pebbles in the form of miniature hearths in the *mpongki*, a piece of ceremonial for which the Lhotas can give no reason. The meat is then all divided up, and the *Wokchungs* and *'Nchukos* first go into the house and cook and eat a little of the meat. Then the guests go in and feast. For this day they are mostly the husbands of women of the sacrificer's clan, with a sprinkling of blood relations and senior men. At night, after much singing of songs in which good wishes for the sacrificer are expressed, the guests disperse and the *'Nchukos* throw away the six small pebbles. Next day about midday two small pigs provided by the sacrificer are speared by the *Wokchungs* outside the house. The hindquarters of one are the perquisite of the parents of the sacrificer's wife. The rest of the meat is eaten in the evening, when all men of the sacrificer's clan in the village who have done the *Shishang* "genna" collect round a fire outside his house and sing and drink his "madhu." The *Wokchungs* and *'Nchukos* each hold a cock and sing songs in which the good fortune of the sacrificer is desired. The cocks are then killed and the meat divided among the guests. The rest of the evening and most of the night is given up to singing and drinking, the old men especially getting happier and happier and more and more boastful of the deeds of their youth.

The Third Social "Genna."

The third social "genna" is called *Etha*. Nowadays the tendency is to combine it with the fourth social "genna" at which a mithan is killed, or even omit it altogether. The procedure is much the same as that of the *Shishang* "genna," except that Humtso, Chami, Kikung, Pathong and Nguli clans claim that they alone have the right to sacrifice a bull, other clans being content with pigs. The performance of this "genna" confers the right of wearing the cloth called *ethasü*.

After *Etha* and all subsequent social "gennas" a ceremony called *osoni-woala* is performed at the granary of the man who has done the sacrifice. The two *Wokchungs* sacrifice two pigs outside the granary, and kill two fowls by knocking their heads against the door. The meat is then divided up and the fowls' feathers are tied to bamboos outside the granary as a sign that the ceremony has been performed there.

The Fourth Social "Genna."

The fourth social "genna" is that at which a mithan is killed (*Tsirotsoala*). The man who proposes to perform this "genna" tells the two *Wokchungs* of his intention. The *Wokchungs* tell the husbands of married women born in the sacrificer's clan, and they (the husbands) in turn give public notice in the village and are called *Wothang* ("announcers"). Rice is pounded, with much singing, and "madhu" prepared. On the day of the sacrifice the mithan, which must be a bull without blemish, is tied up in front of the sacrificer's house, with its horns decked with *rezüyo* leaves. It is given a drink of water and allowed to lick salt out of the hand of the sacrificer's wife. The *Wokchung* touches it on the head with a stick and recites *dranda*. It is thrown, and a spear thrust into its heart by an old man, not necessarily of the sacrificer's clan, who at once runs away while all present pelt him with lumps of earth. After the mithan is dead its nose is pierced by the *Wokchung* and a string of *kuro* bark passed through and tied to a post in front of the house. The man performing the "genna" then takes his dao in his left hand and draws it across the flanks and neck of the animal as if he were cutting up the meat. He then cuts the string and walks widdershins round the mithan up to the door of his house, which he enters after washing his hands and his dao. The meat is divided up as follows: the chest to the clan of the performer of the sacrifice, the hindquarters to his wife's clan, the fore-legs to the husbands of women of his clan (*echantyoi*), the meat of the head to the *Wothangs*, the tongue to the man who helped to buy the mithan, and the lower part of the stomach to the old man who killed it. The performer must on no account eat any of this meat. Probably he will avoid mithan meat altogether for a year, in case an enemy should give him some of his own mithan to eat. The skull and horns must be kept in the "morung" till the sacrificer has dragged a stone, when he is allowed to put them up in his house.

Stone-dragging.

Before the ceremonies[1] begin a man who proposes to drag a stone must build a little shed at the back of his house called *emungrangki*, in which he and the whole household must sleep till the ceremonies are finished. All being prepared and a stone selected, two *Wothangs* announce the date of the ceremony on behalf of the performer, who must allow no strangers from other villages to enter his house, and must remain chaste from the time the stone is dug out of the ground till the completion of the ceremonies. On the appointed night rice is pounded in front of his house with much singing and "madhu" made after daybreak. (Here and throughout, most of the work is done by the *echantyoi*, i. e. husbands of women whom the performer calls "sister"). The "madhu" is put in baskets to ferment and a bunch of green stuff called *soko-mma* ("madhu-forbidding") is put over the door.[2] On the fourth day after this the performer must feed the *Wokchungs* and

[1] The ceremonies described below are those performed in Pangti. The details vary considerably from village to village.

[2] All Nagas put up green stuff over their doors when observing household "gennas," apparently as a signal to strangers not to interfere. There may be some other idea beneath it. A Lhota who passes the corpse of a man who has met with a violent end waves a bit of green stuff to and fro across his face. Mr. Mills tells me that this is to ward off the evil fate (*nyok*) which has attached to the dead man and may infect the passer-by. *Nyok* possibly = Angami *ropfü* (v. *The Angami Nagas*, Part IV.).—J. H. H.

their assistants in his house, receiving their blessing in return. The next day a path is cleared for the stone, the workers being feasted on a large pig. On the following day an old man called *Lungchakdhro* kills a little chicken in front of the house by cutting its throat with a sharp piece of bamboo, and prays that the stone may be carried up safely and unbroken. The chicken is thrown away. Then the *Wokchung* kills a small pig which is cooked by the performer's *echantyoi* in his *mpongki*. Every man is given a piece. The older men eat their portions, but the younger men only touch theirs and throw them down, for it is believed that they would become weak and unable to lift the stone were they to eat this meat. Then all the men of the village, both those of the performer's clan and his *echantyoi*, go down to the stone, which may be as far as two miles away, and make a frame of bamboo, on which it is put and bound with cane and creepers. When all is ready the two *Wothangs* sprinkle a mixture of " rohi madhu," " saka madhu " and *rarakham* in all directions and make a pretence of lifting the stone. These preliminaries over, all take up the frame and carry [1] the stone with much ho-hoing and grunting up to a place on the path called *züchanpen* (" stone-discussing-place "). There they are met by a procession of men in full dancing dress, consisting of all men of the dragger's clan who have dragged stones before, the rear being brought up by the performer himself, followed by two men called *Eso* and *Yuso*, *Eso* being the last man of the same clan who dragged a stone before the present puller, and *Yuso* the last dragger before *Eso* of the same clan. The performer himself carries an axe wrapped in *yutso* leaves, an egg and a chicken. After the inevitable interval for eating, drinking and talking the senior *Wokchung* holds the chicken in his hand and utters prayers for the prosperity of the village in general and especially for that of the performer and his wife. He cuts the chicken's throat with a sharp piece of bamboo and places it with the egg

[1] The Northern Lhotas carry the stone, but the Southern Lhotas drag it up on a rough sledge made of a forked branch, small branches being repeatedly laid in front of it to act as rollers.

Photo by J. H. Hutton.]

"GENNA" STONE TIED ON TO A BAMBOO FRAME-WORK READY TO BE CARRIED UP TO THE VILLAGE FOR THE STONE-DRAGGING CEREMONY

Photo by J. H. Hutton.]

GRAVE OF A WARRIOR DECORATED WITH HIS ORNAMENTS AND A TALLY OF THE HEADS HE HAS TAKEN (NORTHERN LHOTAS)

[*To face p.* 142.

in front of the stone. The two *Wokchungs* and the performer then all hold the axe together and make eight cuts to the right and eight to the left, as if clearing a way in front of the stone. The stone is then carried up to the village and laid in front of the performer's house. The evening is spent in feasting and singing. The performer supplies a bull, which is killed and divided up. The entrails are cooked and eaten by the carriers on the spot. The head goes to the performer and the meat is distributed to all except the performer and his clan and household. The songs sung are called *orrüeya* ("enemy-songs"), and detail the heads taken from every hostile village in the neighbourhood. The next day the *Wokchungs* show the exact place where the stone is to be set up and a hole is dug. All chant a prayer for the good fortune of the performer, holding in their hands curious cups of "madhu" made of folded plantain leaves ornamented with long horns of *rezüyo* leaves, similar to the cups used by the Aos at their big sacrifices. Two boars are then killed and cooked and eaten. A procession now emerges from the performer's house consisting of two old women followed by the performer's wife wearing her *charaksü* cloth for the first time, and another old woman. All four must wear their cloths bound round them under the armpits and not over the shoulders. The four women walk round the hole, which they approach from the side opposite to the Road of the Dead. Each one waves her foot over the hole as she passes. They then wash their faces and hands and re-enter the house. The stone is now tipped into the hole, set up and covered with mats, and the rest of the day spent in feasting and gaiety. In the morning the mats are removed and the ceremony is at an end. Among the Southern Lhotas three days elapse between that on which the stone is dragged into the village and that on which it is set up. During these three days the dragger is "genna." He must not speak to strangers or eat any unclean meat.[1]

[1] Mr. C. R. Pawsey tells me that the stone set up at Pembvo's grave (on the same ridge as Changsung and Ralung but to the south of them, a long-deserted village site) bears a rough incision believed by the local

Occasionally big forked posts (*tsongzü*), ten or twelve feet high,[1] are put up instead of stones to commemorate a mithan sacrifice. The usual reason is that suitable stone is not available, but the Nyimshamo kindred of the Othui clan in Yekhum are a unique example of a kindred which is forbidden to set up stones and must always set up posts instead. The reason given is simply that they have never been allowed to have anything to do with the village *oha*. The kindred came from Yemkha on the Sema border and may represent an immigration of Semas who still retain their own customs, but there is no tradition to that effect.

Birth.

In addition to the articles of food which women are forbidden to eat at all times, there are certain other things which are prohibited during pregnancy. Neither the woman nor her husband may eat tortoise or pangolin,[2] indeed she must not even touch a tortoise, and her husband, though he may touch one, may not bring one into the house or allow anyone else to do so. The wife may not eat bear's meat or the kill of any wild animal, and if her husband eats any of these things he must sleep apart from her the follow-

Lhotas, who greatly cherish Pembvo's memory, to represent the hornbill feathers he used to wear. The incision is in the form of an arc, the convex side upmost, with six lines proceeding from it like rays. I have once seen a stone ornamented with designs in pig's fat; the village was, as far as I remember, Changsung.—J. H. H.

[1] These Y-shaped posts are used as an emblem of prosperity by the Garos, Naked Rengmas, Sangtams, Semas, and by the Hankip clan of Thado Kukis, and were clearly used by the Kachari kings of Dimapur, who have left them in stone instead of wood at Dimapur. Originally they doubtless represent the female organ of generation, in which capacity they are still made and carried in Kohima village at the *Lisü* "genna," and, preceded by an emblem of the male organ, are dragged through the village by chaste boys. Kohima, however, seems to be the only genuine Angami village which either uses the Y-shaped post or performs the *Lisü* "genna" in this way. Possibly the Y-shaped post is to be definitely connected with the Bodo immigration into Assam.—J. H. H.

[2] Lhotas believe that a man who kills a pangolin will die if a scale falls from the skin of the animal. The Phoms of Hukpang have the same belief.—J. H. H.

FORKED POST (*TSONGZÜ*) AT YEKHUM, PUT UP INSTEAD OF A "GENNA" STONE

THE TWO *PUTHIS* OF AKUK COLLECTING RICE FOR THE *TUKU* CEREMONY

Both are carrying *phuis*.

[To face p. 144.

ing night. It is most important that neither the husband nor the wife should kill a snake during this time. Were they to do so the expected child would have a tremulous tongue. Some pregnant women even object to a snake being killed in their presence. It is also forbidden to an expectant mother to cut her hair. Any hairs which fall out are carefully collected and twisted into the hair-band. At the time of delivery the woman lies on her side and is attended to by an old midwife called *Oshangessi* ("thrower-away of afterbirth"). The husband and female relations may remain present. The household goods are only put outside when delivery is delayed. In cases of very painful birth the father either makes fire with a fire-stick and fumigates the woman, or exchanges drinks of hot "rohi madhu" with her. Occasionally the father spits on his fingers and puts a little of his saliva on the woman's stomach. This is regarded as an infallible remedy in cases of difficult delivery.[1] The *Oshangessi*, the moment the child is born, calls it by some name other than that which is to be its real name, in order that the evil spirits (*tsandhramo*) who are listening at the door may be deceived and go away, thinking they are in possession of the real name, which is not given till six days later in the case of a boy and five days later in the case of a girl. The name finally chosen is invariably one which has been borne by a member of the clan before. The false name having been given, the *Oshangessi* washes the child and puts a little boiled rice into its mouth. The navel string is put into a "chunga" and carefully kept by the parents in their house. If it were thrown away and eaten by a dog or pig or otherwise destroyed the child would die. The *Oshangessi* wraps up the afterbirth in bits of rag and *tsampen* (wild lemon) leaves in the case of a boy and *michem* leaves in the case of a girl, and putting

[1] Lhota women wishing for an easy delivery in childbirth catch the little sand lizard called *shamdram*, probably belonging to the skink family, having a very smooth and glossy surface to its scales, and of active habits, and rub it round their navel and abdomen, saying, "Let my child be slippery like you, and come without difficulty." Then they let it go again.—J. H. H. The Hopi Indians of Arizona use a weasel skin for the same purpose (cf. *Man*, July 1921, p. 99).

it in a little basket hangs it up on a *michem* tree, a tree with white flowers, well out of the way of dogs and pigs, who would cause the death or serious illness of the child if they ate it. There is one such tree on the outskirts of every "khel" which is used for afterbirths.[1]

For the next six days in the case of a boy, or five days in the case of a girl, the parents must not speak to any strangers, nor may any strangers come to the house.[2] Freshly killed meat too must not be brought into the house. For these days the child is regarded as in a sense still in the process of being born. The custom until recently was to regard a mother who died during this time as having died in childbirth,[3] and abandon the house and all its contents. At the end of five or six days as the case may be the ceremony of first carrying the child is performed. Into the hands of a son the father puts a miniature "madhu chunga" and wooden dao and says, "If I go on the war-path, if I go hunting, if I go fishing, I will take you with me. Grow up a strong, famous man." He then places the child for a moment in a carrying cloth on the back of the first "carrier" (*Ngaromuchung*), who must be a boy for a male child and a girl for a female child, but may be of any clan. For a daughter the father puts into her hands a miniature weaving sword and belt and says, "If I go to the fields, if I go to pick leaves in the jungle, I will take you with me. Grow up quickly and be strong." She is then given to the *Ngaromuchung* to carry for a minute. For the rest of that day the *Ngaromuchung* must avoid going down the path by which the spirits of the dead leave the village, in case he or she should unwittingly carry the child's soul (*omon*) with her. After the child has been carried by the *Ngaromuchung* the lobes of the child's ears are pierced with a sharp bamboo needle. The *Oshangessi*

[1] Angamis and Semas bury the afterbirth. The Khasis hang it up in trees.—J. H. H.

[2] A similar taboo exists among the Garos; cf. Major A. Playfair, *The Garos*, p. 23.

[3] The Semas and Angamis still do, I think, but they do not abandon the house.—J. H. H.

usually does this, but if she is old and her hand unsteady the father drives the needle through at the place indicated by her. A little plug of cotton wool is put in to prevent the hole closing up.

Boys are suckled for three years as a rule and girls for two, but a little "grown-ups'" food is given from a very early age. Bat's-flesh soup is considered to be a good tonic for a child whom its mother cannot suckle properly for any reason. Within about a month of birth the child is given its first taste of meat. If possible bulbul is given, because this bird twitters so much that by eating it a child will soon learn how to talk. Substitutes are a small fish called *ngolelop*, or a species of cuckoo called *liyosangsü*, which is said to be able to imitate the call of all birds and animals.

As soon as the mother is well enough to take the child out of the house she cuts off a little of its hair and either throws it away or wraps it in a leaf and keeps it. The heads of little boys are shaved except for a little piece on the crown, which is gradually allowed to increase until by the time he can run about his coiffure is like that of a grown man. Little girls have the whole of their heads shaved till they begin to wear a skirt, which is generally when they are five or six years old. It is then allowed to grow, beginning in the spring, "so that it grows with the jungle," as one informant expressed it to the writer.

Marriage.

Girls usually marry between the ages of fourteen and eighteen, and boys between seventeen and twenty-two. The ceremonies are intricate and differ in the northern and southern sections of the tribe. Among the Northern Lhotas the customary procedure is as follows. A man having decided that he wishes to marry a certain girl, he tells his parents, and either his mother or some elderly female relation goes and sounds the girl's parents. If they are agreeable she goes again with a "chunga" of "rohi madhu," which they drink, but by so doing do not bind themselves to give their daughter in marriage. The marriage-price is then discussed and settled by the two families, and the bridegroom gives the girl a rain-shield (*phūchyo*), a small carrying-basket (*eyingkhangdro*) and a dao handle.

These preliminaries being satisfactorily settled, at the next *Pikuchak* the ceremony of *tsoyuta* ("eating and drinking") takes place. The man takes a cock, which he has killed and cooked himself, and some "madhu" rice, and goes to the girl's parents' house accompanied by an old man of his clan called *Hantsen*, and another male relative, a sort of best man. The *Hantsen* enters the house first, then the bridegroom and then the best man. They hand the "madhu" rice to the girl's father, who in turn produces some. The rice of the two families is mixed by the girl and a brew prepared from it which may be drunk by all except the engaged couple. The bride and bridegroom sit side by side on the bed in the *lhurhui*, and the *Hantsen* squats opposite to them, holding in each hand a leaf containing sixteen tiny scraps of the cock which the bridegroom brought. He then swings his hands backwards and forwards eight times, praying that the couple, who by this ceremony are made man and wife, will live long and happily together. From this time the bridegroom will work in his father-in-law's house for about a year.[1] It is forbidden for him to have connection with his wife before *tsoyuta*.[2] To do so would, it is believed, cause the marriage to be sterile. But he may sleep with her when working in her father's house. When the fields have all been cut the bridegroom's relations stack a quantity of wood in the jungle, and bring up one load each to the bride's father's house, receiving a drink of "madhu" for their trouble. Four or five days later the *lantsoa* ("road-making") ceremony takes place. The husbands of women born in the bride-

[1] The same custom obtains among the Kacharis and other tribes of the Assam valley.—J. H. H.

[2] Among the Aos and Konyaks, on the other hand, the usual practice is for a youth to choose as his wife one of the girls whose favours he has been in the habit of enjoying.

groom's clan and their wives fetch up all the wood which was left stacked in the jungle and heap it up in front of his father-in-law's house. The bridegroom kills a pig and gives about twelve pounds of meat to his father-in-law. That night in the latter's house the *Hantsen* strangles a chicken and watches how the excreta fall. If any remains in the vent it is an evil omen indicating that the woman will die in childbirth. The *Hantsen* examines the entrails also, and from them claims to be able to say which will die first, whether the first child will be a boy or a girl, and so on. The chicken is then cooked by the *Hantsen* and taken away as his perquisite. The married couple may watch, but must never say afterwards what the omens revealed. Next day men of the bridegroom's clan distribute the wood heaped up in front of his father-in-law's house among all members of the father-in-law's clan, being rewarded with shares of the twelve pounds of pork.

The bridegroom still continues to work in his father-in-law's house till the next *Tuku* comes round and the *halam* ceremony puts an end to his rather laborious honeymoon. For this the bridegroom builds a small house called *kithandro*, and buys a big pig, which is speared through the heart with a sharp bamboo in front of his parents' house by the husbands of women born in his clan. It is taken to his father-in-law's house and there singed and cut up. The head goes to the bride's father, who also shares with other members of his clan the left fore- and hind-quarters. The chest and right fore- and hind-legs are laid aside. The bride collects cotton from all married women of her clan, and gives them shares of meat from the chest in exchange. In the afternoon all women, married or unmarried, of her clan bring two bobbins of thread each and are regaled with "madhu" in front of her father's house, returning to their houses at nightfall. At night men of the bridegroom's clan make preparations to escort the couple to their *kithandro*, and collect and drink outside his father-in-law's house, the bride and bridegroom meanwhile remaining inside. The drinking over, they put some meat wrapped in leaves and a "chunga" of "madhu" against the house and call out, "Let them come. Any further talking can be done to-morrow. Any further talking can be done the day after to-morrow. It is forbidden to come after cockcrow. If you do not let them come now we will burn your house." After they have been summoned in this way three or four times the procession emerges: first the wife of a man of the bridegroom's clan, then the bridegroom in full dress, followed by the bride wearing her *loroesü* (marriage cloth) for the first time, with the wife of another man of the bridegroom's clan bringing up the rear. The first and last woman must not be pregnant at the time. Before leaving the house the couple each take in their hands a small piece of meat of the pig which was killed earlier in the day and two pieces of thread. The husband waves his spear widdershins round the hearth before leaving the house, a ritual act of which the meaning is not known. They must both maintain absolute silence from the time they take the meat and thread in their hands to the time the *Hantsen* completes the ceremonies at the *kithandro*, whither they are escorted by the bridegroom's male relations. Four of these relations stay behind, and after asking the way to the *kithandro*—a mere pretence, of course—pick up the right fore- and hind-legs of the pig and take them there, having let the bridal procession get well on its way first. The couple find the *Hantsen* waiting for them outside the *kithandro*. He takes the bridegroom's spear from him, jabs the butt into the ground and leaves it standing outside the house. The meat and thread he takes into the house, and having poured water over the couple's hands leads them in. Standing in front of him, the man to the right and the woman to the left, they genuflect to him eight times. They may then speak and he leaves them. The couple sleep in the *kithandro* that night, but sexual intercourse is forbidden, and two small boys of the bridegroom's clan sleep with them. In the morning the boys go down to fetch water, talking loudly all the way, for it would be a very bad omen were they to meet a squirrel or other wild animal on the way. During the day neither of the couple may go to the wife's father's house. On the third day they go with a present of meat, and are feasted there in return.[1]

Three or four days later the ceremonies are completed by the *Ponyiratsen* (" man-and-wife-magicians "). After a drink of " rohi madhu " the couple go into the jungle alone and bring up a load of *yutso* leaves and sixty-four small bamboo " chungas " in eight equal bundles. All are cut on the slant except two in different bundles, which are cut with a level rim and are called *tsungta*. In each " chunga " of the two bundles containing *tsungta* are put eight pieces of *shambuk* pith and eight pieces of *shamburi* pith. When this has been brought the two *Ponyiratsen* are called to the house. They are two old women, wives or widows of men whom the bridegroom calls *aporamo*, and who have dragged a stone. These are given a full " chunga " of " rohi " to drink and proceed to tie up little scraps of pork in *yutso* leaves. They make four parcels each containing four scraps of meat, four each containing six, four each containing eight, four each containing ten, and finally two each containing thirty. These little parcels they put in a basket with a " chunga " of " rohi." Then each throttles a cock and watches the position of its legs when it dies. If the right leg is down and the left up the husband will die first. If the right is up and the left down the wife will die first. If the legs are crossed the couple will quarrel. The excreta and entrails are also examined in the usual way. The husband then singes the cocks and cuts each in half slantwise, so that the head is in one half and the vent in the other. He puts *yutso* leaves on the ground on his right and left, and puts the halves of two different cocks on each. These are wrapped in leaves and put in the load with the pork and " madhu." Then all wash their hands and the *Ponyiratsen* put eight narrow strips of plantain leaf over each ear of the bride and bridegroom, who sit down in front of them, the husband to the right and the wife to the left. The elder of

[1] A somewhat different account of a Lhota wedding is given on p. 74 of Part I. of the Assam Census Report, 1911. In spite of careful inquiries I have been unable to find any Lhota who has ever heard of the marriage song and mock fight there described.

the *Ponyiratsen* next takes a small basket and puts into it a pair of pewter bracelets and waves it in front of the couple, while she mumbles a prayer that they may be happy and have many children. Only women know the right prayer, which is mumbled purposely in order to prevent the husband hearing it properly. The prayer finishes with "hohoho" said eight times, the other *Ponyiratsen* keeping count aloud. From the house the old women go to the *Ponyiratsentung* ("*Ponyiratsen* tree") belonging to the "khel," taking with them the basket containing the parcels of pork and chicken and the "madhu," and four bundles of bamboo "chungas," eight *yutso* leaves without blemish, an egg, and two garments which have been worn by the husband and wife respectively. The old women are supposed to lead away with them all evil spirits. It is therefore considered very unlucky to meet them and their devilish train on their way. When they leave the *kithandro* the wife shuts the door quickly behind them in order to keep out evil spirits and keep in good. Arrived at the tree the elder *Ponyiratsen* divides the "chungas" into two equal heaps and puts the egg between them, with a parcel containing thirty pieces of meat on each side. They then go to the younger *Ponyiratsen's* house, and having divided up the rest of the meat there the elder one goes home. That night the couple for whom the ceremony is being done must sleep apart.

Next day the *Ponyiratsen* come again and take the omens in the same way, except that two hens are used instead of two cocks. After swinging the basket containing the bracelets and mumbling the charm, the elder *Ponyiratsen* lays a bamboo mat on the ground outside the door on the side farthest away from the Road of the Dead. By the mat she lays the two worn garments which she took the day before, the husband's to the right and the wife's to the left. She sits at the right end of the mat, facing her assistant *Ponyiratsen*, who sits at the left end, and rolls an egg along the mat. Omens are drawn from the direction in which the pointed end lies when it comes to rest. If it points towards a hostile village the husband will get heads, if towards the plains money, if towards the house rice. It is a very bad omen if it points towards the Road of the Dead. The assistant *Ponyiratsen* rolls the egg back and the process is repeated eight times. A sickle is then slid along the mat eight times and omens are taken from the direction of its point, just as they were taken from the direction of the pointed end of the egg. When this is finished the elder *Ponyiratsen* shakes the two cloths eight times each to get rid of any evil there may be in them and returns them to their owners, and as she picks up the mat, gives it a flick and sends the egg, which is still lying on it, as far as possible in the direction opposite to that of the Road of the Dead, saying as she does so, "I am throwing away all evil fortune and poverty." She then shakes the mat eight times, and both the *Ponyiratsen* go to their own houses. The wife rolls up the mat and stands it on end inside the door between the *mpongki* and the *lhurhui*. The couple must sleep apart that night, and the mat must not be removed before cockcrow next morning. This ceremony of the *Ponyiratsen* is regarded by Lhotas as a sort of initiation into married life. It is only performed for each individual once in his life. For example, were a bachelor to marry a widow it would be performed for him. Were a married man to take a spinster as a second wife it would be performed for her. But were a married man to take a widow it would not be performed at all.

Among the Southern Lhotas there are certain differences of detail. The first ambassador is usually an old man of the bridegroom's clan. If the girl's parents drink the offered "madhu" negotiations are considered to have begun. Later the old man brings a present of meat and "madhu" and says, "This is so-and-so's meat and 'madhu.' Will you eat and drink it?" If the girl's parents say, "Yes," the couple are regarded as engaged, and the man will help in his future father-in-law's fields and make himself generally useful, though he sleeps with his parents till after *tsoyuta*. For that ceremony the bridegroom prepares "madhu" and kills and cuts up a pig, and goes to the girl's father's house accompanied either by an old man of his clan and an old woman of the girl's clan or *vice versa*. The old woman enters the house first, followed by the old man, the bridegroom bringing up the rear. The girl's parents offer "madhu" to the old man and woman, drinking in turn some of the "madhu" which has been brought. It is not mixed as among the Northern Lhotas. The engaged couple sit on the bed in the *lhurhui*, the man to the right and the woman to the left. The old man and woman sit opposite to them, each holding a leaf containing six pieces of the pork they have brought, and all four swing their arms backwards and forwards, while the old man and woman say, "Live long and have many children." The *lantsoa* ceremony is performed as among the Northern Lhotas. For the *halam* ceremony a few details are different. The bride and bridegroom are accompanied to the *kithandro*, not by two women, but by an old man of the bridegroom's clan and the wife of a man of his clan. The bridegroom does not wave his spear round the hearth, but carries six pieces of meat and six bobbins of thread, while his wife carries five pieces of meat and five bobbins of thread, which the old man takes from the bridegroom's hand, and the old woman from the bride's hand. There is no *Hantsen* as among the Northern Lhotas.

A well-to-do Lhota usually has two or often three wives. Very occasionally a man will have four or even five. All are of equal status, though the oldest wife naturally occupies a position of some authority in the household. The husband usually sleeps with her in the middle room. It is forbidden for him to have connection with more than one wife on the same night. Possibly a vestige of a former system of group marriage is found in the custom of a Lhota who expects to be away from home for some time giving his brother permission to have marital relations with his wife during his absence.[1] On a man's death his widow or widows are expected to go to his brother, who will not, however, receive them into his house till all the ornaments on the dead man's grave

[1] In the case of the Rengmas a younger brother who has a fancy for his elder brother's wife by no means necessarily waits for his brother's absence, nor does the elder brother necessarily object to his younger brother's having intercourse with his (the elder's) wife. I have known the elder brother acquiesce in this even when the younger was married to a wife of his own. This last it was who objected.—J. H. H.

have been cleared away and he has finally gone to the Land of the Dead. A man who thus takes his dead brother's wife performs no marriage ceremony and pays no marriage price. If the woman marries a man of another clan, the late husband's clan realize from the new husband a marriage price equal to the original marriage price. If a woman does not wish to marry again she may keep one of her husband's mithan heads instead of putting it on his grave. This is equivalent to a vow of perpetual widowhood.

The money which is paid by the husband for his wife is known collectively as *oman* (marriage-price), but is divided into a number of items. The first payment of all is known as *chüka*, and is paid not to the girl's parents, but to her mother's father or mother's brother. The amount is Re.1. This is paid as soon as *tsoyuta* has taken place. The second item is *nzuiman* (Rs.8 to Rs.10), paid to the girl's parents as the cost of bringing her up. Thirdly comes *nvaman* (Rs.10), the price of not working in his father-in-law's house. The fourth payment is *kitsoman* (Rs.2), the price of not building his father-in-law's house. The third and fourth items are of course only paid in cases where the bridegroom prefers to pay compensation rather than work in his father-in-law's house. The fifth item is *halamman*, the cost of the pork given to the father-in-law at the *halam* ceremony. The sixth is *tsangchüman* (Rs.2), paid in cases where the bridegroom does not distribute wood to members of his father-in-law's clan. The seventh is *sontsoman* (four annas), paid if the bridegroom does not build a granary for his father-in-law. The eighth is *tsoroman* (Re.1), the price of the bride's breasts, and the ninth *lentamoman* (Re.1), price of intimacy with the bride. Men with land usually let the girl's parents cut one field once. If not, a tenth payment of one rupee or two rupees is made instead. The eleventh item is *otyai-etsoman* (the price of feeding the bride's brothers), the marriage-price proper. This is shared by the girl's father and brothers. It amounts to about two hundred and fifty baskets of rice, or thirty rupees if paid in cash. The rice or money is paid in instalments, often at long intervals. The result is that it is by no means uncommon to find a son paying off the last instalment of his old widowed mother's marriage-price. Should a woman die without children her husband makes a final payment varying from two rupees to five rupees, called *etchhiman* (" price of death "). Once they have received *etchhiman* the girl's parents can claim no further instalments of *otyai-etsoman*. If the woman dies leaving children a payment of one or two rupees, called *mingishi*, is made to her parents or their heirs, who can in this case claim any of the *otyai-etsoman* which may be outstanding.

Divorce.

There is no ceremony connected with divorce as there is among the Aos, and the proceedings are not protracted, the wife generally settling the matter by running away to the house either of her parents or some admirer. In that case all that remains to be done is to discuss the return of the marriage-price. Sometimes the girl's parents return the full amount of the marriage-price which they have received up to date, plus a fine of ten rupees, and sometimes, in cases where the marriage-price has already been divided up and spent, it is arranged that the aggrieved husband shall recover the marriage-price from whoever marries his runaway wife. In cases where the woman runs off with another man the co-respondent has to pay the husband the full amount of the marriage-price, plus compensation amounting to fifty or a hundred rupees. It is very rarely that a man simply turns his wife out. If he does so he cannot recover his marriage-price and has to pay her parents or their heirs a fine of ten rupees. He naturally, therefore, puts up with a good deal from his wife, sooner than lose his marriage-price. Among the Aos the divorced wife can claim a share of the household store of grain. Among the Lhotas she can only claim the thread and chickens she brought with her at her marriage or their equivalent, together with the clothes she wears and all the thread there may be in the house. Any ornaments given her by her husband must be returned to him.

Death Ceremonies.

In cases where the death agony is prolonged the Changs

cut a carrying-string on the threshold of the house in order to release the spirit, but there appears to be no such practice among the Lhotas. At death the nearest relation present closes the eyes and washes the face of the corpse. No hole is made in the roof to let the spirit out as among the Konyaks. A very old man ties a cowrie to a chicken's leg and places it for a moment in the dead man's hand. He then kills it in order that it may go clucking along the Road of the Dead and give warning that the deceased is coming. It is hung by the neck above the head of the corpse, and after the burial the wings are cut off and stuck up on the left wall of the house and the body either thrown away or given to the buriers (*mungpen*) to eat. When the deceased is a man who has taken heads, or killed a tiger, a dog is led into the house on a string and the string put into the hand of the corpse for a minute. After the body has been buried the dog is killed in order that it may go barking down the Road of the Dead and frighten away the ghosts of enemies and tigers slain by the dead man during his lifetime. The flesh is eaten by the *mungpen*. The corpse is buried as soon after death as possible. A grave about six feet deep is dug in front of the man's house. The body is buried fully dressed, and often decorated with all the ornaments worn during life, if the deceased so desired. Nothing of foreign manufacture may be worn by a corpse. A cornelian bead is tied to the dead man's wrist to give to a spirit called *Etchhilivanthamo*, whom he will meet on the Road of the Dead, in exchange for a drink of water. Among the Northern Lhotas a sharp piece of bamboo is also put under the head of the corpse at the time of burial, in order that the soul of deceased may be able to cut any creepers which he may find obstructing his way. The body is wrapped in two or three good cloths and carried out of the house by the *mungpen*. Over it in the grave are put short lengths of bamboo laid crosswise, and on them two planks from the dead man's bed, which are in turn covered with a piece of bamboo matting. In certain villages of the Northern Lhotas rich men were till recently buried in wooden coffins called " boats " (*orhung*), cut out of one log of wood, with a rude representation of a hornbill's head and tail at the head and foot respectively.[1] It is noticeable that they were made in villages which do not make dug-out canoes,[2] or indeed anything more serviceable than a type of bamboo raft which "floats" about six inches under water. These coffins took a considerable time to make and were begun as soon as the illness took a bad turn. If a man recovered after his coffin had been made he was supposed to live a long time.[3]

Stones and thorns are heaped on the top of the grave to prevent pigs and dogs scratching up the earth, and a low fence is built round it. Two bamboo posts are then put up, one at the head and one at the foot, with a cross-bar between them. In the case of a man's grave a basket containing a gourd of "madhu," a little boiled rice and six pieces of meat is hung on the post at the head. His wooden dao-holder, and bear's-hair wig, cloth, cowrie lengta, ivory armlets, etc., are hung on the cross-bar, and his spears are stuck upright on the grave. In the case of a woman's grave only the basket is hung at the head, containing five instead of six pieces of meat. A fire is lighted on the grave. For six days after the death of a man and five days after the death of a woman no member of the household must speak to a stranger or kill any living thing. When this period of "genna" is over the man's possessions are removed from the grave, and imitation spears, or very old ones, put in their place. On the cross-bar above the grave round bamboo basket balls are put to represent the number of times the deceased has done the head-taking "genna." Sometimes roughly carved wooden heads are used. Tigers made from a short length of bamboo, with short bamboo "legs" and "tail," commemorate his prowess in the chase.[4] On this

[1] Some of the Konyaks use coffins of this type, and the Kalyo-Kengyu also seem to use a dug-out receptacle for the bodies of the dead while they are kept in the house during the desiccation process.—J. H. H.

[2] One or two villages situated near the lower reaches of the Doyang where it emerges into the plains make dug-out canoes hewn from a single log. These are admittedly copies of those made by the Assamese, with whom these villages have been in long and close contact.

[3] So the Assamese of the plains believe that if a false report of a man's death is circulated he will live long. The Semas on the other hand believe that it will cause his death untimely.—J. H. H.

[4] The Northern Lhotas build a miniature roof over the grave.

day the wings of the "death chicken" are taken down from the wall, and cut with a dao on the step between *mpongki* and *lhurhüi*, six times for a man and five times for a woman, and a prayer is offered that the dead person will not haunt the house, and in the case of a man who has taken heads a mithan and a pig are sacrificed by his clan. For a woman, or a man who has not taken heads, only a pig is sacrificed. The fire is kept alight on the grave and the offerings of food are renewed until the *tuku emung*, when the dead man is supposed finally to take his departure to the Land of the Dead, and all ornaments being removed the grave becomes part of the village street again.

Offerings to the dead are made not only on the grave, but also by the side of the path from the village which leads to the Land of the Dead under Wokha Hill. Immediately after death two relations, calling upon the dead man to follow them, go down the path, taking with them a gourd of "madhu" and a stick nicked to show the "gennas" the deceased has performed and the heads he has taken. The stick is stuck up by the side of the path and the gourd tied to it. These are to support and refresh the deceased on his way. When the six days of "genna" are over, in the case of a man, a bamboo erection (*nritangpeng*) is put up by the side of the path, with tallies of heads taken and tigers slain such as are put on the grave. On the memorial of one mighty hunter the writer saw two elephants made of black cloth stuffed with straw. For a man who has done no "gennas" a single bamboo pole is put up. On the *tuku emung*, when all ornaments are removed from the grave, the final offerings are made by the side of the path.[1] The relations go out before dawn, and for a man erect a little bamboo platform or tiny altar composed of a small flat stone supported on little bits of bamboo. On it are laid six pieces of meat and some rice and scraps of any favourite

[1] The Kalyo-Kengyu make periodic offerings by the path until the sowing following the death, when the body is broken up. A mat is spread and every sort of grain poured out, and some of all the fruits and vegetables available, together with wooden daos, spears and cross-bows, are put out for the dead, whole baskets of valuable grain being emptied by the road-side for this purpose.—J. H. H.

fruit of the deceased. A new dao-belt, with a miniature dao-holder, is stretched between two sticks, and a little wooden dao and spear are put near it. Sometimes a little bamboo platform (*eno*) with a little notched stick for the ghost to use as a ladder [1] is put up, and on it are laid ear ornaments and offerings of food and drink, and imitation beads made from pith. This offering made, the living have performed their duty towards the dead, and the village can begin a new year with little fear of hauntings.[2]

Such are the usual funeral ceremonies, but under certain circumstances the normal procedure is not followed. An infant is usually buried in the *mpongki*, the reason given being the rather pathetic one that its parents do not like to think of it lying out in the rain and the cold. If a man was killed in war he was buried outside the village and no ornaments were put on his grave. Like all Nagas, the Lhotas regard certain forms of death with horror, as being manifestations of supernatural displeasure.[3] Thus it is that when anyone dies by drowning, or by falling from a tree, or by fire, or by accidentally falling on his own spear, or in childbirth, or is killed by a wild animal, very strict purificatory rights have to be performed, and great care is taken to burn or cut down a tree from which a man has fallen and been killed. Except in the case of a man killed by a tiger or leopard the corpse is buried near the place of death, whether inside or outside the village. An account of the rites following a death by drowning will illustrate the procedure followed. The body is buried by the nearest relations present, no bead being put on the wrist or ornaments on the grave. Anyone who touches the corpse must at the first opportunity throw away all ornaments and clothing he was wearing at the time. Other people present need not do more than throw

[1] The Tangkhuls build a miniature house on a very high machan (for the size of the house) with a tiny notched bamboo for the spirit to use as a ladder.—J. H. H.

[2] For a similar belief among the Garos, cf. Major A. Playfair, *The Garos*, p. 23.

[3] According to Sir J. Frazer the reason is fear of the ghost, vide *Psyche's Task*, pp. 134, 135 (2nd ed.), where the customs of the Shans and Kachins are mentioned and prove to be remarkably similar to those of the Lhotas. —J. H. H. These deaths are known in Naga-Assamese as "apotia."

Eno
Showing wool for ears, and a gourd of "madhu" and a "chunga" to the right.

Nritangpeng OF A MAN WHO HAS KILLED AN ELEPHANT

[*To face p.* 160.

away a thread from their clothes and the cotton wool from their ears, and scrape a shaving off their spears and dao handles. Any fish caught before the man was drowned, if the catastrophe took place while fishing, as is often the case, may be cooked and eaten on the spot, but nothing must be carried away. Each man as he leaves the river flicks the water with his right hand and says, "Take away all evil, O river." As soon as the news of the disaster, for such it is, reaches the village an old man comes out and makes a fire on the path, using a fire-stick to do so. Every man before he can enter the village must step through the smoke of the fire, and hold his ornaments and weapons in it for a moment.[1] Someone is standing ready with a "chunga" of water, and each man washes his hands before he passes on. Even a stranger from another village must do this before he can enter his own village, lest he should bring with him the evil with which he is contaminated. The house and all the property of the dead man are abandoned. His money is simply thrown on the ground and left there. His live-stock cannot be killed, for that would defile the dao. The animals are just left to wander about, or are driven over a cliff if they become a nuisance.[2] No money or debts in kind due to the dead man can be claimed, and his heirs in turn need not pay any of his debts. His house is left to fall into ruins with all it contains. His crops are abandoned and any land he was cutting that year must next be cut by a man of another

[1] In a case that came to my notice at Lotsü, when the *Puthi's* son got drowned when fishing, all the men with the lad threw away all their cloths, weapons, ornaments and everything they had taken with them on their outing. Even the dogs they had with them were killed and their bodies thrown into the jungle. The fact that it was the *Puthi's* son that was drowned probably made the matter much more serious. The misfortune was put down to the anger of Tchhüpfu at the village having failed to "poison" the river with *deo-bih*, but it is possible that this was done in the hope that I would allow that forbidden practice to be renewed.—J. H. H.

[2] Semas sometimes come and ask for them, also for the paddy left to rot in the grain-house. I have known both taken without objection, and I have known Lhotas also object to both on the grounds that in the act of taking them away it would be necessary to move them across the village lands, and that this alone might be enough to bring about some terrible calamity. I think, however, that jealousy had something to do with this attitude.—J. H. H.

clan, though an old man of the dead man's clan may take rent for it. For the purification of the members of the household the following rites are performed among the Northern Lhotas. Friends of the dead man build a little shed and put some clothes and food in it. An old man of his clan, on the day after the death, lights a fire in front of the house and sacrifices a cock. The whole household must then come out of the house stark naked and step over the fire. They then enter the shed, where they put on clothes and remain for six days without speaking to anyone. Friends bring them food, and build a new house for them. Among the Southern Lhotas the usual custom is for the household to remain in the old house for six days. A cock is then sacrificed, and they pass through the fire and wash their hands and feet and go to a little house built for them outside the village, where they remain for six days, being fed by their friends. They then again are made to pass through the fire and change their clothes and wash and have their hair cut, after which they are ceremonially clean. The task of the man who sacrifices the chicken is regarded as a particularly risky one. Lhotas near the Sema border usually call in a Sema to perform this unpleasant duty. The Sema is not over nice in these matters and willingly sacrifices the chicken, receiving as his reward any of the live-stock of the deceased which he likes to kill and carry away. He must not, however, take away beads or money which might pass from hand to hand and eventually reach some Lhota. The people of Yekhum were recently very much distressed because some Semas carried off some money which had been thrown away, and complained that they would not know whether any rupee in circulation was from this tainted source or not. If a man is killed by a tiger or leopard the body is not buried, but is put on a platform in a tree and panjis are set underneath. This is the only example of tree "burial" among the Lhotas,[1] though the Aos invariably lay out their dead on machans, and the Konyaks beyond them actually put their dead

[1] Unless the disposal of enemy heads on the *mingetung* is so reckoned, or the disposal of the afterbirth in trees. Both are buried by the Angami and the latter by the Sema also.—J. H. H.

bodies in trees in certain villages. Such horror have the Lhotas of being killed by wild beasts that if a man who is being chased by an elephant throws down his load and the elephant touches it he may never pick it up again, for it "belongs to the elephant," and were he to take it back some elephant would assuredly take his life in exchange. Similarly the shaft of a spear broken by a tiger may never be used again, or the owner will have to give his life in exchange for the spear. No direct descendant of a man killed by a tiger or leopard may eat meat from a tiger or leopard's kill until he has removed the curse by cutting off the head of a tiger. The wife of a man under this prohibition must observe it, but the husband of a woman under it may eat meat from a kill, but must not give it to his wife. No one may eat the flesh of an animal which has been drowned, or has died in giving birth to young. Were Lhotas strictly logical they would prohibit the eating of meat from a tiger's or leopard's kill. As it is, it is regarded as unclean and meat is prohibited for anyone who has to remain ceremonially clean. Ordinarily, however, it may be eaten, for to forbid it entirely would be a great hardship in a country where such large numbers of live-stock come to this untimely end. Lightning, as is only natural, is looked upon as an instrument of supernatural vengeance. Even if no one be killed, a house struck by lightning is abandoned with all it contains. A tree struck by lightning cannot be cut up for firewood or used for any purpose whatever. Should a field be struck, no crop is cut that year from the place where the lightning fell. The rest of the crop may be eaten, but no seed is kept from that field. The stone adzes which are sometimes found are regarded as thunderbolts and are called *Potsophü* ("*Potsos*' axes"), and no Lhota cares to touch one.

Miscellaneous Beliefs.

Medicine Men.

Some Lhotas say that the peculiar powers believed to be possessed by medicine men (*ratsen*) are hereditary.[1]

[1] The Changs believe that "tiger-men" are confined to the Haki-Ung clan, where the peculiarity is hereditary. They say that at the time of the

Most people hold, however, that anyone, man or woman, is liable to develop the symptoms which are associated with *ratsen*. The person affected falls into a fit at the dark of the moon, and while in this state says that friends are coming, though none of the bystanders can see anything. These fits are liable to occur throughout life at the change of the moon, and are certainly very violent. I myself saw Yimbomo of Rephyim, a well-known *ratsen*, fall into a sudden fit down at the Doyang river when a large number of men were "poisoning" the water for fish. He laughed and shouted incoherently, and kept throwing himself onto the ground with such violence, that two men had to be told off to restrain him. In order to bring a man round from these fits powdered ginger is blown into his nose and ears. When a man shows these symptoms for the first time an experienced *ratsen* is called in to diagnose the case. If he proclaim it to be genuine he strangles a cock, from the head of which he is believed to extract a small stone called *ratse'ha*. This stone he gives to the budding *ratsen*, who is supposed to keep it inside his head, and occasionally even show it to very intimate friends. It is said that a few years ago 'Ntengo of Lungsachung was foolish enough to show his stone to a rival *ratsen* called Khumeshiyo of the same village, who grabbed it and managed to retain possession of it. The result was that 'Ntengo went mad and died soon afterwards.

Every *ratsen* possesses a "familiar" (*sonyo*), which is usually a leopard,[1] but occasionally a snake. The Lhotas are perfectly familiar with the "leopard men" who are found among the Semas, and clearly distinguish them from their own *ratsen*. They say that the soul of the Sema "leopard man" actually enters his leopard, while the *ratsen*

Universal Deluge, when only the highest peaks remained above the flood, the Haki–Ung clan was the only one from which tigers claimed no victims. They therefore became the adopted sons of tigers, and to this day have tiger "familiars." No member of the clan may kill or touch the corpse of a tiger. When a tiger is killed it is believed a member of the Haki–Ung clan will die six days later in a distant village.

[1] In this connection the *Journal of the Royal Anthropological Institute* ("Leopard Men in the Naga Hills") for Jan.–June 1920 may be referred to.—J. H. H.

A MEDICINE MAN (*RATSEN*) IN A FIT
He required two men to restrain him.

A DANCER AT THE REBUILDING OF A MORUNG
He has put on an imitation tiger's tail as a joke.

[*To face p.* 164.

is merely very intimately connected with his *sonyo*, which is an ordinary leopard indistinguishable in form from other leopards. If, however, the *sonyo* of a *ratsen* is killed the *ratsen* will sicken and perhaps die unless he can get another. As the powers of the *ratsen* grow so his *sonyo* increases in size, until in time it may even become unmanageable. This happened to a *ratsen* from Akuk called Mungchemo. His leopard became so big and fierce that he begged the villagers to kill it. They ringed it, but Mungchemo, who was helping, shouted in his excitement and so gave the leopard sufficient warning for it to escape. This failure to get rid of his *sonyo* so weighed on his mind that he eventually committed suicide. Ordinarily, however, the *sonyo* is believed to be under such excellent control that its owner can call it up from the jungle at will. This he rarely does, however, for if another man sees his *sonyo* the *ratsen* becomes ill. There are numerous stories, however, of leopards having been seen actually in *ratsens'* houses. Naturally a *ratsen* ordinarily objects strongly to his *sonyo* being killed, for it may entail his own death. The result is that several villages have told their *ratsen* that since he cannot stop his leopard killing their pigs they cannot allow him to be present when they ring the leopard, for at leopard hunts the *ratsen* is supposed to warn the quarry either by shouting to it or spitting on bits of worm-cast and throwing them towards it. In some places if a *ratsen's* leopard is hunted and killed he lays a cloth over the body as a mark of respect. The fits from which a *ratsen* suffers are believed to be in some way connected with his *sonyo*. They usually occur at the dark of the moon, at which time he has most influence over his leopard, and when he falls in a fit the soul of the leopard is believed to walk over his body. The soul is of course invisible, but visible tracks are supposed occasionally to be left on the *ratsen's* chest.

In addition to the ordinary food taboos a *ratsen* is forbidden to eat bamboo rats, frogs, or king-crows. They are supposed to be able to foretell the future by gazing into "madhu," or water held in a leaf, but their chief occupation in life is to "extract" foreign bodies from the persons of sick people. This is always done inside a house where the bad light makes sleight of hand easy. The patient is rubbed with a leaf, usually a wild lemon leaf, upon which the *ratsen* repeatedly spits. Finally he will show the patient a small pebble or a bit of leaf or hair, which he says was causing all the trouble by lodging in the body. In cases of laboured breathing the *ratsen* says that there is a hole in the lungs. He then by sleight of hand makes a leaf seem to disappear into the patient's chest, and after a few minutes extracts it and announces that the hole is now stopped up. Coughs are usually cured by pretending to extract a lump of hair from the throat. Usually the foreign body which is extracted is simply thrown away anywhere, but in cases of rheumatism, which is regarded as in some way especially connected with lightning, the *ratsen* "extracts" bits of wood from the patient's joints and throws them away near a tree which has been struck by lightning. Into the trunk of the tree he sticks a piece of iron, which he leaves there, and throws down one or two eggs as an offering. Often the *ratsen* will say that the illness is due not to the presence of a foreign body, but to the capture of the patient's soul by an evil spirit. He will then announce the whereabouts of the evil spirit in question, and the appropriate ceremonies must be performed. These have been described under the section on private ceremonies.

Luck-stones.

The Lhota believes that certain stones called *oha* bring good fortune. They are smooth, water-worn stones, varying in size from that of a man's head to that of a walnut, and are kept either under the *mingetung*, or at the foot of the carved post of the "morung," or by individuals in their houses or granaries. *Ratsen*, however, as has been mentioned above, are believed to have the peculiar habit of keeping their *oha* inside their heads. Those kept under the *mingetung* are usually large, and on them the luck of the whole village depends. Those kept in the "morung" affect the prosperity of the section of the village to which they belong. Stones of these two classes have been handed down from generation to generation and are never added to nowadays, though they are believed occasionally to increase spontaneously. But individuals still from time to time find small *oha* in the jungle and bring them home to keep as private luck-stones. The distinguishing mark of an *oha* is that it should be round and smooth, and be found resting on the ground in a little nest it has made for itself.[1] Anyone finding such a stone brings it home, and then notices whether his family increases quickly, or he has good crops, or is particularly successful in trade. He thus finds out what particular form of good luck is attached to the stone in question. Bad *oha* are not unknown. One kind called *ekyulung* ("coughing-stones") causes the owner to fall ill. Yet to throw them away would mean certain death. The possessor of an *oha* which brings luck in trade keeps it with his money. Similarly a rice *oha* is kept in the granary. A famous *oha* is the *Phi-tsong-lung* ("drying-increasing-stone"), which is in the possession of a member of the Othui clan at Pangti. It is said to be a portion of the famous stone at Kezakenoma,[2] called by the Lhotas Ketsarhontsü, which miraculously increased rice dried on it, and was broken off by Rangti, grandson of Longchentang, who according to one tradition came out of the earth and founded the Mipongsandri phratry. This was before the Angamis, Semas, Rengmas and Lhotas split up and became separate tribes. Formerly the Othui clan used to provide one of the *Puthis* at Pangti, and the *Puthi* of the Othui clan always used the *Phi-tsong-lung* as a pounder for husking the rice at the ceremony of eating the first-fruits (*mshe etak*). There are only a few broken fragments of the stone left now, which are kept with other *oha* in the possessor's granary. *Oha* are treated with great respect. The ceremony connected with them at the *Oyantsoa* "genna" has already been described. Before

[1] Among other Naga tribes these stones must be black and heavy for their size, and show a wet smear when rubbed with the thumb. They are nodules of some stone which is not a normal geological feature of the country, and are regarded as distinct from the larger water-worn stones kept to bring fortune to the community, which are definitely of the locality. Cf. *The Sema Nagas*, Part IV. (*Anagha*).—J. H. H.

[2] See *The Angami Nagas*, Part I.—J. H. H.

doing the *Liritang* ceremony at the beginning of harvest a man must make a small offering of meat to his *oha*.[1] At the time of the *Pikuchak* "genna," too, all possessors of rice *oha* must inspect them, taking care to wash their hands both before and after. It is curious that the reason given why the Nyimshamo kindred of the Othui clan in Yekhum cannot set up stones after doing the mithan sacrifice, is that they have never been allowed to touch the village *oha*, when they had to be carried on migration, or indeed to have had anything to do with *oha*. What the connection is, however, between the two kinds of stone is not precisely stated.

Charms. Love potions are commonest in the villages near the plains. I remember a youthful widow of Sanis who was so indiscreet as to get engaged to two men in two different villages at the same time. When the tangle was brought to me to unravel she said she really had only meant to get engaged to one, but the other one had rubbed a love charm on her neck—at least she thought that was what he must have done, though she had not actually noticed him do so.

Certain old women are supposed to possess the knowledge of these charms, which is handed down from mother to daughter. One Amhono of Pyangsa is said to retail a root called *loha*, which has to be ground up and given to the shy loved one with cooked fish.[2] If the suit is hopeless the recipient of the root removes all doubt by being sick on the spot. My informant had never seen the root; he had only heard of it. Another charm is a feather of a bird called *tsentsü*—probably mythical, at least I could never find out what it was. If a man can once touch a woman's hand with this she is his for life.

Witchcraft, in the evil sense of the word, was probably never common among the Lhotas, though the practice used to exist of making a straw image of an enemy in another village, and after addressing it by name spearing it. This, however, could never be done by one Lhota to another.

[1] The Semas and some other tribes rub them with pig's fat.—J. H. H.

[2] It may be noticed that the presentation of fish by a man to his betrothed is the formal sign of the completion of an Ao marriage.—J. H. H.

It is believed to be possible, too, to bewitch a man by calling a stone or bit of wood by his name and cursing it. This belief in the power given by knowledge of a man's name is of course world-wide, and among the Lhotas gives rise to the custom of giving a false name at birth in order that the lurking evil spirits may go away thinking they have the real name. Besides their ordinary name most, if not all, Lhotas have a private name which is never revealed to any but relations or intimate friends. If two men bear the same name they regard themselves as bound together by a particularly close tie and address each other as *akam*. Similarly Lhotas are particular that no enemy should get hold of bits of their hair or clippings from their finger or toe nails. While the Naga Labour Corps were on their way back from France some Lhotas planned to offer to cut some Semas' hair for them, and do "genna" with the clippings when they got home.[1] The plan was only just vetoed in time by one of their own headmen. The commonest charm against evil spirits is a kind of wild mint called *rarakham* (*Ocimum basilicum*).[2] At all "gennas," or when going to a place supposed to be haunted by evil spirits, a Lhota wears a sprig in the lobe of his ear and rubs some in his hair. A small onion (*sandhra*) or a cowrie carried on the person is also considered to be effective.

Apparently the only charm used to make crops grow is a piece of rhinoceros (*molung*) bone hidden near the field.[3] It must be many, many years since any Lhota has killed one of these animals, but I am assured that pieces of bone are still carefully treasured, though they are never shown to strangers.

Ghost stories abound. The following one, which was told me by a man from Rephyim, is typical: "One day I Ghosts

[1] Cf. Apuleius, *The Golden Ass*, Chap. XV.—J. H. H.

[2] *Rarakham* appears to be the same as the Sema *pulakhu*, which, however, was identified for me as *Mosla dianthera*. It is quite likely that both plants are used by Nagas under the same name.—J. H. H.

[3] The Aos erect a stout and tall rice plant on a piece of bamboo and put it by the field to make the rice grow, by its good example, as high from the ground as the top of the uplifted rice plant.—J. H. H.

was coming up from the fields with others when I saw my elder brother's wife coming down to meet us. We called out to her, but she did not answer, only coughed and spat and turned aside into the jungle. When I got up to the village I found she had died in her husband's house while we were down at the fields." Another one, also from Rephyim, runs as follows: "When my brother and I were children we met our uncle on our way up from the fields, but when he got near us he disappeared up into the sky and threw down a big stick and a stone. The stick just missed us, but the stone fell into my brother's basket." A very common story is that of hearing someone cutting jungle near the path, and on going there finding nothing. It is very unlucky to be touched by a ghost (*omon*). A man called Mhomo is said to have been caught by the leg by a ghost and died as a result. If the sound of cutting is heard from a bamboo clump, and it is found that there is no one there, the owner of the bamboos will die in the course of the year. To hear at night the sound of someone stamping down the earth on a grave means that there will be a death in the village shortly. The only ghostly animal I have heard of is a serow said to exist near Okotso. One man's gun is said to have missed fire ten times while the animal stood and looked at him, while another man threw his spear clean through it, and instead of killing the serow was ill himself for a year.[1]

Dreams.

Like all primitive people the Lhota attaches great importance to dreams.[2] In them he believes that the souls of the dead visit him, and his own soul leaves his body and

[1] There is a white serow of supernatural qualities at Seromi in the Sema country, and the Assamese, indeed, call the species *deo-chaguli*, "the spirit-goat," no doubt owing to its exceeding shyness and elusiveness.—J. H. H.

[2] Lobeni, a dream-woman of Phiro, who was an acquaintance of mine and whose dreams of hunting prospects were famous for their accuracy, used to ask for a cloth or handkerchief of her client on which she used to sleep. The same practice is recorded of the Moscoc, dream diviners of Peru. (*Memorias Antiguas Historiales del Peru*, Hakluyt Soc. 1920, p. 60, note.)—J. H. H.

wanders.[1] Thus, if a sick man in his delirium dreams that he is in a certain place he knows that his soul is under the influence of some evil spirit which is drawing it to that place, and takes steps to appease the fiend with sacrifice. Or if a man fights with another man in his dreams he believes that the two souls really meet and fight. To dream of the building of a new "morung" forebodes ill to the village, for the dreamer's soul has travelled to the land of the dead and seen a new village being prepared there for those who are about to die. If a man dreams that he is carrying a child along the Road of the Dead the child will die, and the dreamer may die too. But to dream that he is driven back by dead men means that he will have long life, for the souls of those gone before are not yet ready to receive him.[2] If in his dream a man go to another village he will not live long, for the other village is really that in the Land of the Dead, to which his soul has gone on ahead. Similarly, to kill a chicken in a dream is bad, for the chicken seen is the soul of that which will be killed at the dreamer's death not long after. It is most unlucky to dream of dead men, for it means that they have come to call the dreamer. The only way of averting the disaster is to kill a big boar and give the meat to an old professional dreamer (*hahang*), who offers it to the souls of the dead in his dreams. The night before hunting too it is most unlucky to dream of a successful hunt, for it means that the dreamer's spirit has been out hunting and driven all the game away.[3]

Many dreams are regarded as symbolical. For example, dream water = real crops, so that a vision of a deep pool means a good harvest, but a dry nullah means a lean year. Similarly, dream jungle roots = real meat, so that to dream of digging and finding many roots means that large presents of meat will be received, but unsuccessful digging means

[1] So, too, the Samoans; George Brown, *Melanesians and Polynesians* (Macmillan, 1910), p. 219.—J. H. H.

[2] Cf. the New Britain belief; George Brown, *Melanesians and Polynesians*, p. 193.—J. H. H.

[3] The interpretation of dreams by opposites (cf. Apuleius, *The Golden Ass*, Chap. XXI.) is frequent among Nagas generally, and may no doubt be usually based on this principle.—J. H. H.

small presents. Again, dream fire = real children. A fire which burns up well when the dreamer lights it means a big family, but a fire that goes out foretells deaths in the home. To see an earthquake or one's own teeth falling out is regarded as particularly unlucky and forebodes the certain death either of the dreamer or of one of his family. Anything red, such as a red spear or red goat's-hair, represents man's blood and means that someone will get hurt.

View of the Forces of Nature. The earth is regarded as flat and stretching to an unknown distance in all directions. In the west, where the sky meets it, lives a big snake which sometimes causes earthquakes by moving its body.[1] During an earthquake the meat rack over the fire and the vat in which the daily supply of rice is kept are seized and held by the inmates of a Lhota house. If this is not done it is believed that supplies will fail the next year.[2] The sky is regarded as being hard like a stone, and forming the floor of the world of the *Potsos*, who in turn have another sky and *Potso* world above them, and so on for an unknown number of worlds. It used to be nearer to the earth than it is now, but for some reason not known it has gradually got further and further away. The sun is a flaming plate of hard metal as big as a piece of ground on which one basket of seed rice is sown. It travels along its path in the sky during the day and at night travels back under the earth and lights the Land of the Dead. The moon is like it. In fact, it was once the brighter and hotter of the two, till the present sun, seeing that the earth was being scorched and burnt with the terrible heat, smeared the face of the moon with cow-dung, so that it now gives a very feeble light.[3] An eclipse of the sun or moon occurs

[1] I have found the same belief among the Thado Kukis.—J. H. H.

[2] This belief might be connected with that by which some Nagas explain earthquakes as the spirit under the earth shaking the earth as in a winnowing fan to find out what the crops are like and weigh their quantity and quality.—J. H. H.

[3] Cf. the somewhat similar Garo story; Major A. Playfair, *The Garos*, p. 85.—J. P. M.

Cf. also Col. Gurdon, *The Khasis*, p. 172, where it is to be noticed that the Khasis, like the Semas, make the moon masculine and the sun feminine. The Sema version (*The Sema Nagas*, p. 250) is still nearer to

when a giant dog which lives in the sky tries to eat them.[1] An eclipse means that many great men will die, and the day after one is kept as an *emung*. Stars are little points of fire, and are vaguely regarded as being endowed with life. Shooting stars are the falling dung of stars. The clouds have nothing to do with rain, which is poured down by the *Potsos* from reservoirs in the sky. They are simply the accumulated smoke of thousands of fires all over the earth. The belief with regard to hail is a curious one. The *Potsos* who live in the sky have above them yet another world of *Potsos*, who are evil and try to injure the *Potsos* living nearest to us by throwing down huge lumps of ice on them. But whenever a fusillade begins the lower *Potsos* take care to walk about with the door of their houses held over their backs like rain-shields. The lumps of ice are shattered on the doors and only reach the earth as small fragments which men call hail.

the Lhota, and a similar story (with a "rabbit" instead of dung) comes from Mexico. A geographical link between the two stories is perhaps provided by Japan, where the hare is associated with the moon (*vide* Lord Redesdale, *Tales of Japan*, "The Crackling Mountain," note 1). The Malays also say that the sun and moon were once of equal brightness (Ratzel, *History of Mankind*, I. p. 478). The Nicobarese have the same beliefs as the Lhota both as to the former proximity of the sky and as to the interchange of functions between the sun and the moon (vide *The Indian Antiquary*), August 1921, Part DCXXXV. p. 235.—J. H. H.

[1] This view of the cause of eclipses is in accordance with the common Tibetan account current generally also over at any rate the north of India. It is the form which explanations of eclipses usually take among Nagas, but in contrast to the Angami story, which represents the orb eclipsed as repaying a loan of borrowed light.—J. H. H.

PART V

FOLK-TALES AND SONGS

Folk-tales. LIKE all Nagas [1] the Lhotas possess a great store of traditional tales. The old men tell them and teach them to the younger generation, having themselves learnt them from their forefathers. Every tale is supposed to be told word for word as it has been handed down, but versions naturally vary from village to village. To a tale which most of them must know by heart the audience listens as if none of them had ever heard it before, greeting every joke with laughter and appreciating every point. A very popular class of story is that which explains the peculiarities of various animals. Some of these stories closely resemble those current among the Semas and other tribes. The following are typical examples.

[1] Naga folk-lore in general has much in common with that of other races of Mongolian affinities. Thus the Naga (Angami) and Kachari story of the origin of the domestication of certain animals as opposed to the rest is akin to the Lapp story given by Mr. Andrew Lang under the title of "The Elf Maiden," in his *Brown Fairy Book*. The Angami story is to be found in *The Angami Nagas*, Part IV., the Terhengi Genna, and the Kachari version in Soppitt, *Historical and Descriptive Account of the Kachari Tribes of the North Cachar Hills*, p. 56. Much closer, however, is the resemblance between an incident in the story of "The Fox and the Lapp" (same volume of Mr. Lang's Fairy Tales), and the almost verbally identical incident in the Sema story of Iki and the Tiger (*The Sema Nagas*, p. 319). In the latter Iki escapes from the tiger by pointing to a hornbill flying over and saying, "I made that." The tiger asks if Iki can make him like it, and on Iki's consenting agrees to let himself be tied up, and to undergo an operation entailing his destruction. In the Lapp story the fox escapes from the bear by precisely the same ruse, a woodpecker taking the place of the hornbill. In the same volume of Mr. Lang's is a story called "The Husband of the Rat's Daughter," quoted as from *Contes Populaires*, but apparently coming from Japan, which is identical with the Angami story of "The Rat Maiden" (*The Angami Nagas*, Part V.).—J. H. H.

The Sambhur and the Hanuman Monkey.[1]

This is a tale of the old days before deer and other animals became so different one from the other. The sambhur and the hanuman monkey became sworn friends. In those days the sambhur had a long tail, while the hanuman monkey had no tail at all. One day the hanuman monkey asked the sambhur for his tail and said, "Friend, I want to put on your tail and see how it becomes me. Please lend it to me." Then the sambhur said, "Put on my tail, friend, and see how it becomes you," and gave him his tail. But the hanuman monkey, as soon as he had put on the sambhur's tail, climbed away up into a tree. Then the sambhur said, "Come down, friend, and give me back my tail," but the hanuman monkey would not. Then the sambhur, wondering how he should make himself a tail, pulled out his own liver and made a tail of it and put it on. Men say that that is why even nowadays sambhur tail is so good and tastes like liver to eat.

The Wild Boar and the Tiger.

The wild boar and the tiger were sworn friends. One day when they met in the jungle the wild boar said to the tiger, "My friend, let us two fight and see which will get the better of the other and which will fear the other. What will you take to protect yourself?" Then the tiger said to the boar, "I will take cane and wind it round my body," but the boar said, "I shall smear clay all over myself." They arranged that the fight should take place six days later. Then the boar for six days did nothing but smear clay over himself, letting it dry after each coating, and the tiger did nothing but cut lengths of cane and wind them round his body. Then when the six days were up they fell to and fought. Now whenever the tiger flew at the wild

[1] This and all other stories given are literal translations from the Lhota. My method has been to have the stories dictated and written down in Lhota, and then tested for verbal accuracy before translating them.

boar and bit him, all he got was a mouthful of clay, but the boar, whenever he attacked and bit the tiger, bit through a piece of cane, till he had bitten them all through one by one and killed the tiger. But when the boar was going away after his victory a thin piece of bamboo ran into him. Then he said, "I have killed the tiger. What is this doing running into me?" and seized it in his mouth. But the thin bamboo cut his tongue off so that he died on the spot.[1] Then another tiger came along and saw the body and ate it. That is why nowadays tigers eat wild boars. Yet it is said that because the tiger could not beat the wild boar at first, a tiger cannot catch one now unless he bides his time and stalks it for two or three months.

Rivalling in popularity the stories of animals is a large group of stories about a mythical individual whom the Northern Lhotas call Apfuho and the Southern Lhotas Yampfuho. He is spoken of as having lived in the old, old days when men and animals spoke the same language.[2] In his day, it is believed, there was a terrible earthquake and the whole world became dark.[3] Apfuho clung to a rock, and when light came and the world as we know it had come into being he had been turned into stone. Some Lhotas say that the rock, with Apfuho's petrified dao-holder, can still be seen near Lakhuti, but most people hold that it is not known where he met his end. He corresponds exactly to the Sema character Iki,[4] and many of the stories told of the two are identical. He is always represented as getting in and out of scrapes, and as tricking his fellow-villagers or his friend the tiger, usually in the meanest possible way. The name of his village is never mentioned and there is no tradition as to where he lived. The following are typical stories of his exploits.

[1] All Nagas believe that a severe wound in the tongue causes instant death.

[2] Certain families of the Shetri clan in Pangti claim to be his direct descendants.

[3] The "Thimzing" of the Thados and other Kukis; *vide* Col. J. Shakespear, *The Lushai-Kuki Clans*.—J. H. H.

[4] And to the Angami Matseo, the orphan, pretty closely.—J. H. H.

Apfuho and the Old Woman.

One day an old woman set her rice on the fire to boil and went into her outer room to pound oil seed. Apfuho came along carrying another man's dog which he had killed, and called out to the old woman, " Your rice is boiling over." When the old woman went back into the inner room to look at her rice, Apfuho put the dog which he was carrying on her pounding table and called out, " A dog is eating your oil seed, old woman." Then the old woman came running out to see, and hit the dead dog which Apfuho had put on the pounding table. At this Apfuho cried out, " Oh dear, oh dear, you have killed another man's dog. If you do not give me your pig I will tell the owner." So the old woman said, " I will give you my pig. Do not tell the owner." At dusk when Apfuho came to fetch the pig he fixed lighted torches all along the path, and said to the old woman, " Give me your pig. Look how many men are coming with the owner of the dog, carrying lighted torches in their hands." To this the old woman replied, " I will give you my pig. Go and tell them not to come." So he went and put out the torches and threw them away, and came back and took the pig. But as he was taking the pig away he murmured, " What a fool of an old woman." Her daughter heard this and said, " He called you an old fool, mother." But Apfuho heard her say this and replied. " I only said ' oo,' girl," [1] and the mother said, " Yes, yes, Apfuho only said ' oo '." So Apfuho went off with the pig.[2]

Apfuho and the Tiger.

This is a tale of the olden days when men could understand the talk of animals. Apfuho and the tiger went across a river to hollow out vats from a log on the other side. When they had finished their vats and the time came to return, the

[1] The play upon the words cannot be reproduced in English. Apfuho really said " *emitacholam* " ("What a fool of an old woman ! "), and then got out of his difficulty by pretending he had only uttered the middle syllable " *acho,*" which is an exclamation like the English " Oh ! "

[2] This incident in a very similar form occurs in the Sema story of Iki and the Tiger (*The Sema Nagas*, Part VI.).—J. H. H.

tiger asked Apfuho the best way to carry his vat across the river. Apfuho told him to carry it rim upwards,[1] and the tiger did as Apfuho told him. But Apfuho carried his own vat upside down and was able to cross the river, while the tiger, try as he would, could not cross the river with his vat rim upwards. Apfuho called out, "I will pull you out," but instead of doing so he threw stones into the tiger's vat and pushed him away from land with a forked stick so that he was washed right downstream. Then Apfuho went along to see if the tiger was drowned or not, and found him lower down by the water's edge. When the tiger saw Apfuho he cried, "Here is my enemy," and tried to devour him. But Apfuho espied a hornets' nest by the water and said, "The men of the 'morung' have set me to watch the 'morung' drum, father tiger, and see that no stranger beats it." Then the tiger said, "May I beat it and see what it is like?" and Apfuho replied, "I will ask the men of the 'morung.' You stay here, and if they say you may beat it, I will shout and tell you." So he went a long way off and shouted back, "They say you may beat it." Then when the tiger hit the hornets' nest all the hornets attacked and stung him,[2] and he ran and ran until he fell down a cliff and was killed.

How the Villagers tried in vain to put an end to Apfuho.

The villagers, meaning to put an end to Apfuho, took him with them down to a big pond. Then when they got to

[1] The vat was very heavy, being hollowed out of a solid log of wood, and would soon be swamped if put rim upwards in the water.

[2] This incident in a slightly different setting is found in the Assamese story of the Monkey and the Jackal, the Kachari story of the Monkey and the Hare, in an Angami story and also in an Ao story. In the latter version it is the bear who is thus victimized. For the Kackari story see J. D. Anderson, *Kachari Folk-tales and Rhymes*, p. 27 (Shillong, 1895); for the Assamese story see J. Borooah, *Folk-tales of Assam*, p. 8 [*shial* = "jackal" not "fox"] (Howrah, 1915), and for the Angami story, *The Angami Nagas*, Part IV.—J. H. H.

The Shans, too, relate a similar story in which the Hare induces the Tiger to believe that a swarm of bees is a gong. Milne and Cochrane, *The Shans at Home*, p. 244. An almost verbally identical episode occurs in the Sea Dyak story of the Mouse-deer and the Deer. Gomes, *Seventeen Years among the Sea Dyaks of Borneo*, p. 260.

the water they all began swinging out over the pool on a creeper swing. They made Apfuho use the swing last and went away and left him, thinking he would fall off into the middle of the pond and be drowned. Apfuho kept swinging and swinging and could hardly hold on any longer, when he espied a man and a woman wearing fine ornaments and leading a mithan by a rope. He saw that they were an eloping couple and called out to them, "Who are you? There is a beautiful breeze here which makes swinging very pleasant. Take off your ornaments and put them on the ground and tie up the mithan. Then pull me in with a hooked stick and come and have a swing yourselves." So they did as Apfuho told them, and took their ornaments off and put them down and pulled Apfuho in with a forked stick, and both began to swing.

But when they asked Apfuho to pull them in, instead of doing so he let them fall into the water and drown. Then Apfuho put on their ornaments and took their mithan and went up to the village. And the villagers were astonished and said, "Where have you come from with those ornaments and that mithan, Apfuho?" And he said to them, "In the middle of the pond there are many ornaments and many mithan too. I only brought away these. If you too want to get some you should go and dive into the pond." Then all the villagers said to him in chorus, "Take me, Apfuho; take me, Apfuho." So a few days later Apfuho led the villagers in a body down to the water. There he picked them up one by one and threw them in. Of the men who sank quietly he said, "The ornaments and mithan *he* gets won't be very good." But when people struggled hard, with the water pouring from their mouth and nose, he said, "The ornaments and mithan *he* gets will be splendid." So he let all the people of the village whom he had thrown into the water drown.[1]

Now a blind old woman was stumbling along, feeling her way by the water's edge. Apfuho put an old worn dao in front of her, and when she found it as she groped she said, "Well, if a person like me can find this, people with no infirmities will get a lot." Then Apfuho went up to her and

[1] Cf. the old fairy tale of Big and Little Klaus.—J. H. H.

said, "Now, old woman, you go in too. What are you doing on the edge?" and with these words he caught her and threw her into the middle of the pond so that she was drowned.

The audience always appreciates a play upon words such as occurs in the story of Apfuho and the Old Woman. All Nagas love a pun. A good one is immortal. Ao women—a most pugnacious section of the human race—pun on the names of their adversaries most elaborately. In some Lhota stories practically the whole point depends on a pun. The following is an example.

The Old Man and His Dogs.

Long, long ago, before the Great Darkness came, there lived a man who kept wild dogs, as men now call them. With his dogs he killed and ate many deer. But at last he got so old that he could no longer go into the jungle with his dogs. So he called them all to him and brought them to his house. There he cooked enough rice for each to have a share, but when he divided it up it did not go round properly and the youngest dog got none. Then the old man said, "My dogs, I am very old and can no longer go out hunting with you. But do not forget how I looked after you and cared for you. When you kill a deer, always leave a leg (*ocho*) for me at the cross-roads." When the dogs had gone away they quite forgot what the old man had said to them. Now the youngest dog was angry with the old man because he had given him no rice. So when the other dogs asked him what the old man had said he replied, "The old man said, 'Whenever you kill a deer, leave dung (*ochü*) for me at the cross-roads." That is why to this day wild dogs leave their droppings at the cross-roads.[1]

[1] In the Angami version the man sends a messenger to the wild dog who had run away. The messenger, instead of asking for a leg of every head of game the dog ran down, asked for the whole body. At this the wild dog, quite prepared to give a leg, lost his temper and said, "Bah! I'll give him the hair and leave it on the path for him to find." Hence the dung of wild dogs containing large quantities of hair is found everywhere on paths.—J. H. H.

The types of story described so far have all been more or less humorous. Some tales, however, teach a definite moral lesson; for example, the following.

The Story of the Two Brothers.

There were once two brothers. The elder was poor, but the younger was very rich. The younger brother ignored the elder and kept all his care and affection for his friend. One day the younger brother said to his friend, "My friend, to-day we will go and pick and eat red berries." So saying they went. The younger brother climbed the tree, and while he was picking and eating the berries smeared himself all over with the red juice. Then he called out, "Friend, friend, I am falling," and tumbled out of the tree. His friend climbed down and looked at him as he lay on the ground and said, "You are no relation of mine. I shall not look after you. I will go and tell your brother and get him to come." With these words he went away without attending to him at all. But his brother came and saw him, and looking at him said, "My brother, forgetful one, when you were alive you scorned and neglected me and kept all your love and affection for your friends." With these words he picked him up to carry him, but the younger brother said, "Brother, there is nothing the matter with me," and got up and himself carried his elder brother home. Thereafter the friends were friends no more, but the two brothers loved one another. That is why men say that there is nothing in life equal to the love of one's own relations.

The Widow and the Boys of the Morung.

Old men say that when the Lhotas settled at Nungkamchung [1] a widow had a big pig. One day the boys of the "morung" took the pig, promising to pay for it with rice. But they did not pay, though every day the widow came and said, "Give me back my pig which you bought for rice."

[1] A very old village, once big, but now shrunk to eight houses.

At last she took her iron staff and poured magic powder[1] into it and walked round the "morung," saying, "Give me back my pig which you bought with rice. Give it back. Give it back," tapping the ground with her staff as she went. Suddenly the ground opened wherever she had tapped it with her staff containing magic powder, and all the inmates of the "morung" were swallowed up, only those in the front room having time to jump to their feet and escape. The village all set to work to dig them out, but could not dig out a single man, only a wisp of thatch.

Stories of the Water Spirit (*Tchhüpfu*) are common, and usually describe a visit paid by someone to his lair in a deep pool, as in the following.

The Boy and the Water Spirit.

One day a boy went down to the Doyang to fish. When he did not return home in the evening his parents became very anxious, and in the morning his father took some men down to search for him; but he was nowhere to be found. Then his father was sad at heart and went wandering alone along the Doyang, determined to find at least the dead body of his son. As he went he saw a hair on the ground, and picked it up, thinking it belonged to his son. But it was so long that he only picked up one end of it, and walked on winding it round and round his finger. He went on and on until he had passed eight bends of the river, so long was the hair. At last he came to a Water Spirit, for the hair was one of the Water Spirit's which he had forgotten to wind round his head. Then the Water Spirit cried out, "Let me go," but the man replied, "You have seized my son and taken him to your home in the water. I will not let you go till you bring him out and give him back to me." Then the Water Spirit said, "Let me go and I will bring your son and leave him here. If you do not believe me you may make me swear the most solemn oath known to men." At this

[1] Such is said to be the meaning of the obsolete Lhota word *tiloran*.

the man let him go, and the Spirit gave him a gift of friendship, dried fish and fresh fish and fish paste, and said, "In the morning I will bring your son out of the water and leave him here. Come at the time when men go to their fields and you will find him."

Obedient to the words of the Spirit the man came in the morning at the time when men go to their fields, and there sure enough was his son on the bank. The tale he told his father was this: "I saw a big fish in the water, and dived in and caught hold of it. It dragged me into a hole under the rocks in the pool, where there was no water. There on the dry sand was a hearth made of three human skulls. It was the lair of the Water Spirit." The Water Spirit had not hurt the boy, but had brought him out and left him on the bank, as he had promised to his father. So the father found his son safe by the side of the water and they both went back home. The tale is remembered to this day.

Otherwise tales of supernatural beings are comparatively rare. The story of Sityingo and Ngazo, two jungle godlings, will serve as a sample.

The Story of Sityingo and Ngazo.

Sityingo and Ngazo went to dig for bamboo rats.[1] Sityingo caught many, but Ngazo, though he dug all day, only got one. Then Ngazo said to Sityingo, "I have only caught this and you have caught so many," and showed him the rat. Then Sityingo replied, "Even that you only got because I gave it to you." To which Ngazo replied, "What, I have dug out this rat after digging all day and you say you gave it me!" "Then let it go," said Sityingo, "and see whether I gave it you or not." So Ngazo let it go as Sityingo said, but the rat burrowed into the ground, and Ngazo, though he dug and dug after it, could not catch it again. Then said Sityingo, "You say I did not give it you and yet you cannot dig it out!" At these words

[1] *Rhizomys prunosus*, the flesh of which Nagas regard as a great delicacy.

Ngazo became angry and they fell to wrestling, and Ngazo twisted Sityingo's neck. That is why Sityingo can only look one way. Men say to this day that a hunter towards whom Sityingo looks is sure to get something, but that he from whom Sityingo's face is turned away will get nothing at all.

Stories of human beings being turned into birds or beasts are not uncommon. The following are examples.

How Men became Catfish.

A man took a company of children down to his fields to work. When they had worked all morning and it was time for the midday meal they asked him to give them their rice. But the owner of the field and his family said it was not yet time and would not give them any rice. Then the children said they were going to bathe and all went off, and said, "They would not give us our rice in time, so we will become catfish." With these words they turned into catfish, calling out, "We are catfish, we are catfish." The owner of the field called out, "Come along, I will give you your rice," but the children replied, "You would not give it us before. Now we have forgotten about men's food. We will not come," and swam away in the form of catfish. It is because these children were wearing dao-holders when they were turned into fish that catfish always have a mark on them like a dao-holder—so men say.

How Men were turned into Gibbons.

Once upon a time a man called Kimongthang called his sisters' husbands' relations together and gave them rice beer to drink and said to them, "I have cut a *chentung* tree ready for a sacrificial post.[1] Go and drag it in for me, but do not let a single leaf fall to the ground." So they went and began to drag the tree, but the leaves were half withered and they kept letting them fall. Then, determined not to

[1] Stones are ordinarily put up by Lhotas to commemorate a sacrifice, but forked wooden posts are occasionally substituted if a suitable stone is not available. One kindred in Yekhum always puts up posts instead of stones.

let the leaves fall, they tied them onto the twigs and set to work to drag the tree again. In spite of this all the leaves fell off. Then they were ashamed to go back to the village and meet Kimongthang. So they fled away into the jungle, and the men became mynas and called "*Kyon, kyon.*" [1] But the women ground up rice flour to make rice beer and smeared it on their foreheads and called out, "Woka, woka," and became gibbons. That is why the gibbon now has a white forehead.[2]

Another type of story is that which purports to give an account of some historical episode. Many of them tell of the origin of some particular clan. That relating to the Kithang clan will serve as an illustration. The episode of the hair being swallowed by the fish occurs in Assamese folk-lore,[3] and curiously enough this is the only Lhota story known to the writer in which the Assamese are mentioned, though the Lhotas must have been in contact with them for a long period.

The Story of the Kithang Clan.

One day a man of the Kikung clan named Yanzo took his nine dogs with him and went to hunt deer. But they would do nothing but jump and give tongue round a tree with a hole in it. Then Yanzo, knowing that his dogs would not give tongue for nothing, cut down the tree to see what was inside it, and found in it a jungle man. This man he took home and brought up and called Kithamo. Kithamo had a son called Mering, for whom Yanzo arranged a wife called

[1] *I. e.* "Man, man!"

[2] One version of this story states definitely that Kimongthang was of the Othui clan, and formerly men of that clan were forbidden to eat gibbon. The Changs tell the same story to account for the origin of the Kudámji clan, which is regarded as a gibbon clan.

The Semas have a story of men of the Wotsami clan having been turned into gibbons, and despise that clan as the Changs do the Kudámji, which suggests that it is the Othui clan of Lhotas which ought really to be associated with the Semi Wotsami instead of the Shetri (or, according to Mr. Mills, the Nguli) as is the case.—J. H. H.

[3] "Tale of the Tiger and the Crab" in *Folk-tales of Assam*, by J. Borooah (Howrah, 1915), pp. 54, 55.—J. H. H.

Khamdrio. Now Khamdrio had wonderful long hair—once and a half as long as a man could span with outstretched arms. One day when she was washing her head at the river one of her hairs fell in and was swallowed by a little fish, which went down the stream and was caught by an Assamese. The fisherman was amazed when he split open the fish and saw the hair, and took and showed it to the king. Then the king gave orders that the woman to whom the hair belonged was to be brought to him,[1] and sent one of his councillors with his soldiers to Mering's village. But Mering had fenced his village with a hedge of stinging leaves,[2] which the king's soldiers could not penetrate. Then the councillor ordered his soldiers to pick one of the leaves and take it back with them. And he came to the king and said, "The village is fenced with a hedge of this, so that we could by no means force it." And the king took and put the leaf on his stomach under his clothes to see how it would sting, and he understood how terrible the pain was. Then he sent the councillor to inquire of Mering whether there was anything of which he was afraid. And Mering made answer, "There is nothing in the whole world of which I am afraid. You can only make me afraid by sending up to my village nine elephants with cotton piled on their backs. That will make me afraid." So the king sent up nine elephants to break down the nine hedges of stinging leaves. Then Mering heated his spear red hot, and waiting till the elephants had reached the fence, threw it at the first one. The cotton on its back caught alight, and when the flames reached its body it ran in among the other elephants and set them alight one after the other. Then the elephants fled and trampled many of the men to death. Then the king announced that he would cease to fight with Mering and would trade with him instead. And he called

[1] The incident of the long hair of a girl that caused a king to send men to find her occurs in an ancient Egyptian tale "written down in the reign of Rameses II, about 1300 B.C." *Vide* Sir J. G. Frazer, *The Golden Bough*, vol. xi. pp. 135, 136.—J. H. H.

[2] Broad, shiny leaves, only too common in the jungles of the Naga Hills. The writer has suffered from them more than once. The slightest touch causes intense irritation, which often does not totally subside for ten days.

an Assamese and said to him, "Take a pot of cornelian beads with you and go up to Mering's village. If anyone wishes to buy from you, do not sell, but go on hawking your wares right through the village, and as you go scatter beads in the hedge of stinging leaves. Having done this come down to me again." And he went and did as he was bade, and the men of Mering's village cut down and destroyed all their hedge in their search for the beads which had been scattered there. Then the king sent men into the hills with dogs to hunt down Mering, and Mering fled to Yanzo's village to take refuge with him. It so happened that Yanzo was building his house. He therefore made Mering hide under a heap of thatching grass which was lying ready to hand, and then went and eased himself on the top of the pile. When the Assamese came up with their dogs they began to toss the thatching grass to this side and that in their search for Mering. Then Yanzo said to them, "Your dogs are very clever. Perhaps they are looking for this filth here." At these words all the Assamese were filled with shame and whipped off their dogs and departed.[1] Because of this Mering and Yanzo broke an iron staff and swore [2] on it that they would become one clan and would never intermarry. Afterwards a son was born to Mering whose name was Rapvu. He lived at Nungkamchung, where a bastard son was born to him of a woman of the Kikung clan. This son's name was Lobemo and his descendants still live at Tsingaki. But the legitimate children of Rapvu are the ancestors of the Kithang clan.

Tales valued for their intrinsic merit as good stories of adventure are very numerous, some of them being of considerable length. Examples are the following.

The Story of Lichao and His Daughter.

Once upon a time wild pigs damaged a man's crops very badly, so he went down to hunt them, and wounded one

[1] In an Ao folk-tale a man is chased with dogs and escapes in a similar way.

[2] Nagas regard an oath sworn on broken iron as binding.

with his spear. This he tracked and tracked till he came to the house of Lichao, the old man guardian of wild pigs. There he found two maidens feeding the pig he had wounded. They asked him what he had come for, but he was afraid to tell the truth and say that he was tracking a wild pig that he had wounded, so he replied, "Hearing that there were two beautiful maidens at your house I came to see, hoping that I might take one as my wife." Then they told him to come another day, so he departed.

When the man came a little later Lichao made his slave-girl put on beautiful ornaments and fine clothes, but his real daughter he made to sit all in rags and dirty in the outside room. But the man was not to be deceived. He loved Lichao's daughter and would only take her.[1] Now Lichao used to turn into a tiger and eat human flesh. Therefore he set his son-in-law hard tasks, meaning to devour him if he did not fulfil them. But when she knew this the maiden said to him, "Whatever task my father gives you to perform, tell me and I will reveal to you his purpose." So one day Lichao said to the man, "Go and pick the leaves of *kotyoh* thorns and *koremyoi* thorns, and bring them without a single leaf being torn and without a single scratch on your body. If you do this I will let you depart with my daughter." Then the girl said to her husband,[2] "If you come home with the slightest scratch on your body, or with a single leaf torn, my father will devour you." So her husband went and picked the leaves without a single one being torn and without scratching his body in the least, and rolled them into a very tight bundle and brought and gave them to Lichao. Then Lichao said, "Only that amount will not be enough for us," but when he opened the

[1] Up to this point the story opens in the same terms as the Sema version of the story of Hunchibili, the maiden who is transformed into an orange, a bamboo shoot, etc. (vide *The Angami Nagas*, Part V., and *The Sema Nagas*, Part VI). The *motif* of the transformation of the heroine to and from some form of fruit or vegetable is a favourite one in Assamese folk-lore. *Vide* J. Borooah, *Folk-tales of Assam*. There are also Khasi stories of the same kind.—J. H. H.

[2] Probably the hero must be regarded by now as working off the marriage price by service in his father-in-law's house according to Lhota custom.—J. H. H.

bundle to look, the leaves covered all the ground in front of his house.

A few days later Lichao said, "If you can catch and tie up one of my pigs alone I will let you take my daughter and go," and with these words gave him a length of unsplit cane. Then the man fell to thinking how he could catch one of the pigs, for they were wild pigs; and his wife said to him, "If you cannot catch a pig my father will devour you." At last he caught a pig, and his wife beat the cane on the ground to fray it and gave it to him. Thus holding the pig with one hand he pulled off strips of cane with the other and bound the pig fast. Then Lichao let him take his daughter and go.

So the girl came to her husband's house. But there she could get no human flesh to eat, and soon became so weak and thin that she could not work. One day her husband said to her, "Why are you so weak and thin?" To which his wife replied, "I am thin and weak because I cannot get the food which my parents used to give me." Then when her husband asked what her parents used to give her to eat she replied, "I will send you to fetch a parcel of meat wrapped in leaves from my parents' house. But bring it straight here. Do not open it and look to see what is inside." So he went, and his wife's parents gave him some pieces of human flesh wrapped up in leaves. This he brought straight home to his wife without opening the leaves to look to see what was inside, and when she ate it it made her as plump and strong as ever. But in a day or two, because she could get no more human flesh to eat, she again became so thin and weak that she could not work. Then she spoke to her husband again and told him to go and fetch some more meat from her parents' house. Now her husband was determined to open the bundle and see what kind of meat it was that made his wife get well again when she was so thin and weak that she could not work. But Lichao sent a little bird to go back with him so that he should not open the parcel of human flesh on the way. When the man fingered the parcel which Lichao had given him, having it in his heart to open it, the little bird said to him, "If you open it I shall tell my father; if you open it I shall tell my father." So he did not open it and look inside. But when he had given the parcel of meat to his wife he went and hid and watched quietly to see what kind of meat her father had given him to bring. Now it was nothing but human fingers tied up in leaves that her father had given him to bring. And his wife undid the leaves and roasted the fingers lightly in the fire and ate them one after another. Now when he saw this her husband was much troubled and said, "What meat have your parents sent you? What meat is that you are eating?" But she said, "Nay, I will not tell you. You will only be troubled at heart and filled with fear." But he said, "I shall not be afraid. Tell me." Then his wife said, "I shall turn into a tiger. When I go about the house showing my fangs and roaring you must slip a basket over me. If you cannot slip a basket over me I shall devour even you." With these words she turned into a tiger, and her husband tried to cover her with a basket but could not, so she caught and ate him. That is the end of the story.

The Girl who Married a Tiger.

A woman one day went down to her field to fetch some vegetables. She saw a fine gourd there and was just going to pick it, when a tiger saw her and said, "That is my gourd. Why were you going to pick it? I shall kill you." With these words he caught her, but the woman, who was about to become a mother, said, "Do not kill me, and I will give you my baby when it is born," so the tiger let her go. In due time a daughter was born to the woman. When the tiger heard of this he kept asking the woman if her child was born yet, till at last she told the tiger that it had been born. Soon the tiger asked her if her daughter was strong enough to fetch firewood and water yet, and whether she was old enough to be married. But the woman kept putting him off by saying that her daughter was not yet old enough to carry wood and water and was too young to marry; till at last she saw that she must keep the bargain she had made, and told the tiger that the girl was old enough to work as his wife. But as she sat weaving a cloth for her daughter to wear on her wedding-day she was overcome with grief when she thought how her child would surely be killed and eaten by the tiger, and her tears fell fast on the cloth she was making. Her husband, too, was sad as he worked at a basket he was making for his daughter to carry when she went to her husband's house, and his tears fell fast on the basket. When the girl saw this she said, "Why are you crying, mother?" and her mother answered, "I poked myself in the eye with my bobbin." To her father, too, the girl said, "Why are you crying, father?" And her father replied, "I poked myself in the eye with a slip of bamboo." Then when the day came her parents gave her in marriage to the tiger.

About a year later a little daughter was born to the tiger and his wife. When her mother carried her she never cried, but when her father carried her she cried all the time. So the woman said to the tiger, "Why do you make our daughter cry so much?" The tiger replied, "It is because my beard pricks her." But one day the woman hid herself and watched, and saw the tiger knock his little daughter's head "tap, tap" against a hearthstone and lick up the blood which dripped down. When she saw this the woman resolved to run away from the tiger, and said to him, "I am going to fetch some wood. Hold the baby till I come back." But the tiger said, "I am coming too." And whenever she asked him to look after the baby while she went to get water, or went to the fields or into the jungle, the tiger always replied, "I am coming too," and never let her out of his sight. At last one day she asked him to look after the child while she went down to the spring to wash its carrying cloth.[1] So he took the child and she went down to the spring and set a louse and a flea to wash the cloth, "chuck-chuck, chuck-chuck," while she ran off and made for her parents' house. The tiger, thinking the noise made by the

[1] As the woman would probably take the opportunity of bathing and washing her own clothes, it would have been contrary to Lhota etiquette for her husband to have gone with her.

louse and the flea was his wife washing the cloth, kept calling out, "The baby is crying. Come up and nurse it." But when she did not come up he went down to look for himself, and found his wife gone and the louse and the flea there instead. Then he said, "You would play tricks on me, would you?" and crushed the louse with his thumb-nail, but the flea jumped and got away.

Then the tiger set out to search for his wife and asked everyone he met whether they had seen her pass. All replied that they had not seen her, till at last he came to the *sangalia* creeper, who said she had just gone by that way. Then he chased and chased her till he came up with her at dusk at the door of her parents' house. The woman cried out, "Mother, come out of the inner room and open the door for me." But her mother replied, "Who is that? I have no daughter. My daughter disappeared long ago," and would not come out and open the door. Then the woman said again, "I am your own daughter, mother, whom years ago, when I was little, you hit on the head with the pigs' food ladle. Do you not know me now?" With these words she began to squeeze through the little opening by the door left for the dogs, but the tiger seized her legs while her mother seized her head and shoulders. And they pulled and pulled till she was torn in two and the tiger was left with her lower half and her mother with the upper half. Then the tiger took his half to his house and kept watch over it with a whisk so that not a single fly should settle on it, and buried it. And he wept, saying, "O my wife, when you were alive I loved you so much that I was careful always to give you good meat to eat as relish with your rice. You never had to eat leaves and such-like poor fare." But her mother said, "Why do you weep so? We have torn her in half. Now we will cook and eat her." And she cooked a little of the flesh from the upper half of the girl and offered it to the tiger, who refused it, saying, "How can I eat the flesh of the mother of my daughter?" But at last he ate it. Then he said, "Human flesh is good," and went and dug up the portion he had buried and ate that too. That is how the tiger came to eat human flesh, and that is why to this day tigers sometimes kill and devour men.

The ordinary Lhota believes the founders of the tribe came out of the earth, and does not worry his head as to how they originated in the world below. The following story, however, is an example of the widely spread myth that the world was populated by the offspring of a brother and sister.[1]

Lankongrhoni and the Villagers.

In the days of our ancestors there lived a woman called Lankongrhoni. She had a son who was very handsome. His name was Arilao. All the girls admired him only and wished to marry him. They cared nothing for the other men. So all the men of the village planned to kill him treacherously. They agreed that on any day when they should all go down to the river to poison fish, whoever failed to come was to be fined a big pig. Two or three days later they went down. Then Arilao's mother said to him, " Son, do not go." But he said, " Do you want us to lose our big pig, mother ? " and went. And the men felled a tree on the river bank and hewed a trough out of it and said, " Let every man lie in the trough in turn and see if he looks a fine man." So they each lay down in turn, but as each man lay in the trough the others kept repeating, " You don't look nice, you don't look nice." At last they said, " Let Arilao lie down," and made him get into the trough, and calling out, " Arilao looks nice; we are pounding up Ariloa, we are pounding up Arilao," they pounded him up with the fish poison. Now Arilao had a friend, and he was very sad because Arilao had been killed that day, and waited weeping further down stream. Soon the finger-nail of his friend Arilao came floating down and lodged against him. Then he said, " Is this all there is left of my friend ? " and with

[1] Cf. Perry, *Megalithic Culture of Indonesia*, chap. xii. The Vuite clan of Kukis are also sprung from Dongel and his sister, and the Kukis, like the Lhotas, have a legend of a period of great darkness and floods over the earth and fires (The *Thimzing*), during which the greater part of mankind was drowned.—J. H. H.

these words lifted the nail off the water, and wrapping it in a leaf slipped it into his belt. The villagers made a fine haul of fish, but Arilao's friend was so sad that he did not trouble to catch a single one. When the villagers trooped off up towards the village he hung back to the last.

Now Lankongrhoni came to meet her son on the way and asked each of her fellow-villagers, "Where is your companion?" or "Where is your friend?" or "Where is your younger brother?" or "Where is your elder brother?" And each man replied, "He is coming behind, laughing and talking with the girls. He is just coming." At last came Arilao's friend, weeping and very sad. When Lankongrhoni asked him where his friend was he said, "The news would make you sad, mother. I will not tell you." But she replied, "Do not give way to grief, my son. Tell me." Then he said, "Mother, this is all that is left of my friend," and gave her his friend's nail which he had carried up in his belt. Then Lankongrhoni was very sad, but she hid her grief, and a few days later gave notice to the village saying, "To-morrow bring all the children to my house. I am going to kill my big pig and give them a feast there." So the next day the villagers brought all their children to Lankongrhoni's house and left them there and went down to their fields. Then Lankongrhoni killed her big pig and feasted the village children on it. Afterwards she made the children remain shut up in her house while she went outside and said, "Children, tell me where there are holes in my house," and they replied, "There is a hole here, granny," or "There is a hole there, granny," and she stopped up the holes as the children told her of them. At last she called from outside and said, "Are there any more holes, children?" And they replied, "There are no more holes, granny." Then she said, "I want to light my pipe now. Give me a brand." So they gave her a brand and she set fire to the house and burnt all the children to ashes. But she herself climbed away up a thread thrown down from the sky and disappeared.[1]

[1] The version of the story given here is that current among the Northern Lhotas. In the Southern Lhota account Lankongrhoni escapes into a porcupine's hole, from which she is afterwards dug out and killed.

Now the villagers knew nothing of what had happened. But a crow went from field to field and hopped about in front of the workers dressed in a skirt like a little girl, and said, "Arilao's mother has utterly destroyed the children of the village." Then the villagers said, "What does it mean to-day, a crow behaving like that? Surely something has happened," and so saying they all went off home. And when they saw that all their children had been burnt up, each said to his neighbour, "This is your fault, this is your fault," and they fell upon each other and killed each other so that they all died. But two orphans, a brother and sister, were frightened when they saw this and climbed up into a fowl-house and hid. Afterwards, all the villagers being dead, there were none for them to marry, so they became husband and wife, and from these two, even from their fingers and toes, were born all the men there are in the world. This is one of the stories which men tell.

A few stories like the following are found which purport to give the origin of some common saying.

The Woman with a Caterpillar for a Husband.

A man and his wife lived together. Now at night the husband was a man, but in the day he turned into a hairy caterpillar. His wife did not know this. One night before she went to sleep she said, "To-morrow I am going to gather some leaves to eat." Early in the morning her husband left the house first and turned into a caterpillar and nipped off the leaves and waited at the place. Then the woman came and at the sight of the leaves exclaimed, "Strange, a caterpillar has nipped off the leaves. I will take them and go." So saying she took the leaves and went. But that night when they were in bed she said to her husband, "To-day I found that a caterpillar had nipped off the leaves I went to gather." Then her husband said, "It was I." At these words she was greatly troubled, and when he was asleep she gently pushed and pushed her husband till he fell off the bed into the fire and was burnt. After that the woman swallowed caterpillar hairs with her food, whenever she ate, and coughed and coughed till she died. Therefore nowadays if anyone coughs much people say, "You should not burn a caterpillar."

The forces of Nature form the subjects of several folk-tales, as the two following stories show.

The Sun and the Moon.

At the beginning of time what is now the sun was the moon, and what is now the moon was the sun. In those days when what is now the moon was the sun it was very hot, so that all the leaves and the trees in the jungle shrivelled up and died, and men suffered torments from the heat. Then what is now the sun said to the moon (which was the sun in those days), "Why do you shine so fiercely that you make all the leaves and trees in the jungle shrivel up and die, and cause men to suffer torments from the heat? You by being the sun are making men and leaves to die from heat and the world will be destroyed. Therefore from to-day I will not let you be the sun." With these words he smeared the face of what is now the moon with cow-dung, and what is now the sun become the sun. Therefore men say that the dark marks on the moon are where the sun smeared cow-dung on its face.[1]

The Wagtail and the Owlet.

Long, long ago, about the time that the Great Darkness came upon the earth, all the birds—for in those days the kinds were not as different as they are now—met in council

[1] In the Sema version a man throws cow-dung at the sun and turns it into the moon. In another Assam version ashes are thrown. In a Mexican version a hare or rabbit is thrown. In all the effect is the same. The hotter orb is turned into the cooler one. I have not met the story among Angamis, who describe the marks on the moon's face as a tree or as nettles.—J. H. H.

to decide how night should follow day. With one voice they called on the owlet to give his opinion. Then the owlet said, "Let there be nine days' darkness and nine days' light." "No, no," said all the birds, and smacked him on this side of his head and on that. That is why nowadays the owlet has a flat head. Then all the birds said, "Who will speak now?" And the wagtail said, "Listen to me, then; I will speak. Let us make darkness and light alternately, day by day." "Yes, yes," said all the birds, and stroked the wagtail [1] all over. He used to be as big as a village cock, but because all the birds stroked him so much he is now very small.

Finally, there is the story of the hero Ramphan and his dao. According to one tradition Ramphan is supposed to have lived when the Lhotas and Rengmas were still one tribe, and some Rengmas from Themokedima once even came to Akuk and claimed the dao, which is still preserved there as an heirloom. It is a long, thin piece of iron about two feet long and three inches broad. The spike of the haft is long and evidently protruded through the wooden haft, which probably existed once. It is rarely shown to strangers, and never to Southern Lhotas, on the ground that they approach Akuk from the direction of the Land of the Dead. The story given below is that told by the present possessors of the dao, and places the scene of the exploit at Longcham, an abandoned site on Wokha Hill, whence the Lhotas are supposed to have spread into the country now occupied by them.

The Story of Ramphan.

When the Lhotas were living at Longcham a tiger caused them grievous loss. One day it killed all of a party of nine women. Among them was Ramphan's wife, who was about to become a mother. At this disaster all clamoured to abandon the village, but Ramphan said he would go and face

[1] In one version the sun-bird is substituted for the wagtail.

the tiger. First he put on each of his fingers a section of thin bamboo. Then he took his long dao and lay down among the corpses of the nine women and waited for the tiger. Soon the tiger came and went to each corpse and ate a little of the flesh and laid it on one side, saying as he did so, "This one I killed on her way to the fields," or "This one I killed when she went to cut wood," or "This one I killed on her way to fetch water," or "This one I killed when she went to pick jungle leaves," or "This one I killed when she went to get vegetables," or "This one I killed when she was going down to fish." At last he came to Ramphan and said, "This one I do not remember," and picked him up and laid him aside, and then settled himself down to sleep. Then one by one Ramphan began to snap the pieces of bamboo on his fingers to see if the tiger was asleep or not. But at each snap the tiger pricked up his ears. At last when he had snapped nine of the pieces of bamboo and there was only one left, Ramphan thought to himself, "If the tiger is not asleep when I snap this I am done for." But when he snapped the last remaining piece of bamboo the tiger did not prick up its ears, for it was fast asleep. Then Ramphan rose up and cut off the tiger's head with his long dao, and climbed with it up to the top of a high spur and shouted the shout of a warrior who has taken a head. But he was sad when he thought of his wife lying dead in the valley below. And he called to his village men and said, "I have slain our enemy. Do not desert your village. Wait for me." But when he reached home he found that the villagers had already abandoned the place. From far away they shouted back to him, "We have sprinkled the back of one of our sows with rice husks, which fall as she walks. Follow the track of that and come." Now as Ramphan followed the trail of rice husks he caught up on the path a woman who was a leper. And the woman, whose name was Mangtsilo, said to Ramphan, "What does this mean, father? A poisonous snake here said, 'Snake-plant, snake-plant, Mangtsilo,' and glided over my leg. What does it mean?" Then Ramphan told her to crush up some leaves of the snake-plant and lay them on her leg. And she did as he told her and her leprosy was cured.[1] Then Ramphan took her as his wife.

One day when Mangtsilo was weaving outside her house, Ramphan's slaves began to spin their tops near by. They made Mangtsilo's brothers join in, and drew them on and on till they came close to her house. Then one of the brothers recognized his sister Mangtsilo, and went and told his parents that he had seen a woman exactly like his sister. But his parents said, " Your sister was lost long ago. Her very bones have rotted away by now. How could you have seen her ? " But he said again and again that he had seen a woman exactly like his sister, so that at last his parents went to see and found that it was indeed Mangtsilo. Then they demanded her marriage price from Ramphan, but Ramphan said, " First give me the marriage feast and then I will give you the marriage price." So her father said, " What can I do ? Make and give me only a bamboo spoon and a bamboo rice-stirrer." So Ramphan made and gave him only a bamboo spoon and a rice-stirrer. That is why Ramphan and Mangtsilo only had one son and one daughter born to them.

[1] The Kabuis have a similar story of a cure for leprosy being revealed by a snake; cf. T. C. Hodson, *Naga Tribes of Manipur*, p. 129.

SONGS

Not only have the Lhotas a number of traditional songs, but they are also experts at making up topical songs about any events of local interest. The singing is unaccompanied either by instrumental music or dancing. The following is given as an example of a traditional song. It is sung by men lopping the branches off trees when clearing jungle for new jhums. The Lhota version with a free prose translation is given, as no verse translation would give any idea of the swing of the song. It runs as follows :—

Ana echangcho locho
Sena hambong eshonile.

Ana echangcho locho
Reching hambong eshonile.

Ana echangcho locho
Yizem hambong eshonile.

Ana echangcho locho
Süng chomani yingkale.

Zükitacho yakpowo echilato,
Zükitacho yakwoina elhyu.

The interpretation of this song is as follows :—

On the tree that I am cutting
May a cock minivet perch.

On the tree that I am cutting
May a cock hornbill perch.

On the tree that I am cutting
May a cock king-crow perch.

On the tree that I am cutting
May taro and vegetables grow.

The " madhu " is his who climbs to the top,
The " madhu " grows at the top of the tree.

The music of this song will serve as a specimen of Lhota harmony. I am indebted to Mrs. Hutton for the notation.

INTRODUCTORY CHANT.

SONG.

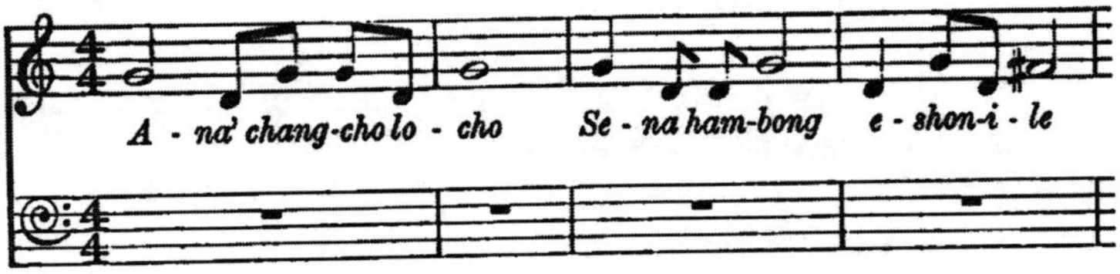

FINAL CHANT.

The introductory and final chants precede and follow each verse and are sung on the syllable *a*.

Another traditional song is the following lullaby sung by a widow to her child :—

Ole iyi le he-e,
O iyi e he-e,
O kakao ntitscona chitata chonchiato ?
O iyi e he-e,

O zükitacho niyuhungcho chonchiato ?
O iyi e he-e,
O zükitacho khencheng soko niyutokoka.
Chitata tichonchia,
O kakao.
Ole iyi le he-e,
O iyi e he-e,
O ango o-o,
O ntitscona chitata chonchiato o ?
O iyi e he-e,
O ntena chitata chonchiaka a.
O iyi e he-e,
O kiyonipo etchhi tyengro ekamochina.
O iyi e he-e,
O elaniki shiato nichamkao maka.
O chitata tichonchia a,
O iyi e he-e.

This may be translated as follows, omitting the meaningless chant of *Ole iyi le he-e*, etc. :—

" My little one, why are you crying so much ?
Is it because you want a drink of ' madhu ' that you are crying ?
I will give you well-kept ' madhu ' to drink.
Do not cry so much.
O my little one,
O my child,
Why are you crying so much ?
Even if you cry like this
Your father, who has become a young brave among the dead,
Cannot come back and call you and take you in his arms.
O do not cry so much."

Songs composed to celebrate some particular event are meaningless to anyone who does not know the full details of the circumstances to which they relate. An interlined and much expanded translation will help to explain the following specimen. It tells of the various people who were concerned in the founding of the new village of Japfu from Mekula, a migration which greatly annoyed those who remained in the old village.

Ho holo iye hele,
Ho holo iye hele,
Ho yanthan yanra Pithango.
(Ho for Pithango plotting to found the new village of Japfu.)

Ho holo iye hele,
Ho holo iye hele,
Ho yangen yanra Renowo.
(Ho for Renowo of the old village plotting to stop them going.)

Ho holo iye hele,
Ho holo iye hele,
Ho chapha Tsirenthang.
(Ho for Tsirenthang as fat as a carrying basket.)

Ho holo iye hele,
Ho holo iye hele,
Ho oyam phanka Zaremo.
(Ho for Zaremo, who went because he could never say No.)

Ho holo iye hele,
Ho holo iye hele,
Ho maorale Konchiyo ho esonlanicho.
(Ho for Konchiyo, the old man, burrowing into the scheme like a beetle in straw.)

Ho hati lishomo kamiki.
(He has become as fond of heavy jungle as a giant tortoise.[1])

[1] One is reminded of the reported use of "tortoise" by the Chinese as a term of mild opprobrium.—J. H. H.

Ho holo iye hele,
Ho holo iye hele,
Ho Japfu lantyulo ho epyu kalamo?
(Will you creep on all-fours up to Japfu on the height?)

Ho holo iye hele,
Ho holo iye hele,
Ho nthang tera Rishamo.
(Ho for Rishamo as handsome in the eyes of Rensali as a red flower for the ear.)

Ho holo iye hele,
Ho holo iye hele,
Ho panka tera 'Nseno.
(Ho for 'Nseno, no longer young, like a withered flower for the ear that looks best at a distance.)

Ho holo iye hele,
Ho holo iye hele,
Ho okap echü Rensali.
(Ho for Rensali who keeps her love for Rishamo so carefully hidden.)

Ho holo iye hele,
Ho holo iye hele,
Ho woro kurri Yanchano.
(Ho for Yanchano as bald as a chicken.)

Ho holo iye hele,
Ho holo iye hele,
Ho juzü kurri 'Nrio, penching chenpen 'Nrio.
(Ho for 'Nrio with ugly curled hair like a buffalo's forehead, 'Nrio as black as pounded oil-seed.)

Ho holo iye hele,
Ho holo iye hele,
Ho Kikung loroe Tsensolo.
(Ho for Tsensolo, fair woman of the Kikung clan.)

Ho holo iye hele,
Ho holo iye hele,
Ho Kithang tyengro Mangsamo.
(Ho for Mangsamo, buck of the Kithang clan, who stole Tsensolo from her husband.)

Ho holo iye hele,
Ho holo iye hele,
Ho yantsowotsenle ho woro nungratoksi.
(What did it matter if you paid a fine? The money, not Tsensolo, had the pain of parting from you.)

Ho senka tehrru nikhioalo, sithesiyu nikhioato?
(You are barren and useless as a wife. Did he take you to make of you a post for his house or rafters perhaps?)

Ho holo iye hele,
Ho holo iye hele,
Ho ntithana nirhanchoato ho yanaloio?
(Why did he marry you, woman?)

Ho holo iye hele,
Ho holo iye hele.

The recruiting of the Lhotas for the Naga Labour Corps, and their service in France and return have been celebrated in song at Pangti. A free translation of the song runs as follows.

O Hutton Sahib, young man of a foreign race,
What is that letter which has come for you from abroad?
O Hutton Sahib, young man of a foreign race,
The letter you got so quickly
Is it to call us to go to the German War?
Look how in every village
The bucks plan each with his friend to go.
Oh, we will go to the German War.
Let not a word of the letter fall fruitless.
We men of the Mountains, we the bucks

Have routed the enemies of the Sahib.
Let us return quickly, us the braves of the Mountains.
Let our women-folk at home hear the news,
Let them hear that we have routed the enemies of the Sahib.
We braves of the Mountains are coming back.
Let our women-folk at home hear the news.
Let them meet us with drinks of "madhu."
Bid them come and meet us on the road.
Tell our two [1] Sahibs to send word to them.
They have given us money as countless as the grains of ash on the hearth
But he who gives thought to it,
Only he will keep his money.

[1] *I. e.* the Deputy Commissioner of the Naga Hills and the Subdivisional Officer of Mokokchung.

PART VI

LANGUAGE

SIR GEORGE GRIERSON, in his *Linguistic Survey of India*, places [1] the Lhota language in the central sub-group of Naga languages, together with Ao, Tangsa,[2] Thukumi [3] and Yachumi. The Lhotas have no script of their own, though they have a tradition that they once possessed skins with writing on them. Being hungry they ate the skins and have been illiterate savages ever since.[4]

The grammar of the language has been described by Dr. W. G. Witter of the American Baptist Foreign Mission Society in his *Outline Grammar of the Lhota Naga Language.* I propose to confine myself, therefore, to a brief note founded on that work.

There are two dialects, the Liye and Ndrung, spoken north and south of the Doyang respectively, which differ but little save in the pronunciation of certain consonants. For example, Liye *tüng* (seven) becomes *küng* in Ndrung; similarly *otyak* (basket) becomes *okyak; otyam* (needle) becomes *opyam*, and so on.

Vowels.

A long as in " father."
A short as *u* in " but."
E long as *a* in " pay."
E short as *e* in " then."

[1] *Linguistic Survey of India*, Vol. III., Part II., pp. 284 *sqq.*

[2] The name of an Ao-Konyak village.

[3] A Sema name for the Sangtams.

[4] A similar tradition is to be found in many Naga tribes as well as among the Padam Abors and possibly other tribes on the north bank of the Brahmaputra.—J. H. H.

Ī long as in " machine."
Ĭ short, a little longer than the *i* in " sin."
Ō long as in " bone."
Ŏ short as in French " dot."
Ū long as in *oo* in " fool."
Ŭ short as in " pull."
Ü as in " turn."

Only syllables which are strongly long or short have been so marked.

Diphthongs.

There are no true diphthongs. The separate sounds of vowels which occur together can just be distinguished, though often very faintly.

Consonants.

B as in English.
C never used alone.
Ch as in " church."
Chh as *ch*, but with more aspiration. Sometimes approaching " *ts* " in sound.
D as in English.
F as in English.
G never used alone. When it follows *n* it is pronounced as the *g* in " singer," not as the *g* in " finger."
H as in English " hen." Aspirates the consonant with which it is combined.
J not used.
K as in English.
Kh as in " funk-hole."
L usually as in English, but sometimes pronounced almost like *n*.
M as in English.
Mm like *m*, but with the sound held longer.
N as in English. A final *n* often only gives a nasal sound to the vowel it follows.
Nn like *n*, but with the sound held longer.
P as in English.
Ph as in " tap-house," not as *f*.

Q not used.
R as in English, but rather more rolled.
Rr as *r*, but much rolled.
T as in English.
Th as in "hot-house."
V as in English.
W as in English.
X not used.
Y as in "year."
Z as in "zebra."

Grammar.

For the indefinite article *mătsanga* is used both with persons and things, and *nchyua* with persons only. The article is, however, usually omitted unless there is some special emphasis on the singleness of the person or thing spoken of. The place of the definite article is taken by demonstrative pronouns. Article.

There is no distinction of gender except in the case of animate objects. For human beings *epue*, "male," and *elue*, "female," are added when the sex is not otherwise indicated; e. g. *ngāro*, "infant," *ngaro epue*, "little boy," *ngaro elue*, "little girl." In the case of animals, *ōpong*, "male," and *ōkhu*, "female," are used; e. g. *wōkō*, "pig," *wokopong*, "boar," *wokokhu*, "sow." Gender.

The plural termination is "*ang*," affixed to the demonstrative pronoun *chi* or *shi*. "The men have gone": "*Kyonchiang yichaka*." The word "*ōni*" is used as a form of dual. "We two," *eni* (i. e. *e-oni*). "My father and your brother came yesterday": "*Āpo nā nīta oni nchü roa*." Number.

The subject of a transitive verb takes the suffix *nā*, which is also that of the instrument. In the case of two or more subjects the suffix is attached to the one nearest Case.

the verb. When the subject is followed by an adjective qualifying it, the suffix is attached to the adjective.

Etsi-na	*sōko*	*yūchaka.*
The Sahib	"madhu"	has drunk.

The object immediately precedes the transitive verb governing it and is not inflected.

E-na	*soko*	*yuka.*
We	"madhu"	will drink.

The direct object precedes the indirect.

Ōtsi	*Chongsĕmo*	*pia.*
Rice to	Chongsemo	give.

The noun is not inflected for the genitive. The possessor precedes the thing possessed.

Yănăsao	*'tsi*	*Chongsemo*	*pia.*
Yanasao's	rice	to Chongsemo	give.

Place and time are rendered by postpositions such as *i*, "to," "in"; *na*, "from," "with"; *lo*, "to"; *theni*, "with," "from," and many others.

Shi-na	*ora-i*	*wo.*	*Ā-ki-lo*	*woa.*
He the	jungle-to	will go.	My-house-to	go.

Eng-iya-thang-na.
Sun-coming-time-from (*i. e.* "from dawn").

Adjectives. Adjectives follow the nouns they qualify and take the suffixes instead of the noun.

Ōtūng	*săpo-lo.*
Tree	tall-on.

When a noun is used as an adjective it precedes the noun it qualifies.

Ora kyon.
Jungle-man.

To form the comparative an adjective takes the suffix "*wo*," or sometimes for euphony "*mo*."

Yanasao Asao sapowo.
Yanasao (than) Asao (is) taller.

In interrogative sentences the adjective plus the comparative suffix *wo* is repeated first with the interrogative suffix *alo*, and then with the interrogative suffix *ela*.

Yanasao sapow'alo Asao sapow'ela?
Yanasao taller Asao taller? (*i. e.* Which is taller, Yanasao or Asao?)

The superlative is formed by adding the suffix "*wo*" to the adjective as in the comparative, and putting some word meaning "all" before the noun representing the things among which comparison is being made.

Lănga 'tung shi sapowo.
All trees this taller (*i. e.* This is the tallest tree).

The cardinals are as follows:— Numerals.

1. *Ēkha* (only used in counting, otherwise *matsanga* or *nchyua* is used).
2. *Ēni.*
3. *Ēthăm.*
4. *Mēzü.*
5. *Mungo.*
6. *Tĭrok.*
7. *Tiing.*
8. *Tīza.*
9. *Tŏkū.*
10. *Tāro.*
11. *Tarosi ekha* (lit. "ten-with one").
12. *Tarosi eni.*
13. *Tarosi etham.*
14. *Tarosi mezü.*
15. *Tarosi mungo.*
16. *Tarosi tirok* or *mezüna mekwi mpen* (lit. "by four twenty not making").

17. *Tarosi tüng* or *ethamna mekwi mpen.*
18. *Tarosi tiza* or *enina mekwi mpen.*
19. *Tarosi toku* or *ekhana mekwi mpen.*
20. *Mekwi.*
21. *Mekwisi ekha.*
30. *Thămdro* (i. e. *etham taro*).
40. *Zūro* (i. e. *mezu taro*).
50. *Tüngya.*
60. *Rokro* (i. e. *tirok taro*).
70. *Ekha tüng* (*i. e.* "seven times once the sum of fingers").
80. *Ekha tiza* (Liye), *Zaro* (Ndrung).
90. *Ekha toku.*
100. *Ekha taro.*
1000. *Thanga.*

Fractions :—

$\frac{1}{2}$ = *poko.*
$1\frac{1}{2}$ = *matsanga-si poko.*
$\frac{1}{3}$ = *Echu etham chuche matsanga* (*i. e.* "One part of three parts").

Counting is done on the fingers, and reckoning is kept by little bundles of sticks. It is a common sight to see, say, five little bits of bamboo stuck up in a prominent place in a wayside granary, or five notches cut in a log. This means that the owner will claim Rs.5 from whoever damages the granary or misappropriates the log.

There are no true ordinals.

First = *ōvūngōchī* (the one in front).
Second = *ovungochi sīlāmo* (the one behind the one in front).
Third = *ovungochi chito oni silamo* (the one behind both that one and the one in front).

Ordinal adverbs are formed by the prefix *echo* or *echung.*

Once = *echoa* or *echunga.*
Twice = *echoni* or *echungeni*, etc.

The personal pronouns are as follows :— Pronouns.

First person	Singular	*A, ai, aiyo, akha.*
	Plural	*E, eten, eyo.*
Second person	Singular	*Nna, nno, ni, yi, i.*
	Plural	*Ni, nino, nte, yi.*
Third person	Singular	*Mbo,* and the demonstrative pronouns *hi, shi, chi.*
	Plural	*Oten,* and the demonstrative pronouns *hiang, shiang, chiang.*

Personal pronouns take the same suffix as nouns.

A mokthata.
I am tired.

A-na pīka.
I will give.

As in nouns, the possessive is formed by placing the possessor before the thing possessed.

My house = *Āki* (= *A-oki*).

The demonstrative pronouns are as follow:—*Hi* or *shi*, "this," *chi*, "that," *hiang* or *shiang*, "these," *oten* or *chiang*, "those." They follow the noun they qualify and take suffixes as do adjectives.

A-na oki-shi-lo otsi tsōka.
I house-this-in rice will eat.

The interrogative pronouns are as follow :—

Who ? = *ochi, ocho.*
Which ? = *ocho, kuwe, ko.*
What ? = *ochi* or *ocho* (referring to persons); *ntio, nyu, nyuwo* (referring to things).

Nno ntio chonala ?
You what are wanting ?

A relative clause in English is usually rendered in Lhota

by the verb followed by *wochi* (lit. "go that"), often pronounced *mochi* for euphony.

A-na	*echo-mō-chi*	*a-pia*
I	wanted-one-the	me-give

(*i. e.* give me the one I wanted).

The interrogative pronouns are, however, sometimes used as relatives.

A-na	*kuwe*	*chonana*	*chi*	*a-pia.*
I	what	wanted	that	me-give.

The Verb. The verb is not conjugated for person and number. Certain suffixes are used to express tense. They are as follow :—

-a = perfect or future, the context giving the sense. It is also the termination of the imperative. Thus, from the verbal root *tso* = eat—

Ana tsoa = { I will eat. / I have eaten.

Tsoa = eat.

-ka is the ordinary termination of the future—

Ana tsoka = I will eat.

-cho is the ordinary termination of the preterite—

Ana tsocho = I ate, I have eaten.

-ala is the ordinary termination used to express continual action, and is apparently a form of the verb *lia*, "is"—

Ana tsoala = { I am eating. / I was eating.

To express habitual action the verbal root without any termination is used.

Ana otsi tso = I eat rice.

The verbal root followed by a faint *v* sound expresses future action.

Ana tsov = I will eat.

Further shades of meaning are expressed by a large number of verbal modifiers which are added sometimes to the verbal root, and sometimes to the verbal root plus the termination *-a*. These modifiers are followed by the suffixes already mentioned. The commonest are as follow :—

(1) *vān* indicates continuance. Alone it means "stay," "remain," "live."

Ana tsoavancho = I continued eating.
Ana ochi vana = I live there.

(2) *kam* also indicates continuance.

Ana otsi tsoakāma = I am eating rice.

(3) *chak* implies completion.

Ana atsi tsochaka = I have eaten up my rice.

A reduplicated form of *chak* is also sometimes used to express the English pluperfect.

Ana atsi tsochakchaka = I had eaten up my rice.

(4) *sāla* implies immediate future.

Ana tsosala = I am just about to eat.

(5) *tok* has a causative, or permissive sense.

Ana shi tsotokala = I am making him eat.
Shi tsotoka = Let him eat.

(6) *hng* is a verbal root meaning "wish."

Ana tsohnga = I wish to eat.

(7) *pvu* is added to the reduplicated verbal root to express frequency.

Shina tsopvu tsopvu vanala = He is always eating.

(8) *lan* or *lam* expresses repetition.

Shina rolancho = He came back again.

(9) *ten* or *tem* indicates the first doing of an act.

Ana tsotencho = I ate first.

(10) *ta* indicates that several people are acting together.

Otena tsotala = They are eating together.

(11) *khān* signifies absolute completeness.
Ana atsi tsokhancho = I have eaten up all my rice.

(12) *nhyu* indicates incompleteness.
Ana otsi tsonhyua = I have eaten part of the rice.

(13) *s* = " more."
Otsi apisa = Give me more rice (*pi* = " give ").

(14) *hrak* = " got."
Ana otsi tsohraka = I got some rice to eat.

(15) *kok* = ability.
Ana oso tsokoka = I can eat meat.

(16) *che* or *cheyu* also = ability.
Ana otsi ntsoche = I cannot eat rice.

Imperative Mood. The following examples show the shades of meaning of the terminations in use.

tsoa = eat.
tsosa = eat more.
tsoalo = go on eating.

Participial Clauses. The sense of English participles and participial clauses is given by postpositions and adverbs added to the verbal stem or the verbal stem plus *a*. Examples are as follow :—

(1) *-na* " from," " by," the instrumental postposition.
Ana otsi tsona . . . = { I, if I eat rice. / I, by eating rice. }

(2) *-i* = " at."
Shina amhungi atapcho = { He at seeing me struck me. / He struck me as soon as he saw me. }

(3) *thang* = " at the time of."
Ana tsoathang shina atapcho = He struck me when I was eating.

(4) *-le* = "at the time of"—usually added to verbal modifier *van*.

Ana tsoavanle shina atapcho = He struck me when I was eating.

(5) *sanati* = "immediately after."
tsosanati woa = Go as soon as you have eaten.

(6) *si* or *sa* = "after."
tsosi woa = Go when you have eaten.

(7) *leha* or *chakla* denote concession.
Ana otsi ntsoleha woka = Though I have not eaten I will go.

Certain prefixes are added to verbs of motion to indicate direction. **Directional Prefixes.**

(1) *chung* = "up"; *chungwoka* = I will go up.
(2) *cho* = "down"; *chowoka* = I will go down.
(3) *thre* or *thro* = "in"; *threyia* = come in.
throwoa = go in.
(4) *chi* = "out" = *chiyia* = go out.

A conditional clause is usually expressed participially by means of the postposition *-na* added to the verbal stem. Another method is to add *-wo* to the verbal root of the protasis and *-katola* to the verbal root of the apodosis. **Conditional Clauses.**

Otsi hello liwo ana tsokatola [1] = If rice were here I would eat.

Purpose is usually expressed by adding the postposition *-lo*, "to," to the verbal root. It may also be expressed by the prefix *e-*, either with or without the postposition *-lo*, or by the suffix *kiatto*. **Purpose.**

Ana tsolo rŏcho.
Ana etsolo rocho.
Ana etso rocho.
Ana tsokiatto rocho.
} I came to eat.

[1] Dr. Witter gives *-katola* as the suffix of the apodosis. I am myself inclined to think that the word *tsokatola* is the ordinary future form *tsoka*, plus a suffix *-tola*.

Negative. With the imperative the prohibitive prefix *ti-* is used.

Titsoa = Do not eat.

In the other tenses *n* (or sometimes for euphony *m*) is prefixed to the verb.

Ana ntso = I do not eat.

Interrogatives. The following suffixes are added to the verbal root plus the termination *-a*.

(1) *-ke.*

Nno tsoake = Do you eat?

(2) *-nüng.*

Nno tsoanung = Do you eat?

(3) *-la*, with a reduplicated verbal root.

Nna tsotsoala = Do you eat?

(4) *-ela*, with a reduplicated verbal root. This form is only used when speaking of past time. The termination *-a* of the verbal root is elided and disappears.

Nno tsotsoela = Did you eat?

(5) For double questions *-lo* is suffixed to the affirmative verb and *-la* (or *-ela*) to the negative verb.

Nno tsoalo ntsoala = Do you eat or not?

(6) *-ne* is used in asking permission.

Ana tsoane = May I eat?

Voice. There is no passive form of the verb.

I have eaten up my rice = *ana atsi tsochaka.*

My rice has been eaten up = *atsi tsochaka.*

The latter appears to be really a case in which the subject is understood.

Verbal Synonyms. As in other Naga languages, different verbs are used for variations of the same act. Dr. Witter gives the following list as an example.

Ephyopala = to wash in general.
Etsiala = „ „ clothes.
Süala = „ „ dishes.
Myuala = „ „ face.
Phiala = „ „ feet.
Ntsakala = „ „ hands.

Adverbs.

The following are typical examples. Many are composite words formed from a noun or pronoun and a post-position.

Always	= *echung.*	Perhaps	= *kanyu.*
Formerly	= *nkolo.*	Probably	= *kache.*
By day	= *engilo.*	In this way	= *heto.*
Last night	= *nsamo.*	In that way	= *chito.*
To-night	= *osamo.*	On the right	= *amymwe.*
To-day	= *nching.*	On the left	= *aiyiwe.*
To-morrow	= *ochü.*	Ahead	= *ovungwe.*
Yesterday	= *nchü.*	Behind	= *silamwe.*
Now	= *nthanga.*	There	= *ochi.*
Suddenly	= *ekhiapa.*	Here	= *hello.*

Post-positions.

Several have been noted in connection with the verb. Examples of others are as follow:—

Among	= *onungo.*	Towards	= *we.*
Below	= *okapi.*	With	= *pana.*
Between	= *yite.*	Near	= *nthango.*
From, with	= *theni.*	In front of	= *mhatungi.*

Syntax.

In a simple sentence the subject comes first and the verb last, with the object between them.

Ana otsi tsoka.
I rice will eat.

Adverbs usually come first.

Ochü ana otsi tsoka.
To-morrow I rice will eat.

Interrogative adverbs, however, often follow the subject.

Chongsemo	*kothang*	*rov?*
Chongsemo	when	will come?

Possessive nouns and pronouns precede the thing possessed, but adjectives follow the noun they qualify.

Ana	*Chongsemo*	*'tsi*	*mhōna*	*tsoka.*
I	Chongsemo's	rice	good	will eat.

In compound sentences the principal clause stands last.

Ochi	*nyanya*	*vāna*	*ana*	*ntsiala.*
There	a goat	is	I	know.

In reporting the words of a third person the actual words spoken are placed with the particle *to* immediately in front of the principal verb.

Thus "Chongsemo said he would go" would be in Lhota—

Chongsemona	*ana*	*wov*	*to*	*ezocho.*
Chongsemo	I	will go	thus	said.

If the actual words of the speaker are not used the indirect discourse is placed after the principal clause and its verb takes the affix *-lato.*

Chongsemona	*ezocho*	*omona*	*wolato.*
Chongsemo	said	he	would go.

The following specimens of the language with literal translations will serve to illustrate the grammar and syntax.

I.—The Story of the Cuckoo and the Crow.

Păngpăng-to	*nā*	*kāshāk-to*	*ōni*	*ōkămo*	*tscōtăcho.*
cuckoo	and	crow	they-two	friends	became.

Ole	*pangpang-chi-na*	*kashak-chi*	*ēzōchō*	"*Ā-kăm,*
Then	cuckoo-that	(to) crow-that	said	"my-friend,

nnā-hā ōnyu-shi-ki mhōna ā-rānīke ana-ha
you-too gum-this-with well me-ornamenting I-too

onyu-shi-ki mhona i-ranika." to
gum-this-with well you-will ornament." thus

ezoa mhona eranitokcho. Chi-silōcho
having said well made him ornament. That-after

kashak-chi-na pangpang-chi ezocho "A-kam, nna-ha
crow-that (to) cuckoo-that said my-friend, you-too

mhona a-ranike ana-ha mhona i-ranichoka."
well me-ornamenting I-too well you-will ornament."

to ezoa onyu-chi picho. Ole
thus having said gum-that gave. Then

pangpang-chi-na "A-kam, a-pfu-na a-tsāla,
cuckoo-that "my-friend my-mother me-is calling,

a-pfu-na a-tsala," to ezoa onyu-chi-na
my-mother me-is calling," thus having said gum-that-with

kashak-chi kŭrri-lo tyankaisi tsancho.
cuckoo-that head-on having poured out ran away.

Chī-tsōkō-nā nhūnga-cha kashak-cho nyīkā-lā.
That-reason-from now-till crow-the black-is.

Hochi-na pangpang-cho kashak khyūa engo
That-from cuckoo-the crow fearing (by) day

n-sāmphina zāmo-thăng-tai "pangpang pangpang."
not-wandering darkness-time-only "cuckoo cuckoo."

to khua samphiala.
thus crying wanders.

Translated into ordinary English the story runs as follows :—

The cuckoo and the crow became sworn friends. One day the cuckoo said to the crow, "My friend, you ornament me prettily with this gum and I will do the same to you," and got the crow to do as he was asked. The crow then made the same request to the cuckoo and gave him the gum. But the cuckoo cried, "My mother is calling me, my mother is calling me," and poured the gum all over the crow's head and ran away. That is why the crow is black and the cuckoo is so frightened of the crow that he only wanders about at night, calling, "Cuckoo, cuckoo." [1]

II.—How Children were turned into Monkeys.

Onpoi-na	*otsoi*	*epue*	*'ts*	*ekha*	*elue*
man and wife	children	male	child	one	female

'ts ekha to	*pōki*	*vāsi*	*elue-chi*	*tchhīcho.*
child one too	having got	having been	wife-the	died.

Tole	*epue-chi-na*	*elue-chi*	*tchhicho*	*silo*	*elue*
Then	husband-the	wife-the	died	after	wife

ethăn	*soa*	*vāncho.*	*Ole*	*elue*	*ethan-chi-na*	*elue*
new	took	remained.	Then	wife	new-the	wife

etchhio-chi	*'tsoi*	*t'-oni-chi*	*n-nzām*	*elăm*	*kangshi*
dead-the	children	two-the	not-pitying	much	trouble

ntsonshicho.	*Osi*	*nchōkāchō*	*mbo-na*	*nūngri-t'-oni*
gave.	But	one day	she	(to the) children-two

"li-nhyako	*wota,*	*otsi-cho*	*a-na*	*eng-aku*	*ni-'ni*
"field-to watch	go	food	I	day-every	(for) you two

hāntokmūngka;	*oki*	*ti-yitake."*	*to*
will have taken down;	home	do not come."	Thus

ezoa	*wotokcho.*	*Chi-silo*	*mbo-na*	*otsi*
having said	made to go.	That-after	she	food

kīlāto	*zīro-chü*	*hōno-chü*	*māku-to*	*tai*
calling-it	rat-dung	chicken-dung	husks-too	only

[1] The Kayans of Borneo tell a similar story in which the argus pheasant and the coucal take the place of the cuckoo and crow (*The Pagan Tribes of Borneo*, How and McDougal, Vol. I., p. 247). The Greenland Eskimo give a similar account of how the raven became black. Cf. "The Raven and the Goose," in *Eskimo Folk-tales*, by Knud Rasmussen and W. Worster, p. 66 (Gyldendale, 1921).

nkapnkapi *nungri-t-'oni*
having tied up in leaves (to) the children-two

hantokmungcho. *Tole* *nungri-t-'oni-na* *eng-aku*
had carried down. Then children-two day-every

mbo-na *otsi* *kilato* *ziro-chü* *hono-chü*
she food calling it rat-dung chicken-dung

na *maku-to* *nkapnkapi*
and husks-too having tied up in leaves

hantokmung-chi *lānphelānphei*
having had taken down-that which having opened

zesi sicho. *Chi-silo-cho* *nungri-t-'oni-na* *kyon*
saw. That-after children-the two man's

etsoyu *n-chămcheo* *ora-i* *tsangti-*
food and drink not-remembering jungle-in nuts

longpen-tai *hlotso-hloyuta* *vancho.*
berries-only picking eating-picking drinking stayed.

Ole *nchokacho* *opo-na* *otsi* *hānsi* *wo*
Then one day (their) father food carrying going

" *oyi,* *otsi* *tsota.*" *to* *ezoa* *tsale*
" come, food eat." Thus having said calling

nungri-t-'oni-na " *A-po,* *eyo* *nhungo* *kyon*
children-the two " my-father, we now man's

etsoyu *n-chamche* *kama* *yākso*
food and drink not-remembering having become monkeys

kamayiala." *to* *ezoa* " *wu-wu* " *to* *khuta*
are becoming." Thus saying " wu-wu " thus calling

yakso *kamayicho.* *Chi-silo-cho* *opo-na* " *Toka*
monkeys became. That-after (the) father " Then

ni-ni-na *yakso* *kama* *yi-na* *oyan*
you-two monkeys having become being-from village

mung-thang-mungri *eli chepya* *'yam-li* *penchü-muchü*
emung-time-keeping is seeing village-fields seeds-roots

shotso	*shoiya*	*yitake,"*	*to*	*ezoa*
scratching up	digging up	will go,"	thus	having spoken

yitokcho.	*Hochi-na*	*nhunga-liya*	*yakso-na*	*oyan*
let (them) go.	This-from	now-till	monkeys	village

mung-thang-mungri	*eli*	*chepya*	*'yam-li*	*penchü-muchü*
emung-time-keeping	is	seeing	village-fields	seeds-roots

shotso	*shoiyala*		*to*	*rutala.*
scratching up	digging up	are	thus	(men) say.

The interpretation of the tale is as follows :—

A man and his wife had one son and one daughter. The wife died and the man married again. But the new wife did not love her step-children and ill-used them. One day she said to them, " Go down and watch the fields. I will send food down for you every day. Do not come back to the house." But instead of food she only sent down rat-dung and chicken-dung and rice husks tied up in leaves. When the children opened the leaves they saw that their step-mother had sent them down filth instead of food. Then they forgot what human food was like and took to picking and eating berries in the jungle. One day their father brought down some food and called them to come and eat it, but they said, " We have forgotten what human food is like, father. We are turning into monkeys." With these words they called out " wu-wu " and turned into monkeys. Then their father said, " You have turned into monkeys, and now you will watch for the days when the villagers are keeping *emung* and cannot go to the fields, and will scratch up the roots and seeds they have sown." That is why to this day monkeys scratch up the roots and seeds in the fields when they see that the village is keeping *emung*.

Abuse and Nicknames.

The figurative expressions used by Lhotas in jest or for purposes of abuse are so apt and to the point that they deserve brief notice. A dwarfish person is called either *hampochütang* (fowl's-dung) or *zitsenaro* (mouse). A woman of loose morals is called *nyanyavu* (she-goat) or *ntsingo* (a small fish with the reputation of taking any bait thrown to it). The expression *wokomhi* (pig's tail) is applied to a fussy man who is always running backwards and forwards. *Nangkinangka* (chrysalis) denotes a sulky man. *Shamakok* (wasp) is a man with a very small waist. *Potak* (duck) is a man who waggles his posterior as he walks. In a quarrel a man will sometimes address his opponent as *sakaptso* (" born under the verandah of the house," *i. e.* bastard), and will be called *songkoptso* (" born under the granary ") in return. A man with no teeth is nicknamed *okingkham* (open door), and so on.

Baby Language.

An English mother who says to her baby, " Didums wantum's bottleums denums ? " uses language sufficiently like that in ordinary use to be intelligible to a mere bachelor, but the Lhotas have a curious custom, when addressing small children, of using words which are in no way connected with the speech of every-day life. For instance, " boiled rice " is called *mama*, " madhu " is *koko*, " rain " is *tsetse*, " eat " is *hamto*, " go to sleep " is *shoboto*, " get up " is *hoksi*, " sit down " is *phato*, " go along " is *tsatsato*, " I will smack you " is *khakto*, and so on.

The origin of this baby dialect is unknown, but it is noticeable that the Aos use almost identical words in addressing their children.

PART VII

APPENDICES

APPENDIX A

THE LHOTA CALENDAR

THE Lhota divides the year into twelve lunar months,[1] which are named as follows :—

Ndri (February). " The month of the *ndri* flower."
Emhu (March). " The blowing month."
Ephi (April). " The dry month."
Cheshi (May). " The watching month," *i. e.* all watch to see if the crops will sprout well.
Oten (June). " The month of millet " (*teni*).
Nnung (July). Derivation unknown.
Chikanika (August). " The month of quarrels," because poor men have come to the end of their resources and try to borrow from rich men, who refuse to lend.
Ndrangtso (September). " The bursting month," because the pots are bursting with new rice.
Rongorongyi (October). " The going backwards and forwards month," *i. e.* carrying the crop up to the village.
Chopuk (November). " The month of ease."
Shotokuk (December). " The month of ceremonies."
Echon (January). " The spreading month," *i. e.* the rats scatter the straw about the abandoned fields.

In order to correct the calendar an extra month or part of a month called *Chotantsu* is put in after *Echon* whenever

[1] Opposite each month I have given the traditional derivation of the name. The correspondence with the English months is only approximate, of course.

necessary. The months being periods of the agricultural year the whole Lhota country is not in the same month at the same time. The inhabitants of a cold village where the crops are late may be struggling through *Chikanika* while those of a warm village are enjoying the peace and plenty of *Ndrangtso*.

APPENDIX B

MENSURATION

THERE is no standard of weight in use throughout the tribe, but in every village there is kept a stone (*ephwa*) which is used in apportioning the shares of meat at feasts. The weight is generally nine to ten pounds. For trade a balance of the bismar type is used, notched to weigh in Indian seers and fractions of seers.

The standard measure for rice is *chukoluk*, which is regarded as one man's wage for a day and usually weighs about six pounds. The table would be as follows :—

2 *chukolukruso*	=	1 *chukoluk*.
3 *chukoluk*	=	1 *sitsi*.
1½ *sitsi*	=	1 *enokyak*.

Two baskets (*etek*) are regarded as going to one *enokyak*. The size of the baskets varies from village to village, and the buyer must accept the standard of the village from which he buys.

Though nowadays Lhotas occasionally try to state distance in English miles, the real measure is by *echen*, the distance between one temporary granary and that at the next stage on the path up from the fields. It varies from village to village. On an easy slope it may be a mile and a half, on a steep slope it will be a mile or even less.

The depth of water is either measured in *echam* (the height of a man) or *eshi* (kicks). That is to say, if a man having dived to the bottom of a pool has to kick his legs three times before he reaches the top, the pool is reckoned as three "kicks" deep. A tree is spoken of as so many *phunchap* (ladder-steps) high.

Just as fingers and toes are the usual counting apparatus,

so the Lhota uses the distance between the various parts of his body as standards of measurement. The distance between the tips of the fingers of the outstretched arms is called *ntiya*, and that from the middle of the chest to outstretched finger-tips *monyak*. A cubit is *kecha*. The spans of the thumb and first finger and thumb and middle finger are *ekohundro* and *ekosüpo* respectively. The breadth of a finger is *yingro*. These measurements are used for all conceivable purposes. The size of a mithan, for instance, is not stated in terms of its height at the withers, but in terms of the length of its horn in *ekosüpo* and *yingro*. Similarly, to measure a pig you pass a long slip of bamboo round its chest and measure the bamboo. Thread is never measured by length or weight. If it is in a skein, the thickness round the skein is taken, the circles formed by thumb and first finger and thumb and middle finger being called *etsokhundro* and *etsoksüpo* respectively. If it is in a ball, the ball is reckoned as a *keraksüpo* (big handful) or *keraktero* (little handful).

APPENDIX C

HUMAN SACRIFICE

MAJOR BUTLER gives the following account [1] of a human sacrifice: " About the 27th July, 1850, Lieutenant Vincent succeeded in effecting, for thirty-seven rupees, the ransom of Tooleram, a Cacharee boy, who had been carried off from the village of Loongee-jair on the 18th February by a marauding party of Angahmee Nagahs. Two other children were at the same time carried off, but had been sold to other villages; a little girl was sold to some Nagahs at Beereh-mah, but could not be traced. The fate of the third boy was horrible; he was purchased by the adjoining tribe of Lotah Nagahs, and a man of the village having died immediately after the purchase, it was considered a bad omen, and that ill luck had befallen them on account of this captive child. They therefore flayed the poor boy alive, cutting off his flesh bit by bit until he died. These cruel and superstitious savages then divided the body, giving a piece of the flesh to each man in the village to put into his *dolu*, a large corn-basket. By this they suppose all evil will be averted, their good fortune will return, and plentiful crops of grain will be ensured."

Nagas are always ready to give garbled, not to say scandalous, accounts of the customs of their neighbours, and there can be little doubt that Major Butler was misled by his Angami informants. Lhotas, in common with other tribes, believe in a vague sort of way that the taking of a head brings prosperity to the taker's village, and the boy was probably killed and his body cut up and distributed, as was done more recently in the case of the Nankam slave

[1] *Travels and Adventures in the Province of Assam*, by Major John Butler, p. 189.

bought by Akuk. But there is no tradition that it was ever the custom to torture victims before death, and I think the Lhotas must be acquitted of this charge. It would, further, be clean contrary to their customs to put pieces of human flesh in their rice, which would thereby become polluted rather than blessed.[1]

The story goes that long, long ago a rich Lhota was very ill. In vain pigs, cattle and mithan were slaughtered. Finally he had one of his slaves sacrificed in cold blood, in the hope that the slave's life would be accepted in place of his own. The man died, however, in spite of this last sacrifice, and Lhotas, seeing that it was unavailing, have never imitated his example. This tradition and the practice of spearing the *opya* at the *oyantsoa* "genna" point to a time when human sacrifice was practised to avert evil fortune, but it would be safe to say that within historical times no such custom has been followed by them.

[1] As the keeping of paddy in large corn-baskets is an Angami custom, and not followed by the Lhotas, the account given to Major Butler is clearly inaccurate, and I agree with Mr. Mills that it is probably a sheer invention of the same nature as the Semas and Aos are in the habit of making with regard to the hostile tribes to the east of them.—J. H. H.

NAGA-ASSAMESE GLOSSARY

As far as possible Naga-Assamese words have been avoided. For the following, however, no convenient English equivalents exist.

apodia. From the Assamese āpăd ("misfortune"). Certain forms of death by misadventure are spoken of as "apotia" deaths (see p. 160).

chunga. A section of bamboo with a node left intact at one end. Used as a drinking vessel or for carrying water.

dal. Lentils.

dao. A heavy bill used by Nagas both as a weapon and for agriculture.

deo-bih. Literally "spirit-poison." The juice of a certain root formerly used by Nagas for poisoning fish. The practice is now prohibited.

genna. A very common Naga-Assamese word and one used in various senses. (1) A Naga ceremony; (2) = "forbidden" (*e. g.* "It is genna to take the head of a man of your own village"); (3) = "tabued," as Angami *kenna,* of which the word is a corruption (*e. g.* "my house is genna to-day").

jhum. Naga cultivation (see description on p. 45). Also used = a field which has been cultivated in this way.

khel. A division of a village (see description on p. 24).

lengta. The small apron worn by the men of most Naga tribes.

machan. A bamboo platform.

madhu. Rice beer.

mithan. *Bos frontalis* (domestic) and *bos gaurus* (wild).

morung. The "bachelors' hall" in which the boys and unmarried men of a khel sleep.

pan. A leaf which is chewed with betel nut and lime.

panji. A bamboo spike stuck in the ground to impale enemies or game.

MAP SHOWING LHOTAS AND NEIGHBOURING TRIBES

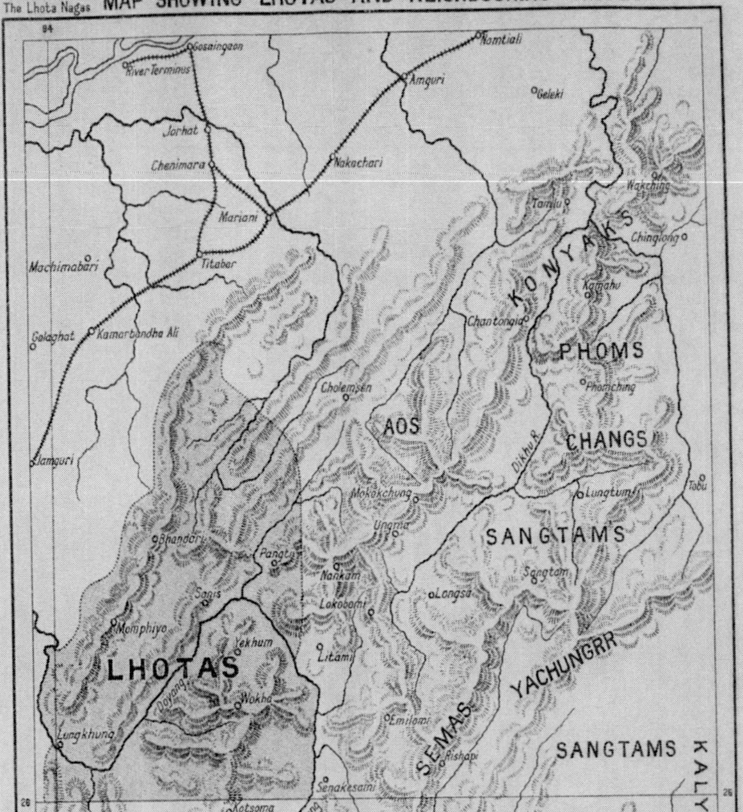

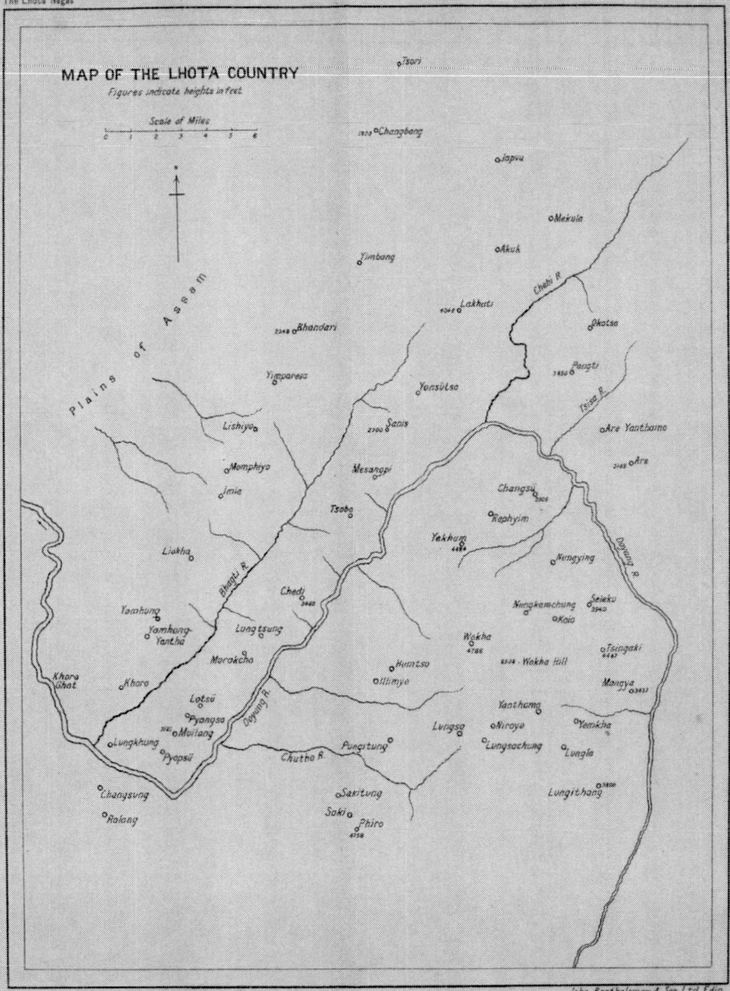

John Bartholomew & Son, Ltd. Edin.

INDEX